EDUCATION AND THE TEACHER

EDUCATION AND THE TEACHER

Janardan Prasad

M.A. (Philo., Socio), M.Ed., ND. (Art), Dip. in Wd. Working
Former, Lecturer in Education (Art)
Central Institute of Education, Department of Education,
University of Delhi, Delhi

KANISHKA PUBLISHERS, DISTRIBUTORS
NEW DELHI-110 002

KANISHKA PUBLISHERS, DISTRIBUTORS
4697/5-21A, Ansari Road, Daryaganj
New Delhi -110 002
Phones : 2327 0497, 2328 8285
Fax : 011-2328 8285
E-mail : kanishka_publishing@yahoo.co.in

Education and the Teacher
Edition: 2016

PRINTED IN INDIA

Published by Madan Sachdeva for Kanishka Publishers, Distributors, 4697/5-21A, Ansari Road, Daryaganj, New Delhi-110 002, Typeset by Sunshine Graphics, Delhi, and Printed at Rajdhani Printers, Delhi.

Dedicated

to

Late Professor, P.K. Roy

Former Principal

Central Institute of Education, University of Delhi,

Delhi.

Foreword

Teacher is an important player in the process of teaching, learning in the field of education, which lead the youngs to socialization, moralization and enculturation. From the times immemorial the teachers have been playing a vital role in educating the youths and moulding them for leading a sane axiological social life. In olden days the Indian teachers (the Gurus) have been the beacon lights for the youths, in the society, as they have been moulding the youths for saneful living. Then main aim of education was to socialize the youths for living a saneful and spiritual social life.

Now, the solitary aim of present system of formal education is to prepare the students for annual examination which breeds cut throat competition in the society. This process does not have any place for the enculturations of the youths. As such, socialization, co-operation sharing, joint family system and national culture are disappearing from the society day by day.

Shri Janardan Prasad, because of his long experience of working in Central Institute of Education, University of Delhi, has tried to highlighten the main core issues of the present formal system of education, such as teaching profession, the process of formal education, curriculum construction, co-curriculum activities, art activities, teaching as a profession and role of an ideal-teacher.

I appreciate the efforts of Shri Janardan Prasad which he is doing after his retirement. I hope his efforts will be helpful for the teachers and improve the present state of school education, and this book will be helpful for the teachers.

Shri Suryanarayan Sharma
M.A. M.Ed. Ph.D. (B.S.)
Former Dy. Director of Education,
Delhi.

Preface

My inner consciousness forced me to write these pages as my heartiest tribute to Late Professor P.K. Roy and to Central Institute of Education, Delhi. Prof. P.K. Roy who was a dedicated, fair, honest, kind hearted, soft spoken and able educationist. He was also an able, non-inclinative and just administrator. He had helped me a lot. He had encouraged me to do M.A. in Philosophy and M.A. in Sociology. He had appointed me as an Artist in Audio-Visual section of the C.I.E. I am very grateful to the departed soul (Former Principal Central Institute of Education, Delhi).

I am also very grateful to many of my teachers and colleagues at the Central Institute of Education, Delhi who had helped and guided me to self-educate myself while working in C.I.E. Prominent amongst them where Late Shri H.A. Gade, Late Shri K.D. Bakshi, Late Prof. E.A. Pires, Prof. R.P. Sharma and Shri S.P. Tyagi. I am also very grateful to Late Prof. J.R. Bimbhraw, former Head of the Department of Mechanical Engineering, Delhi, College of Engineering, who had always inspired me to self-educate myself. Before joining C.I.E., while I was serving as an Instructor in the Industries Department, U.P. Government, Late Prof. B. Biswas, Head Chemical Engineering, Hercourt Bulter Technological Institute, Kapur, U.P. had also inspired me for self-study and, under his guidance. I had done intermediate, B.A., Certificate in Carpentry and Diploma in Wood Working. Late Prof. E.A. Pires, former Principal, C.I.E. (Government of India) had inspired, encouraged and permitted me to do N.D. Fine Art (A.I.C.T.E.) seven years Part time Course from College of Art, Delhi and allowed me to do B.Ed. as a teacher candidate. Later on Prof. R.N. Mehrotra encouraged me to M.Ed. I found C.I.E. family where I could find a very congenial atmosphere otherwise for an artisan it would have quite impossible.

Any academic contribution is impossible for a person like me, but as a gratitude to C.I.E., so far, I could contribute (1) Education and Society (2) Art Education (3) Audio-Visual Education. I am also working on. (1) Indian Socioscope (2) Vishwakarma Artisan of India (3) Education and the Teacher (4) Family (परिवार) and (5) School Education. I had also written book on Wood Working. I am also thankful to Shri R. Padamnabhan, Librarian C.I.E. for allowing me to use C.I.E. library when I needed.

JANARDAN PRASAD

Contents

1

Introduction

Education is a process of bringing or moulding a young for living a congenial and comfortable life. Since times immemorial the man has been bringing up or educating his offsprings for living a sane social life. And since times immemorial the educational objectives have been based on this principle. In ancient civilization and Mohan-jo-daro and Vedic civilizations in India, education was imparted on this principle. In all civilizations like Greek, Mesopotamia, Hebrew in Eastern Europe and Mohan-jo-daro and Vedic Civilization in India and in Chinese Civilization educational aims were framed and education was imported in familial way. Education was first imparted in which the mother was the prime teacher of the child. Even in Gurukulas the familial type of educational system was followed. Some Gurkulas were named on this principle as Taxila was named. Taxila means a moulding place. Still in many tribal areas the familial education is in practice. The main aim of education in these tribal areas is to mould the child according to their tribal culture. Many tribals train their youths to be sane, specialized, moral, co-operative and responsible persons.

The main aim of Vedic education and Brahmanical education, though it was imparted to two upper varnas, was to socialize and to prepare them to guide and protect the rest of the population. This was done through the religious, discourses and social services by inculcating a same moral behaviour in all citizens. This type of education was based on homogenity.

Hereclitus said that the change is inevitable, he it a social or economic or cultural or epistemic change. As the time passed on, there has been a change in all areas. Man's nature is acquisitive being a greedy living being, the necessity is mother of invention for new things. The man has been continuously trying to exploit the natural resources for his use and comfort. He invented many things. Due to the development of Science and technology there has been a remarkable progress in all fields. Industrialization took place which entailed modernization, hedonism and xenophilism. Even though the thrust of man did not satisfied. The man started capturing the lands of other people and made these people his subjects. After this the man overtly or covertly tried to keep the captured territories under this control. He tried to force his will through improving his language and culture on his subjects. The weak always surrender before the strong. The people of the captured counties accepted the language and culture of their masters and their system of education and language. This brought cultural diffusion and the people of the captured countries got acultured.

The same thing happened in India. English people imposed their system of formal education for killing the Indian culture and keeping the Indian slave forever. Everybody knows what has happened due to the imposition alien system of education. What is condition of Indian social milieu. We Indians more or less totally renounced over national culture. We are now totally accultured. Our present formal system of education has not any place for exculturation of the Youth. The Indian society has totally become materialistic. The industrialists always aspire for their own interests. The corruption has become so rampant that nobody is safe. In the past we used to worship the virgin girls. Now-a-days they are the prime victims of molestations, rapes, dowry deaths, kidnapping of girls for ransom has become common feature. Joint family system has been totally crumbled, Neighbourly sociability has been totally vanished. There is no respect for the elders. Parents are always found in rat-race of money earning for making their hedonistic needs and demands. They do not have any time for educating and enculturating their children.

Our present system of education is entirely based on examination system which breeds cut throat competition. There is no place in school curriculum for enculturation, moral building and sociability. The school principals are forced to show good examination result. If any school fails to show good examination results, the school is warned. Only there is a craze for excellent marks. The parents also are always for good examinations results. The political parties which are governing the never think of national culture. Now the only hope lies with the teacher to save our youngers from the virus of acculluration. Keeping the fact in view it has become necessary to improve our educational system and give due place to the teacher in our educational system.

2

Education

"What sculpture is to a block of marble, Education is to the soul".

—*Addition*

Education is a recovery, Mere passing of information can never be education. Joetibhai Desai said that "a child can not be taught, he/she can be brought up" so education is a process of bringing out the hidden potentialities of the child. Therefore, for educating the children, a process should be applied which may innovate and motivate them to think, reason, comprehend, analyze and finally learn by upsurging and bringing out their hidden knowledge. While doing so the teacher should use the torch of freedom, which should be carefully nurtured and passed on to the younger generation, so as to enable the students to prove their dedication, sincerity, integrity, devotion and eradication in learning and knowing thing. For detailed knowledge about education it is necessary to know further.

GENESIS OF EDUCATION

By studying dictionaries and encyclopedias we come to know the etymology of the word 'education'. The English word 'Education' is a derivation of Latin words—'Educare', meaning to help in 'coming up' or 'to raise' or 'to dig out', or 'to bring up'. Likewise the Sanskrit word 'vidya' has come out from the Sanskrit word 'vidh' meaning 'raising' (उभारना). The word 'Siksha' has come out from the Sanskrit root 'Sikhs' meaning to bring up from within. Also the Arabic word Talim = Ta+alim means 'self learning from within.

From the above descriptions it can be inferred that 'Education is a process of leading out or bringing out what is already with in.

But the question arises what is to be brought out, from where it is to be brought out or raised? There are mythological descriptions and interpretations in our Hindu and Greek mythologies about the concept of 'education', which also have been repudiated by later empirical thinkers. Aryans believed that the human soul is immortal. It does not die when physical body of the person dies. In Hindu 'Sankhya yoga Darshan' (संख्या योगा दर्शन)it is stated that every social which is embodied in a physical person is part of a 'Bigger soul' which is termed as 'Paramatma' or a 'Transcendental Person'. So, there is a duality of 'soul'. One is a 'Transcendental soul', that is, 'Paramatma' (परमात्मा) what we equate or presume with Almighty God. Another is 'Atma' (आत्मा) or individual soul (जिवात्मा) which is embodied in every physical persons body. It is believed, that the individual soul is part of a bigger. 'Whole', that is, 'Paramatma' (परमात्मा). When the physical body of a man gets exhausted and goes old the atma (जिवात्मा) leaves the body and after some time it comes to another body. This process is termed as transmigration of the human soul, which is termed as rebirth (पुर्नजन्म). And the soul (जिवात्मा) is immortal.

The Atma or soul (जिवात्मा) while embodied accumulates the experiences gained by it through the sense organs of the body in which the soul is embodied. What we remember, we remember, what was experienced and stored by the soul. According to Greek thinkers, the recovery of these accumulated experiences, which has been stored by the soul in its previous embodied life and previously further supplemented through experiences, is a process of Education. This recovery is done through educating or getting out these experience through the process of teaching done by the teacher.

It is also believed that the Greeks came to know about the immortality of the soul from Indians. It is believed as described by a Russian mythologist; it may be true or a mere hunch or a pure imagination, that during the rule of Greek king Perciles (543 B.C.), the Spartans used to create troubles for their neighboures as many of the countries are still doing in the present days. Ultimately war errupted between Greeks and Spartans which continued for 27 years (431-404 B.C.). This war is known as Pelosenian war. Perciles made military service compulsory for all able bodied Greeks between the age of 18 years to 40 years by imposing law of conscription. This was a kind of an emergency declaration.

There existed individual difference in all times, some Greeks liked to fight some did not. Some went to war front unwillingly. Those who did not dare to go to war front tried to escape. There was one Greek sophists (name not known) who escaped from military duty and fled to Egypt where he tried to know why people fight each other. Getting no satisfactory answer he went to Mesopotamia (present Iraq) from Egypt where he was advised to go to Taxila in India for getting a suitable answer. From Mesopotamia he finally came to India via Aryana (present Iran) and Gandhara (present Afghanistan). Both these countries were Aryan Countries and had blood relations with India. He stayed at Taxila for about eight years. He studied all Hindu scriptures, that is, all Indian philosophical Hindu theistic schools i.e. Sankhya-yoga, Naya vaishishka and Vedant and Advitvedant and all atheistic schools i.e. Buddhism, Jainism and Carvaka, all Upanishads, Arynakas (आर्यनाका), Brahmans, Ramayana, Mahabharata and Shrimad Bhagwat Gita. He participated in all Gurukula activities at Taxila and finally he came to know that the human soul is immortal as various Indian philosophical schools adhere to.

According to Indians the human soul is permanent, invisible, imperishable, indestructible and is part of the permanent soul which is called 'Paramatma' (परमात्मा). All individual souls (जिवात्मायें) are part of a bigger 'whole', that is Parmatma or God. Therefore, all individual souls (जिवात्मायें) are immortal. Prime or Supreme Soul is present in all bodies, as such all human beings are true representations of God and are equal. This is why Indian society rests on the foundation of equality and is a homogenous society. The individual's soul or Jiwatma (जिवात्मा) takes work from the body. It acquires experiences through the sense organs of the body and accumulates these experiences with it. Bringing out these experiences from the human soul or brain is called 'Education'. As for digging earth some instruments like spade (फावड़ा) are required, for bringing out old human experiences some methods like teaching and using teaching aids are required.

The Greek Sophist after staying at Takshila about eight years, and knowing that human soul is immortal and never dies, this is why Arjun after listing sermons of Gita from Bhagwan Krishna fought and won Mahabharta war, he went back to Greece to participate in Pelosenian War. He went to king Perciles and offered himself to go to the war front. He told to the king that the human soul neither dies nor is destroyed. Only human body dies. Therefore, there is no reason to be afraid of war. With this adhoration the Greeks got encrouged. They fought the war against Spartans. They not only defeated the spartans but totally eliminated them. And the terror of Spartans was eliminated for ever.

This message was picked up by other Greek Sophists and philosophers. They started thinking why individuals soul (जिवात्मा) or Jivatma does not die and is immortal? Socrates (470-399 B.C.) was an original thinker, speculator and philosopher. He used to think speculate himself and discuss all ontological, teleological, epistemical, metaphorical axiological and sociological problems with his disciples in the street corners. Plato, Crito, Socrates, Hereclitus, Isocrtes and Paremdes were his some important disciples with whom he used to discuss all important matters. His wife Xentippe did not allow Socrates to permit entry of his disciples or any outsider in his house. If any body dared to enter the house, she used to power a full pot of cold water over his head. Socrates was very conscious to know about the reality of Indian concept of immortality of the soul, so he discussed such a ontological question with his disciples in the street corner before his house.

Indians merely said that the human soul is immortal. It can not be destroyed. But no concrete proof about the immortality of the soul is available in Indian scriptures. Also, no concrete proof in this regard has been advanced by the later seers. The Greeks were eager to know why the soul does not die along with the human body? Socrates discussed this ontological question at length with his disciples and finally came to believe that the human soul is actually immortal. Later on his disciple Plato after the death of his teacher Socrates compiled the dialogues of Socrates with his disciples. These dialogues covered all problems mentioned above relating to truth beauty, justice, ontology, epistemology, axiology. The dialogues which covered immortality of the soul and consequent emergence the concept of education at length and three proofs were advanced proving the immortality of soul. These are: (1) Law of Contrariness, (2) Law of Form and (3) Law of Reminiscence.

Law of Contrariness

Every thing in this world comes and goes. One who was born and brought up will positively die. Like sun rises in the morning and sets in the evening, and everyday is taken by another day, every might is followed by another night. And all living beings, plants, flora and fauna come and go. The life of a person comes and ought to go. As such, life follow death and death follow life. There is continuous circle of coming and going. And this circle always entail contrariness. There is some transcendental element which keeps this coming and going continued, and gives life to physical world. This transcendental element is nothing but soul (जिवात्मा) which is part of omnipresent, non-visible and indestructible 'whole' and is immortal. This is 'Paramatma' or Super Soul or God. Therefore, soul (जिवात्मा) is immortal.

Law of Form

Since every thing in the world is temporary, illusionary and perishable; this temporiness has a permanent base or image else where; this idea is analogous to Indian idea of 'Maya' and 'stirtha' (Permanence). The things or lives which we see in this world are all temporary, illusory and perishable. And a permanent base of these things or lives resides else where, which is invisible, permanent and Transcendental Form. This idea of permanent Form is analogous to Indian idea 'Supreme Soul' (Parmatma) or God, which has imbibed all individual souls. In other words, all individual souls are parts of a bigger 'whole', that is Almighty God. The individuals soul, which is paramount, governs the human body.

Law of Reminiscence

We remember many things. How do you remember? What is the power that makes us to remember? It is the soul (जिवात्मा). Since it does not die, it keeps the experience stored with it. It is due to enlightment of the soul we remember all past experiences. Therefore, the soul is permanent imperishable, undestroyable and immortal. The process of education is nothing but remembrance of the past experiences. It is a recovery of what is already with the soul.

In Indian 'Naya Vaishiska Darshan' (philosophy) a more advance convincing argument is available in this regard. The Naya Vaishiska Darshan argues that we only remember till we are alive. A dead body can not remember. We remember what we had experienced through sense perception in the past. We perceive through our body parts, that is sense organs—ears, nose, touch, taste and smell. But, the moment the human body dies, that is, sense organs neither perceive nor the human brain or head remembers. Then what is the force behind remembering? It is nothing but human soul. Till the human soul resides in the human body, the body can see, hear smell, taste, touch and ember. When the body dies the soul goes with the already acquired experiences and resides in other body. Taking out these already acquired experiences is nothing but 'education'. This is done through remembering.

Various thinkers have defined 'education' on these lives, though they do not attribute creditability to he soul for all of our learning and education. Even Plato did not attribute direct creditability to the soul for the emergence of education. He said that education is the result of sense perception plus comprehension. Sense perception leads to comprehension, learning and knowledge. Aristolle laid stren on the analysis of the matter. Rene' Deserts believed in innate ideas and laid stren on thinking for taking out the innate ideas which are possessed by the human body at he time of birth. He had faith on thinking. He believed that he existed due to "Cogito Ergo Sum:", that is, thinking and reasoning. British Empiricist, philosopher John Locke repudiated the rationalistic theory of Rene' Descartes. He believed that the mind of the child at the time his/her birth is blank like a blank 'Tabula Rasa' (slate). As child grows, he/she perceives and gets primary and secondary ideas through perception. As such, the individual is born without any previous knowledge or experience. He perceives and gathers knowledge. At the time of birth individuals mind is like a blank state. As such, John Locke's thinking is against the hidden knowledge stored by the human soul. For him main source of knowledge is experience. And the teacher while teaching the students should provide experience sincerely and strictly. And John Locke termed this process as hardening in education. A few quotation of thinkers on education are given below:

"Education is a training which leads you " to hate what you ought to hate" and "love what you ought to love"

—Plato

"Educations is the creation of a sound mind in a sound body."

—Aristotle

"Educations is defined as a natural harmoneous and development of man's inmate powers."

—Postalozzi

Education is defined as a process of development which consists of passage of human being from infancy to maturity, the process by which he adapts himself gradually, in various ways, to his physical, social, spiritual environment.

—T. Raymont

"Famous art theorist Herbest Read has also exposed the same views on education."

"Education is the manifestation of perfection already in man"

—Swami Vivekanand

"By education I mean an all round drawing out of the best in child and man, body, mind and spirit. Literacy itself is no education."

—M.K. Gandhi

"Education is the development of capacities which enable man to control his environment."

—John Dewey

"Education is to equip man to understand truth, beauty and goodness."

—Socrates

"Education is to create humbleness of blind"

—Dr. Arnold

"Education is to know what one does not know and behave well."

—John Ruskin

"Education is thought that leads to bodily expression."

—R.N. Tagore

"Education of the child should be according to nature. When the child is born he is free but after his birth he finds himself in chains. There should not he social restrictions on the child."

—*J.J. Rousseau*

"Child's education should be based on play."

—*Madam Montessori*

"Child's feeling should not he hurt. Education should lay stress on emotional development of the Child."

—*Friedrich Froebel*

As such, viewing the above opinions, it can he assumed that education is a process of development of latent or innate potentials or capabilities enshrined in the child or student; Mere passing of information or imposing one's knowledge to the students can never he education. Every child or student has his/her innate capacities and capabilities. The development of the capacities and capabilities is education. The child or a student is not an ignorant client. The nature has gifted every child or student with especial unique capabilities and capacities. In comparison to other living wings, human child or student has been rewarded with a bigger brain to think, reason, comprehend and take a decision for action. He has been rewarded with moving hands for acting and flexible feet for walking. Other animals lack all these. He can not be dictated to accept the diction of the teacher, as a patient of a doctor accepts the prescription of a doctor, or a client accept the legal advice of the lawyer. Therefore, it is essential to educate the child or student in a proper, logical manner and in congenial atmosphere while teaching, so to develop his innate capacities.

3

Educational Processes

Any kind of activity, be it social, economic, cultural theological and educational, entails a functioning process. Even the human life, which has long continuum entails a process. The child is born, brought up and encultured. He/She is made to share biohetogenity and live united with opposite life long. As such, man passes through varied stages of life—as a married householder and finally and old man or woman. Like wise education is also a perennial life long system and processes. The educational system also affected by biological, social, economic, cultural, political and in many case by theological factors; and human life is affected. As such, for successful implementation of any type of educational process there is a need for a careful study of the past history of the educational system of the country and also country's present sociological economic, cultural, political and theological structures, of the society. Then only appropriate educational process can be thought of and adopted.

The process of learning in the whole animal world starts from the very early stage. Generally, education is imparted, from the very beginning, non-formally and informally in familial way and finally formally. It we peep into the educational history we find all these processes. Familial education starts in the family at a very early stage. In old cultures and civilizations the familial education was prominent. The mother of the child used to play a prominent role in familial education. the informal education also starts very early within peer group. It is seen that not only human beings, but also animals, birds, insects and bees educate their younger once informally. Thereafter non-formal education is imported by the family elders. In non-formal education, the youngers learns a lot through per. se. (perceptions). All artizens and service class train their youngers in their family occupations non formally. Because India is caste ridden society, occupations are followed on caste lines. A son of carpenter till now, used to follow his hereditary occupation. As such, the wards of hereditary artizens used to be highly skilled artizens. The wards of artizens used to learn in a perspective spectrum, in which they used to observe their elders while working. they used to observe all kinds of raw materials and tools used in making of things. One of the top-most advantage of hereditary way of non-formal education was availability of regular employment. Hereditary non-formally trained artizens did not require to knock the door of employment exchanges. Due to the concept of upper castes and lowest castes and related concept of purity and pollution and, resultant consequent concept sanskritization, the wards of artizen castes evaded their familial non-formal hereditary training and shifted to another occupations. The hereditary trained artizens are very few in the society now. Indian non-formal system of Indian education was not only liked but was appreciated by many foreigners in olden days also in the recent past. While Lord Macualey was trying to impose the western type of formal education on the Indians, the then Governor of Punjab (now half has gone to Pakistan) had objected to formal education. He supported the Indian old system of education i.e. non-formal education for the artizen castes and formal education for the upper castes. He said that by these system the Indian would retain their culture.

These are three recognized process of education, (1) informal education, (2) non-formal education and (3) formal education. Not only in India but in the whole world the formal education is predominant. All educational institutions follow the formal system of education is few achieving a stipulated national educational aims. What are these aims will be discussed later on. First it is necessary to know what is a 'form'? A form is a structured shape. The word form is a derivation of French and Latin words 'forma' meaning a configuration of physical things or a 'shapes' given by a man or men by composing different things together. In other words a 'form' is composition pr configurated shape of a thing. By putting or joining physical things together a form is created, which has a desired shape is form. Formal process is also applied in many fields—such as in forming social, political, theological structures in addition to educational system. In social structure formal system is applied to make a sane society. In political field the politicians apply formal system develop a curtsy of loyal followers. But in education field the rulers want to create any army of loyal followers who could follow and adhere to the ideology of the rulers. Recent dilemma of N.C.E.R.T. books published for school children has exposed this tendency. Besides the rulers want to create army of loyal works. For achieving these ends the school formal education is designed accordingly. As such the formal education is a system of shaping the future guardian as per need of the day. As such 'formal system of Education' is an applied system of education. By formal method of education the educator tries to shape the future guardian according to the suitable norms which may fulfill the desired ends.

The theory of formalism immerged in early twentieth century. First impact of formalism can best be seen in the field of creative aesthete things. Later on the concept of formalism covered he hedonistic things. When an artist creates a thing he gives a shape to it. In the beginning the shape was given by the artists for his emotional satisfactions without any material inclination. The art form is a combination of some symbols. The symbols are composed together to represent some ideas in shapes. The shapes have virtuality. It can be said that form is a structured shape. In other words a 'form' may be said new creation. It can be a self creation or an impositions. Due to industrialization art form are commercialized. Because of this change of formalism in art, in other areas also the original forms are changed. Due to flux in formality the rulers and administration designed the system of education through which they could materialize their objectives. As such, in education social, cultural and spiritual objective are generally ignored. Formal and hedonistic objective are thought or chalked out in advance and preferred and according to these activities school curriculum is planned in advance and the students are taught according in schools. The school system of formal education is the latest process of education which is done through teaching. The teaching is done by the teacher. The syllabus of the school is so heavy that it keeps both the students and teachers very busy. The teaching process in school in school is more or less information passing process. The teacher is always at the giving end and the students are at the receiving end. Whereas, the teaching should be a two way process through which the teacher could ignite a thought process in the minds of the students. The school should create a situation which may expose the students to epistemic atmosphere and the students may be innovated and motivated to think, reason, and analyse; and then can learn through inquiry. For an inquiry, thinking is essential. Thinking, leads to reasoning. If we look to the etymological aspects of education, education is nothing but bringing out which is already there.

Therefore, it is essential that while educating the students, both at school and university levels teaching should be improved keeping in mind the bringing out hidden perspective. This can he done if teaching is based on activities. At the school level it is essentials. Because activity based teaching always motivates for thinking, reasoning and comprehending. A the university level it is also necessary. The students should be encouraged to do self-learning and inquiry. It is necessary, that the teaching at school level, being the starting point of learning, should always he primarily be educative which can be done through igniting thinking process. For educative teaching thinking is essential. And for educating learning for things are essential (1) the motivation of the students for self-learning (2) their involvement in activities relating to subjects they intending to learn (3) the mode of presentation during the course of teaching should be elicitation oriented based on healthy and cordial teacher taughts interaction and (4) the students should not be mere receivers they should be givers also. In addition to this there should be a system of feed back. Therefore, if is essential that the mode of presentation in the class room should always be based on bi-polar communicative system. Necessary care should be taken that system of education should be so designed that no deserving candidates he denied expression. Good education is that which apply deductive process and allows students to contribute in the knowledge development. Such process of education will always satisfy the ego of the students. When a student contributes and does a new thing in the class room during the course of teaching process, he/she is not only satisfied but is over thrilled and overwhelmed with his/her achievement. This also ads to the personality development of the students. For such an educational recovery it is necessary to use some tools skillfully. What are these tools? These are nothing but audio-visuals aids. The use of teaching aids always entail rapport between the teacher and taughts. Education is two way process which should always involve active participation of both the teacher and taughts. It is, therefore, effective participation of both is necessary.

In fact all teaching processes involve the communication of ideas, through sense perception and through the medium of speech, and also by use of written or printed material. Our sense organs are gate way of knowledge. All of our sense organs help us in understanding the environment around us, and thereafter lead us to comprehending it. Hearing and seeing are most important in this respect. We understand and learn by both. But by seeing we learn quickly. So providing direct experiences in educating the children are necessary. These help in completing the triangular process of learning viz. motivation, stimulation and comprehension possible. These further help in establishing a channel between the learner and things that are worth of learning. The assumption in learning is, what we understand through hearing we forget bit by bit. It is considered important in the field of education.

If we look etymologically, to both the concepts, the teaching and education, though have different meanings, are supplementary to each other and go hand in glove. Without teaching education can never be possible and without education teaching is fruitless.

For this end deductive approach is to be applied while teaching, which would entail correct use of teaching methods and proper application of teaching aids. Above all re-organising and revitalizing of present curriculum will be necessary. Our present educational approach is only examination oriented. The life building approach in our present educational system does not get priority and is missing. Along with learning and knowing, essential approaches, like self-searching or introspection, socialising and moralizing for amicable living in society all are necessary. For this there should be a space for enculturation in our educational system.

What is seen in the present society is that the man is mad after material gains. The axiological aims are always ignored. Our educational system only aims at good examination results and which is not for sane future citizens. This is why we daily notice, loot, dacoities, burglaries, molestations, rapes and murders in the society. Our educational system is blind to these problems. This situation has emerged because of blind modernization due to westernisation and consequent acculturation. This has brought mechanized industrialization. Westernization has devastated

Indian cottage industries which had a hoary past. Due to all this, our old social institutions like joint family system, brethern community life and moral life are disappearing day by day. We are bankrupt in our cultural development as our enculturation process is disappearing day by day. Our educational system only aims at producing the younger generation in a way as factories produce nuts and bolts. If our educational structure is not re-organized and educational aims are not reformed, we will totally loose our culture which has already been damaged to a large extent by alien system of formal education imposed by Lord Macauly nearly one hundred and seventy two years ago. So our present educational system needs immediate reformation.

The teacher is a main functionary in the process of education of our children. The education is as old as society. The present teacher is the successor of our old Gurus, who were the enculturators and social builders of the nation. They were epistemic. Our present teacher should be grateful to the old teachers and should repay the debt to the old teachers. This can be done by using the professional ethics of the teaching profession. The present teacher should be epistemic like our old Gurus. They should proficiate, should take care of their clients, that is, students. Above all they should be non-inclinative as were our old Gurus (teachers). For achieving this the present teacher should use better teaching methods supplemented by the use of teaching aids. The teacher should keep in mind that they are not only servants of teaching institutions. They are more than that they are the builders of our future guardians. They should realize that the area of their teaching job is much more wider. It is not limited upto teaching only. They should try to enculturate students by inculcating axiological and sociological values in the children. They should apprise the students about simple living and high thinking.

Now-days there is a wave of instantivity in achieving material gains in every sphere of life. This is because of advancement of science and technology and thereby unprecedent increase in production of consumer goods resulting a hedonistic way of life. So present system of education affected badly the important aspects of life like cultural, sociological, religious and political. For material and hedonistic gains man has totally forgotten the tenets of religions. Daily prayer are missing. These are replaced by weekly *Satsangs* on the western pattern of weekly prayers in churches service as was designed by St. Calvin in the wake of industrialization. For material gains the man, day by day, is loosing humanity and is adopting animal nature of irrationality. He is becoming more and more greedy, irrational, self-centred, orthodox and fundamentalist, which generate unbreakable tension in the society as well as in the nations. What is happening in the world we all very well know. The terrorists activity by czechish in a Russian school resulting death of 400 innocent school children is proof of this. True and sane education can solve all such barbaric problems. Indian old education solved such problem not only in India, but in Asian Countries like China, Japan, Indonesia, Sri Lanka and other east Asian countries.

Uptill early twentieth century the formal education was imparted by the teacher to the student directly. The mode of communication was verbal and that too was one way. The teacher was considered a man of knowledge, a man of character having limited needs necessary for his subsistence. As such, the teacher was devoted to his profession. He used to acquire knowledge by reading library books and from his own experience. Through there were chances of interaction between the teacher and his disciples, but due to alien concept of formal education this was minimum. as such more or less they students used to be passive listeners. And there was very little scope for the students to think, reason, and comprehend to what was taught to them. On the country our old Brahmanical system of education was based on 'Vad' and 'Vivad', that is systematic discussion, between the learned people, the teachers (Guru) and the students. As such our present formal process of education has no place for informal as well as non-formal processes of education. It is bookish. Its products are mere receivers and cramers. Our formal process of education has also made our teachers and educational administrators formal. They have to performed their duty in mere formal way as other governments servants do, setting aside the life building process. They can, in many cases, be compared with the workshop machenics who deal with the lifeless material.

Not only the teachers and educational administrators have become formal but the parents have also become formal. They have forgotten that its home where the education of the child starts in informal and non-formal ways. They only aspire to earn more and more. Husband and wife both go out of home for doing jobs. With the result they have to push their young children to creches and day care schools. When they come home tired they try to use the electronic media T.V. and radio for mitigating their long fatigue. How can they stop their children to see unnecessary T.V. programmes? Our educational system can not he improved until the craze for undue earning is stopped and mother is motivated to do familial education. The mother should carry on familial education till the child is ready to bear the burden of living alone.

No doubt, the present formal educational process is good for good performance in examination, which is suited to get employment in present technological competitive industrial age. But one should not forget that an individual besides an earning member is also a member of big social whole, that is society. He/she, can only survive, if the social whole that is society, survives. For the survival of the society there has to be certain rules, regulation, customs tradition, institutions and culture. One can not survive without these social requirements. Without these the man will go back to the barbarous age. Nature in the entire animal world has rewarded the man with some special human faculties that is bigger brain for thinking and reasoning and comprehending and also future planning. Nature has also given man movable hands and erect posture for acting and walking. But the man has also been loaded with too much greed and acquisitiveness than other animals. Therefore, there is a dire necessary to educate the man and woman for saneful living. Our educational system should have a process to educate the future guardians for warding off the present social evils like unsociability, material craze corruption. The educational system should generate harmony through love and affection. Therefore, our educated system should be so designed which should bring cultural homogenity in the society for harmonious living. It should generate an atmosphere of economic prosperity. Also education should create conditions for individual dignity, integrity, honesty, social security, freedom to adhere individuals own traditions, customs and religious beliefs. The dominant sections of the society should not impose their will on the weaker sections of the society. Education should also generate a sense of tolerance, team spirit brotherhood, unity. These aim can only be achieved with a sense of simple living and high thinking.

Acquisitive possessive and individualistic human personality is the gift of capitalistic society. This has damaged the humanistic values. Proper education can relieve our youngsters of this human evil. The education process should nurture a spirit of diligence, professional competence and, also a spirit of human care in younger generation. All these will create a social consciousness in them. The explosion of knowledge added more burden on the school teachers and, as well as, on the children. In view of all this, the quality of education needs reformation and the teacher will have to bear the burden of it.

The teachers have to work in hostile educational atmosphere, excluding cynism, despair and unrecognition. Even the students in many cases do not respect their teachers. These days the teaching profession do not get due recognition in the society. Inspite of all this the teachers should be proud of teaching profession. Professor Amrik Singh said that modern teaching community suffer from self-inflicted wounds. The educational historical and evolutionary growth added the miseries of the teaching community. Main trouble lies in teaching and learning process. The teaching should look to the creative teachers like S/Shri R.N. Tagore, Shri Aurobindo, C.V. Raman, J.N. Kapoor, Pandit Madan Mohan Malviya, Mahatma Gandhi, Dr. Zakir Hussain, Sarva Palli Radhakrishnan J. Krishnamurti and many other creative teachers who had adopted innovative and creature methods in teaching. Also the teacher preparation institute like Central Institute of Education, Delhi should be established on large scale in the country. The teachers in such institutes should follow the foot steps of late Professor A.N. Basu and Late Professor Dr. E.A. Pires former Principals of the Central Institute of Education, Delhi. Education should be self-propelling force. Edward shills in his paper "Academic Profession in India" remarked that "Indian Community has shown its incapacity to do hard work in doing persistent academic work to build up an academic community. They lacked academic professional ethics which could have brought a social change."

As such, the teacher is the builder of the nation will have to play a vital role in revitalizing the present rottened alien and unsuitable formal educational structure, so as to bring a dynamic desirable social change in Indian society through appropriate educational process of teaching. The teacher is the epicentre of enculturation. The teachers can revive the Indian Culture.

But the teacher alone can not reform the present crippled alien formal process of education. The rulers, the parents, the administrators and the whole society should examine the present alien educational process and find out its merits and demerits and should take necessary steps to reform and improve the present educational system. It is the result of the present system that our sportsmen could not do anything in Olympic games in Athens 2004. They returned home with shame. This happened because in our present educational process does not give any due place to the sports. Likewise, there are many activities like art activities which are necessary for enculturation do not get proper place in school curriculum. Due to examination fever extra-co-curricular activities also do not take place in schools and students remain unaware about the national culture.

4

Evolution of Teaching in Education

Education of the young, by teaching, existed in all times, at all stages, and in all societies. As a matter of fact the education is inherent in animal blood, and there is an inbuilt system of learning. As such, educating the youngs is found not alone in human beings, but also in other animals beasts, birds and insects. Since human beings are rational animals they are more conscious and concerned for the growth and development of their future guardians. This is because, human beings are prone to their dependency on their offsprings, in their old age and also in unhealthy stages in their lives. They have an intense desire to bring up their youngers from the very begging very carefully. So the teaching in human societies is as old as human evaluation.

In the earlier stages of human evolution and the evolution of human society there existed parental or familial education through teaching. And earlier civilizations as of Mesopotamia, Egypt, Greece, Israel, India and China were the product of familial education. With the passage of time, the human society became more complex, the other elders of the community started teaching the children of those who were unable to teach their children. So, the parents, elders, peer groups priests and wisemen have traditionally been teaching the younger generation. They took teaching as their pious duty by passing on their knowledge and skills to next generation. As, Aristotle put it, the sanest sign of human wisdom is one's ability to teach what he knows. According to Hindu traditions 'teaching is one of the best giving (Dan दान) and knowing is the safest wealth which can not be stolen. Knowing, doing, teaching and learning were considered pious activities in many societies. And these are still important activities in all societies. These are indistinguishable from one other. In all societies, the induction of the youngs into acting doing, feeling, thinking, reasoning, comprehending, learning and believing were the features on which social progress depended. These epistemic features were passed to youngers by the elders informally through personal contacts, by sharing common activities, through myths, legends, folk feelings and beliefs, customs, art and crafts and culture. Formal ceremonies as 'yogopavita dharan' paved the way acquiring the skills from the elders by observing and imitating the elders. And the young used to enter the tribal life and participate in day today activities.

Formally, the schools were established in City (Sloles) in Greece. In India also such formal schools existed in the form of Gurukulas. Many of these Gurukulas like Taxila, Ujaini, Vikaramshila, Sandipti, Vallabhi etc. were famous learning centres. These Gurukulas existed prior to Greek schools. In these schools neither the teachers were trained nor any particular prescribed methods of teaching were applied. The teachers of these Gurukulas were learned, epistemic and sincere to teaching profession. Their prime aim of education or teaching was to pass on their entire knowledge to their Shishyas (students) without any inclination. Also such condition continued in other civilized countries for centuries through out the world. Prior to 19th Century a little attention was given to the teaching methods as distinct form and the textbooks. Right from the Gurukulas till 18th century generally the teacher was not required to obtain a degree neither in subject nor in teaching, though the institution of University existed earlier and, the institution of school came into existence much later. Only the exposition of the teachers' ability was necessary which was usually developed and discovered through seminars discussions and debates. This reinforced the necessity of the teacher. In medieval world this necessity was felt more and efforts were made for evolving the methods of teaching and organization of knowledge. In older times, in the west, the qualifications and functions of the teacher were decided by the Church. Likewise the abilities of the Guru (the teacher) in Gurukulas in India were decided by the Kulacharyas of the Gurukulas. Later on, in Muslim period the abilities of Talibs (Teachers) in Madarsas were decided by the head/Walid of the Madarsas. Now it is the duty of the state. In the West Church Bishop used to decide about the certification for the teacher. In 1559 Queen Elizabeth I extended it to England

and issued a notification prohibiting any one from teaching with a required. Certificate from Bishop which was granted only after an examination of the applicants learning and dexterity in teaching. In addition to this sobriety, honesty, communication, skills personal qualities were necessary. After the industrial revolution schools emerged as distinctive institutions for mass education.

Now, what is essential for most of the societies in Europe, America, Africa and Asia is to provide a substantial period for formal education for all and, not for a small proportion of the population, who generally become political, social and religious leaders in the society. Our Gurukulas system of education was by and large was a scheme of education for such a small segment of population. The logic behind such a segmental scheme of education was social stratification on caste lines. The artizen castes or business castes or service castes were deprived of Gurukula education. They were trained in their respective trades and vocations by their elders and parents non-formally involving the youngsters in their hereditary trades. In the west too, only rich feudal and rich affluent classes could get a chance for higher education. The people involved in technical trades used to get training in guilds, working with guild masters.

Now the situation is altogether different. Every child is entitled to go to school when he/she attains the age of fire and remains at the school until 17 or 18 years of age. Not only this there are many commercial educational shops as creches, nursery schools, preparatory schools where children of two to five years of age are admitted. Now-a-days children do not get time to play. The variety of educational patterns require trained teachers in all fields. The government spend a substantial amount on teacher training. Many social voluntary organizations of the society also contribute in this novel enterprise, but under the tight control of the State.

The 'teacher' means, one who teaches and work in school. The schools are establishments for teaching for education in the areas considered necessary for upbringing, socialising and enculturaring the youngsters. Such education is given in school upto the age of 18. Thus, the education refers to the structure, or institutions where the future teachers are trained for teaching profession. There are various categories of teachers as—necessary school teachers, primary school teachers, secondary and senior secondary school teachers, technical teachers for industrial training institutes and

Polytechnic, Lecturer, and Profession of Colleges, Technical Colleges and I.I.Ts. Teacher training, therefore is one of the most important activities in the field of education as teacher is considered a national builder.

Modern structure of teacher education is the gift of the west. Evolution of teacher and training had started there. Almost all western countries had adopted the system of formal education after industrialization. Many have opened schools for teaching the children 3R's, so the demand of teachers had also increased. As the infrastructure of the school increased. Many of the schools are going to be commercialized under the formal education, so the demand of teachers increased. As such, the teacher preparation has also increased. Many teacher training institutes have also emerged.

The present formal education is the gift of western countries. Due to industrialization these countries first searched the markets for the sale of their industrial products. Thereafter, these countries got hold over the countries where their goods were sold. Later on these countries were forced to accept their culture of which education was one of the important tool for acculturation. The western industrialists continued to search the new markets for their industrial products which entailed formal education and thereby the process of acculturation, which was necessary for the consolidation of their power. Due to this, ultimately system of formal education and formal teaching became a permanent feature throughout the world. And for this the teacher and school became most important tools for spreading the formal education. The present process of formal education is nothing but a copy of the western system of formal education. Our schools function in western style. And the teachers for the schools are trained according to this style. In the beginning there used to be one teachers training school in each district which was called 'Normal School'. The contents of the 'Normal Schools' for teacher training contained: (1) educational theory, (2) educational psychology, (3) elementary history of education (4) methodology of teaching younger children and (5) some elements of extra co-curricular activities and, sports which had 'Kabadi', wrestling and hockey. The day's teaching started with morning assembly which also contained a common prayer. After the dyarchy system which allowed some freedom by the Britishers in 1935 some elements of handwork, (6) spinning by Takli, some clay work and weaving was introduced under Basic Education. This was what, the writer had experienced when he was a student in his village primary school in Uttar Pradesh in late thirties of the nineteenth century before the World War II. The teachers were awarded J.B.T. certificate by National Schools. They were appointed in District Board Administered primary schools. Some Basic Teacher's Institutes like one at Patna, one at Wardha, Jamia Millia Islamia, Delhi and a few at places were established. These basic education institutes became redundant after the death of the Father of the Nation. Late Shri M.K. Gandhi as the then Government headed by Late Pt. Jawaharlal Nehru followed the formal education imposed on India by the alien British rulers. Basic education prepared by Gandhiji was based on co-relation, morality, co-operation, homogeneity and manual work. These were supposed to bring self-sufficiency and enculturation in the society. Such a good scheme of education was buried by then Government along with the cremation of the Father of the Nation Late Shri M.K. Gandhi. The then rulers could not anticipate the dire consequences of formal education.

The British Government, in order to spread their scheme of formal education for achieving their desired ends of acculturation and raising a faithful class, established High Schools and Intermediate Colleges, atleast one in each district. These schools were governed by the Director Public Instructions in every province stationed at provincial Head Quarters. After independence the Directions of Public Instructions were redesignated as the Director of Education. But their infrastructure and functioning remained the same as it was earlier. The number of schools increased in due course of time. The schools functioned in old style. The requirement of teachers also increased.

After 1857, revolt against East India Company by the Indians for ousting the Britishers, the Indian administration was taken over by the British Govt. through an ordinance issued by Queen Victoria which was later approved by the British Parliament, and the Queen of England became the Emperroress of India. And thereafter the British Government introduced many reforms including educational reforms. Few Universities were established. The Universities of Calcutta, Madras, Bombay, Allahabad and Punjab (Lahore now in Pakistan) were established to provide bureaurucrats for government offices. Some of the graduates of these universities preferred teaching. These universities opened teacher training departments which awarded degree of Bachelor of Teaching (BT) which enabled the successful candidates to be appointed as teachers in government schools.

Immediately after the independence Late Shri Maulana Abul Kalam Azad took an innovative step in teacher training. He felt that old traditional methods of teaching will not serve the purpose. He visualized the need of a modern educational institute in India which could serve as a beacon light in the field of education and teacher training and, thereafter in service teacher refresher course training. He also felt need of enculturation impetus in teacher training programme. Main dream in Maulana Azad's mind was to nullify the virus of acculturation impact created by our school system which is the result of formal type of alien system of education imposed by Lord Macaulay in 1833 A.D. to keep Indians loyal to Britishers for ever. And to mitigate this foreign virus Late Maulana Abdul Kalam Azad thought of Central Institute of Education, Delhi. He laid the foundation of this Institute on 19th December, 1948 at Old D.R.D.O. Office, 33 Chhatra Marg, University of Delhi, Delhi-7. In the beginning 'Bachelor of Teaching' was started which was later-on named as Bachelor of Education in 1952. In due course of time Master of Education, Doctor of Philosophy (Education), Master of Philosophy, Diploma Vocational and Educational Guidance and Diploma in Textbook Research were also introduced. Central Institute of Education was managed by the Government of India upto 31st August 1962. And while it was under the Government of India, it was considered one of the top most educational Institutes of Asia. It had Department of Educational and Vocational Guidance, Department of Text Research, Department of Extension Services, Department of Art Education, Experimental Basic School and Mini-workshop for making audio-aids, teaching crafts and for designing school equipments and furniture. All these departmental infra-structure was the result of vision of Late Prof. A.B. Basu and Late Professor E.A. Pires former principals C.I.E. When the Institute was transferred to National Council of Education Research and Training on 1-9-62, Professor Pires resigned and joined U.N.O. Since then the C.I.E. is where every body knows. C.I.E. culture was praised throughout India. When once Late Dr. Piers, when he was educational advisor to U.N., visited C.I.E. and addressed the C.I.E. staff and students he said that "one student of C.I.E. is equal to one hundred students of any training Institute of Asia". Central Institute of Education, Delhi had functioned well till its merger with N.C.E.R.T. on 1-9-62 and later on with the Delhi University on 1-5-74. Under the leadership of its two former Principals Late Professor A.N. Basu and Late Professor Dr. E.A. Pires and also. Later on under the leadership of Late Professor P.K. Roy it functioned very well and tried to fulfill the dreams of Late Maulana Abul Kalam Azad. Now it is functioning under University of Delhi as Department of Education and its original name has been prisioned. There has been many additions and deductions in the wings of C.I.E. since then, which is true in view of Late Hereclitus who had said that every things is in flux. May God give strength to the wings of the Central Institute of Education again which is now named as Department of Education, University of Delhi. In many Universities in India Departments of Education were established which produced teachers.

In this materialistic commercial age this fact can not be denied that many universities of the country in late twentieth century got commercialized. With the help of few politicians these universities opened correspondence courses. Those deserved to get B.Ed. degree had joined the B.Ed. correspondence courses in these universities. These B.Ed. correspondence courses were mere a formality and no concrete instruction were given. Practicals like practice teaching was also a mere formality. No practical work like art activities cultural activities, training in making of Audio-Visual Aids had any place in B.Ed. correspondence. The products of these course were not aware about what is black board. So the students, who were working teachers used to remain ignorant about all these pedagogic norms. Only some theoretical aspects of teacher education like (*a*) principles of education or education theory, (*b*) psychological of education (*c*) methodology of teaching (*d*) educational history were taught through correspondence. There was no space for extra-co-curricular activities which are necessary for enculturation, whereas many teacher training like C.I.E. lay stress on these activities. Finally, the National Council of Teacher Education banned the B.Ed. Correspondence courses throughout the country. Our teacher training programmes run by various Universities needs a close review. Teacher training it should lay stress on steps which could produce teachers who could infuse character building in younger generation and make them sane citizens. He/She could enculturate the students. The teacher in modern times has great responsibility when the joint family system has totally crumbled down and both the parents, because of their involvement in jobs, do not have time to enculturate their children. All cultural traits traditions, social norms of socializations, customs and spirituality are to be infused by the teacher. Therefore teacher is supposed to be a trend setter, enculturator and on the whole a builder of the future guardians. Therefore, it is essential to include a substantial programme of culture building in teaching, for which the teachers should be trained. The school authorities should give equal importance to cultural and artistic activities along the academic activities which may make the students, who are our future guardians, moral, honest duty bound, co-operative. In otherwords, through these programmes students will be enculturated. Society expect that our teachers should be duty bound and trend setters as Indian teachers were in olden times. Such exceptions can only be materialized if our educationists, and administrators also take some positive steps in this regard, set some exemplary traditions in this regard and help the schools and teacher training institutes.

Since our present system of education is an imitation of western system of education, it is necessary to peep into the historical development of evolution of the teacher education in the west. As per western teacher education evolutionary perspective, we find that it can be divided (*a*) pre-service and (*b*) in-service training. Pre-service teacher education includes all stages of education and training that precedes teachers entry to paid employment. The earliest formal arrangement for teacher preparation introduced in some German states in early 18th century which included pre-service and in service training. A seminary or normal school for training teachers for elementary school was first established, which preceded with some senior normal schools or superior normal schools for the preparation of senior teachers. These schools aimed at additional attainments as (1) acquiring knowledge of human mind, (2) principles of education as a social science (3) methods of teaching as an art. By the end of 18th century there were many such institutions in operation in Germany. The systematic teacher training was linked to an equally systematic process of certification control of teaching condiiions and in service study and training. All public teachers were required to attend a series of meetings to enhance their practical knowledge. The conference used to take place in districts bimonthly in summer, and a circle conference twice a year, annually and departmental conference once a year. Each conference was responsible for devising repetition courses for experienced teachers who want to refresh and add more to their knowledge.

In nineteenth century, development pertaining to teacher education, in U.S.A., Britain, France, Belgium and Japan owed much to the pattern that had been established in Germany. In France efforts were made, after 1792, to set up system of normal schools. In 1908 Napoleon had established the 'Ecole Normal' (Normal school) to trained teachers. But until 1833 A.D. an uniform system of teacher training could not be stabled in France.

During the first 30 years of 19th Century, teacher preparation in U.S.A. and elsewhere was dominated by monitoral methods introduced by Andrew Bell and Joseph Lancaster. In the simplest terms the method evolved a 'master' introducing the senior pupils or monitors who then passes on their newly acquired knowledge to large number of pupils. Such methods of teaching were cheap, simple, wisely delivered, believed to be effective. These required a necessary emphasis upon facts, drill, repetition, mechanical learning in each such teaching. By 1820 A.D. there were such twenty Lancasterian schools in the state of New York where the system had official recognition and status until the middle of 19th century. Large number of pupils were educated by monitorial system. It was managed with less amount, and as matter of fact it established maximum level of literacy. But this system was also criticized.

Among those who were impressed by the Lancasterian system was David Stow, who in 1834 A.D. founded Glasgo seminary, from which trainees were called graduates after training. They were appointed as teachers in schools in Scotland and in many British Colonies. In U.S.A., Horace Mann founded Massachusetts National School. Horace Mann became famous for similar developments in Connecticut, Michigan, Phade Island, Iowa, New Jersy and Illinois. In England Voluntary organizations were in force first in establishing Training Colleges. In 1850, similar development happened in Austria.

In western world more efforts were made to organize the human knowledge in more diverse and scientific ways, with the result a new discipline of secondary education was expanding. The early pedagogic systems also were failing into disfavour. Reconcilement for teachers need was felt. And professional for class room teaching, woven into pedagogic considerations was also felt. And on these points there occurred liberal agitations in France and USA. Patriotic missionary role teacher was considered necessary in Japan. And generally emphasis was laid on practice teaching and practical techniques in school management. This also entailed a discussion, which of these should get importance.

Some educators felt that the syllabus of the Normal Schools should be academic depending upon the future teacher training needs, nothing more than the knowledge of conventional subjects soundly taught. Others opined that the teacher training should have a purely professional functions, only such knowledge what the teacher would teach in the classroom. Some argued that there should be a harmonized approach while imparting general and special professional knowledge during the course of teaching. The work of Derwart Coleridge, Principal St. Mark College, London, who admitted that he took his models not from pedagogical seminars held in Germany but from the Universities of Oxford and Cambridge. He exemplified through an attempt to introduce a large bent of general knowledge. Sir James Kary Shuttleworth founder of another college emphasized the knowledge of subject matter; he held that "not only the subjects of instruction but also the methods of teaching or instruction should be so ordered, as it is to be in itself a preparation of the future vocation for the teachers. On this account the oral function of classes in a normal school is greatly to be preferred to any mode of teaching.

In U.S.A. Horace Mann supported the value of a training in common branches of knowledge as means of mental discipline. The views of Derwart Coleridge, James Kay Shuttleworth and Horace Mann, with those of many other educators of the time reflected social as well as pedagogic considerations. Horace Mann failed to recognize the Persian system of education, that so impressed him, was one that which took lower class pupils and trained as teachers of the lower classes, was a system which was already under fire from the German educators.

In Belgium in 1870, and by the end 1890 legislations were

enacted in a number of countries to systemize and broaden the work of normal schools. In Japan through an ordinance in 1886 many higher normal schools were established for providing training in teaching courses for boys and girls who had completed 8 years of elementary education. A French law enacted in 1879 A.D., established a nationwide system of colleges for training women as primary school teachers. In Russia a statue on teachers seminaries was promoulgated in 1870 A.D., and with in five years there emerged fourteen statue for training of the teachers of higher grades. In Scotland Universities of Edinburg and Andrew established chairs in Education in 1876 A.D. In U.S.A. a number of Universities set up Departments of Education. In some of them, the beginning combined with the preparation of teachers and systematic research studies.

The Departments of Education in U.S.A. universities owned a great deal to the efforts of men like Henery Bernard who had worked as Schools' Commissioner in Rhode Island from 1845 to 1849 A.D. He had stimulated local interests in Education, that also led to the creation of Department of Education in Brown University. Henery Bernard wrote influential series of books on pedagogy and teacher education. And later on, as President of Columbia University, he inspired Nicholas Murray Buller and others to establish a Teachers Training College in 1888 which soon became a foremost University School of Education in U.S.A. It incorporated two schools and teaching laboratories enrolling children from Kindergarten to College age. An announcement was made in 1901 made it clear that it was not restricted to any on level of professional preparation. The purpose of the College was to afford opportunity, both in theoretical and practical fields for training of teachers of both series for kindergarten, elementary and secondary education school teachers, principals, supervisors, specialists in normal development as briefly described below:

Until 1890, "theoretical elements in teacher preparation were of two kinds (1) the study of certain principles of teaching and school management as exemplified in textbooks written by experienced school men and were published in many countries during the second half of the 19th century and (2) instructions in mental and moral philosophy, history of education, psychology and pedagogic. Some of the most important influential works such as Roxncartze's philosophy of education which was translated in

English in 1870 made little distinction between philosophical and psychological data. But in 1890, psychology and sociology began to crystalize as more or less distinctive areas of study, so students of education had a wider and more clearly structured range of disciplines to draw upon for their data and perception (Visualization) and to provide scientific pedagogic principles.

In the middle of 19th century the ideas of Swiss educator J.H. Pestalozzi and of the German educator Friedrich Froebel inspired the objective thinking, defined in 1878 by Alexander Bains in his widely studied 'Education as a Science'. It was an attempt to provide a 'range cover' to all utilities of life and all process of the nature. The works of these pioneers who led to a clear recognition of the developmental needs and character building of the childhood. Later on the contribution to the 'crops of ideas' that underline the process of teacher education continued to provide philosophical, sociological and socialization justification for particular views of the nature of education and teacher training, and also had a greater or lesser influence on the methods to be employed in teaching in classroom.

The work of the German philosopher J. Friedrich Herbart (1776-1841) was of particular importance in this respect. Herbart wrote a number of pedagogical works during his teaching career at the universities of Gattengen and Konisburg along with Herbartian lines became established in European Countries, in America and in Japan. Herbertianism provided a complete systemic, philosophical theory, a set of educational aims, a rational psychology of education and system of pedagogical teaching. It held that the teacher should build an educational process on what the child already possess or knows and should inculcate a spirit of knowing and learning through appropriate materials, in accordance with formal steps—of preparation, presentation, comparison, generalization and the application. Herbartian doctrine had and, still has, an educational consciousness. The present concept of lesson planning may be an outcome of it.

The influence of Darwinian evolutionary ideas upon pedagogy was very much marked as evolutionary point of view emphasized the process with regard to individuals adaptations to environment, as their influence was conservative, as per teachings of English philosopher Herbert Spencer. Evolutionary ideas were embodied in the child as per theory of American philosopher Standley Hall, who said that the stages of individual development or growth recapitulated through social growth, therefore, distinctive status and character of childhood must be respected. American philosopher William James emphasized on the process and circumstances which channelise the creative process and help the child to grow and become a creative being. William James emphasizes, however was not so much upon adaptations of circumstances to shape and change to meet the needs. William James formations of associations, the building up useful habits, systems, had implications for the study of learning, that the teacher educators were guide to recognise and that were made more significant by the later experiments of American philosopher Edward L. Thorndike (1874-1949) by his experiments on animals, stand at the beginning of a tradition that still continues. The laws of learning he formulated for long have been staple of Teacher psychology as the genuine base of pedagogy, and he claimed that as chemistry, botany depend on the experimentation, so the art of education depends on physiology and psychology. He argued confidently that "A complete science of psychology would tell every fact about every ones intellect and character and also behaviour. It would also tell the cause of every change in human nature, act of every person that has changed any other person, or agent or himself."

The greatest influence on teacher training curricula in USA and in many other countries was exercised not by the experimental psychologists but by the pragmatist philosopher—John Dewey. He began with the conception of scientific method that he generalized in the specific pedagogic approach. This method was popularized by other methods like 'Project Method'—an enquiry based learning. This is combined with child's interests and capacities of learning and life experiences, and nature and importance of democratic learning values and nature of different types of subject matter. This is all taught in social context of the school. Psychologist education gave importance to the individual development. John Dewey said that the school is an embodiment of community's and society's ideals, and is spearhead of social reform. Thus the teacher education should give full attention to the school also. Also, John Dewey's views invited some criticism.

Inspite of the fact that John Dewey pleaded for all round development which should be in complete social perspective. But he did not suggest any sociological norms or qualities in his pragmatistic approach of education. If any educational programme does not generate moral values in the young, and only lay stress on individualistic growth, the products of such educational scheme will be staunch individualistic and human values will have no place in his mind. And such a person can do any unethical deed for his personal gains. We find that the father of Indian nation Late Shri M.K. Gandhi conceived such a similar scheme of education during Indian freedom struggle for the development of Indian youths and Indian economy. And this scheme of education was named as Basic Education. But the unique scheme of education launched by the father of the nation had a complete axiological individual relationships. Main aim of the basic education was enculturation. But after the death of Late Shri M.K. Gandhi, our westernized and accultured leaders who were at the helm of power did not like it and allowed formal education to continue. The scheme of Basic Education was further designed by Late Dr. Zakir Hussain former President of India. This unique scheme of education had got an applause in Indonesia and Kenya where it continues till to day.

Due to variety of pedagogic views as per various social structures in the world there exists contrary views about role of teachers, teacher training as well as teaching methods and; these can be termed as conservative and progressive view points. Conservative views lay stress on teaching subject matter, i.e. effective instruction, regular and orderly class room discipline. According to conservative view point, it is believed that this will encourage children to learning subject matter diligently. It will enhance scholarship, and scholarly achievements. Such a view is teacher created and teacher overled. It makes the teacher's role predominant. The teacher becomes an authority. He is a giver and student is the receiver. Under the conservative pedagogy view, these is no chance of effective teacher taught interaction. As such, there is very limited chance for thinking, reasoning, analysing, doubting and comprehending based on perception. As such, there is no chance of self-learning or self-education under the conservative method of teaching.

On the other hand, progresses view of teaching and teacher training lay much stress on child centred approach in teaching. The teaching process is supposed to apply innovative and motivative approach in teaching imbibing curiosity, interests to learn the child. So flexible patterns of teaching which ignite and urge the students to learn are used in the class room. The teacher is required to establish rapport between him/her and clients, that is the students. He/She tries to recognize the individual differences in the students. Under the progressive method of teaching the authority of the teacher is negated and is replaced with a kind ear and a kind a heart. The teacher is supposed to be ever sincere to his clients that is, students. The progressive teaching recommends minimization of verbal communication and replacing or supplementary if be non-verbal communication. The teacher is required to establish a bi-polar communication between him/her and students. Under the progressive teaching scheme of education, the teacher is required to judge the capacity of he students to learn first, and then start teaching. The progressive teaching is required to be based on the on self-bearing, self experience and not on verbal one way communication. As such the teaching should be integrated, that is, with verbal narration, subject matter should entail thinking, doubt and comprehension. The basic scheme of education visualized by the Father of the nation and later on planned by Late Dr. Zakir Hussain was infact a progressive education. Under this scheme of education, the teacher was supported to apply progressive methods of every step and the child was also always found in learning vicinity.

As such conservative and progressive ways and methods of teaching have roots in different conceptions of the nature of man, his belief and social structures of the societies. Both perspective got wan and wave in accordance with the time. In Vedic period, in Brahmanical system of education, those who ever in system of education supremacy managed to keep their hold on masses, by alienating those who were doing constructive jobs in the society like Vishwakarma artizens who have been dumped to the lower strata of society through Varna Card. We find that the Indians were fighting amongst themselves at the cost of national security. This was because of lack of rationalization. In U.S.A., fear of loss of technological supremacy encouraged conservative critics to promote child centred education. In the same way meaningless one way education experienced by many especially by poor, coupled with wide spread alienation education. Many educationists did not subscribe either to conservative or to progressive ideas, which influenced the teacher preparation and the development of methodology of teaching.

Many ideas influenced the curriculum construction and the teacher preparation during the last decade of 19th century and first years of 20th century. The dynamic psychology of Edmund Sigmund Freud, Gestalt psychologists conception of 'whole' and other methods of increasing human abilities, that were developed in France, U.K., Germany and U.S.A. Jean Jacques Rousseau played a prominent role in highlighting naturalism in education. Likewise religious ideas also played a dominant role in the preparation of the teacher and developing teaching methodologies. Roman Catholics and Muslims in some theocratic states did what favoured to their religious. Some dictator states moulded the teaching in their states which favoured their ideologies. Spartan in eastern Europe, four thousand and five hundred years ago in the past had imposed terrorist ideology in their educational system. The Marxists in Soviet Union had imposed communist ideology which did not have any place for axiology and individual freedom. All these affected the teacher preparation and teaching methodologies at all leads. Social, economic and democratic commitments in U.S.A., as exemplified by John Dewey, have boosted a sense of national upliftment, which also proved a boon in the field of teacher preparation and development of teaching methodologies.

The new commitments also affected the processes of learning, measurement and assessment of abilities of students through examination system. This reflected a specific diagnosis for learning problems. For teaching there should be planning for teaching the children in homogenous way by distinguishing ability groups. The emphasis should be laid on problem solving. This can be done by project method and perceptive method. These problems should be reflected in teacher training programmes. And the teacher should also made aware other problems like enculturation.

Organization of teacher preparation improved a lot in 20th century. The social, political, economic, demographic, democratic and technological changes imposed new conceptualization and legitimized new processes in the field of education. Urbanisation, reduction in child mortality and improvement in child health, and also better economic conditions enabled the families to afford longer schooling. Centralization of educational schemes, availability of audio-visual teaching aids helped in improving the teacher preparation. Due to ideological, political and social variations still exists various levels of teacher preparation in the world which produces teacher as per their needs.

LEVELS OF TEACHER PREPARATION

Arrangements of teacher preparation widely vary from country to country. Some countries still continue to have monitor system. Still some teachers receive short courses of training, through they shall have teach large number of students under classroom system. These teachers are trained in normal schools. In U.S.A. and in some developed and developing countries including India the teachers are university graduates. These teachers are trained after graduation for secondary or senior secondary schools and after senior secondary for junior schools.

The second level of teacher preparation may be called J.B.T. Such preparation begins after completion of senior secondary examination. A new course has been recently introduced named B.El.Ed., Bachelor of elementary education. This course provides combined academic and professional training. The duration of this cause is four years. This course provides concurred study.

Finally, at the university level teacher preparation is undertaken for those who have completed graduation or post graduation for B.Ed. degree course. Generally B.Ed. Course is of one year duration. It is a comprehensive, covering (1) philosophy of education, (2) psychology of education (3) history of education, (4) teaching methodologies and (5) specialization in any one of the fields as: (*a*) audio-visual education (*b*) art education (c) library education (*d*) physical education (*e*) co-curricular activities, (*f*) education guidance etc. etc. Besides, all these the B.Ed. students are trained in teaching in any two subjects. The students have to do teaching in a school atleast for three months. And above all teacher training institutes try to train the B.Ed. students in extra-co-curricular activities so that they may enculturate the students in school while teaching. After doing B.Ed. the teacher can do M.Ed. The above qualifications are considered necessary for employment as teachers in schools at various levels.

Until the middle of the 20th century the normal school pattern applied to students preparing for primary work in schools in European Countries—Austria, Belgium, Spain, France, Italy,

Ireland, Netherlands, Switzerland and Turkey. In India also normal school used to train primary and middle schools teachers. Also in some Asian and African countries which were under the domination of western countries the system of normal school was applied for the preparation of teachers. No such training was thought of for University Teachers.

ISSUES AND PROBLEMS OF TEACHER EDUCATION

In almost all countries courses of Normal Schools, Colleges and Universities contain three elements: (1) First elements of study of one or more than one academic subjects, cultural or aesthetical subjects for the purpose, both enhancing their knowledge and using it for enculturation too, (2) The second element is the study of educational principles, increasingly organized in terms of social science discipline such as philosophy, sociology, psychology and history. (3) Element is professional courses and school experience. Primary school teachers may also receive instructions in the contents and methods of subjects other than their own specialities that figure in the primary curriculum. In normal schools and universities these three elements run parallel to one another, and the students are professionally committed from the outcome of three course, to it. Elsewhere, the study educational process and professional work, including school experience may follow the completion of period of study that the students have begun without any prior commitment to the teaching career. There are still advance courses in countries when the possession of a university degree, without any qualification in education is sufficient basis for the award of qualified teacher status. In England and Wales, for example, compulsory training for graduates, comprising two terms (1) six months for professional and theoretical studies, (2) further three months for school experience was scheduled to come into effect only in 1973.

General Education

Sequencing of balance between content organization, general education, and special academic course in education has been a subject of discussion and criticism among the academic specialists and defenders of liberal cultures. The grouping range of speculation and empirical data generated by burgeoning social sciences, philosophy and history. These have provided a rich base from which those responsible for teacher preparation mined the material they needed for the construction and legitimation of the pedagogic systems and principles. But this could not provide any systemic theory of teaching.

STUDY OF SYSTEMIC EDUCATIONAL PRINCIPLES

There arose a dispute whether educational principles are to be seen as part of liberal element in the teacher training course or general education or personal development can be part of professional sequence. Study of philosophy, sociology, psychology and history should be part of teacher training with great emphasis or not? These provide a systematic same human conduct. It is also said that it can not be easily well done due to paucity of time as correlating of child's learning should also be there.

PRACTICAL TRAINING

Practice has always been important in every field. It is formally done in a model practice teaching atmosphere in a school, especially chosen for the purpose. The practice teaching school should be situated in the neighbourhood of teachers training institute. But it is also noticed that some practice teaching schools are not sufficiently co-operative and do not provide a teaching atmosphere. Some schools tend to be more academically oriented and prefer only conservative teaching; whereas pupils should be oriented in progressive teaching methods also. These schools do not co-operate and refuse to undertake experimental roles by the students. Variety of experiences are very helpful to the pupil teachers. Some practice teaching schools consider practice teaching is a kind of academic disturbance. Practice teaching involves dual work for university teacher-supervisors. And sometimes the school teachers do not co-operate with the University teachers training College supervisors. Formal school education is examination oriented and the school teachers find it difficult to give sufficient time to the pupil teacher for practice teaching. They feel that practice teaching will hinder in covering the prescribed school curriculum content. It is also seen that some times the few supervisors deputed to supervise the pupil teachers while during practice teaching remain a merely a formality. Either they do not attend at all or they hardly contribute, as they should have done, in practice teaching. Since school teaching is largely considered for getting good marks in annual board's annual examination, some senior secondary school principals consider the practice teaching as the killer of school time, and they do not like it. As such they do not cooperate, as they should. Some elderly pupil-teachers sometimes become meglomanious and they find it difficult to digest the suggestions of the practice teaching supervisors. Finally, it has also been observed that teachers institutes take practice teaching a mere formality and these institutes do not take it seriously.

APPOINTMENT PROCEDURES OF TEACHERS

In India, in olden times the teaching was considered a pious, honourable, respectable and distinguished social service, because through educating the old Indian teachers used to do a remarkable social service without any inclination. The gurus used to teach in Gurukulas. Main aim of the old Indian education was to prepare the two upper castes for educating the masses through social up bringing by inculcating in them spirituality, morality, brotherhood and co-operation. This was done by giving religious sermons and through it passing to the masses axiological, epistemological, teleological and sociological knowledge. The main purpose of Indian education was to build a homogenous society even under the strict caste social structure. As such the teachers (Gurus) used to be the builders of the nation. They were highly educated and knowledgeable persons. Vidyadan was considered the best pious donation. The highly educated and knowledgeable persons, after their own introspection, and with direction from their inner consciousness and with the commend and full determination of their soul, they used to offer their services voluntarily for teaching the young 'divijas' "Brahmacharyas' in Gurukulas. Their offer for teaching never entailed any material requirements or emoluments etc. They used to do teaching for mere vidyadan or knowledge donation, as it was considered best sacrifice. They were only provided free food and shelter for their survival. The food was provided by Gurukula Kitchen which was run with social donations. In the older days in European countries, in Middle East, in China and Japan and in the east similar was condition.

With the social change, due to scientific and industrial development throughout the world—first in the west and later in the rest of the world, formal education became a necessity, through out the world. So the education which was in the past a perogative of the few, with the passage of time became a universal necessity of common people. Perogative of few to education became right of every body, so to say of every common man. In the past, in India two upper Varnas, that is Brahmans and Kshtriyas were entitled for Gurukulas education. In some part in the west, also only feudal class used to get education. Because of this social change, the educational institutions like schools, universities and technical institutions came into being. These institutions require teachers of varied abilities. So, the teacher preparation and their appointment in educational institution became a necessity. For this, a proper selection procedures have been evolved. And appointing or selecting agencies like State Public Service Commission, Union Public Service Commission and Selection Boards have emerged.

The teacher selection procedures differ from country to country according to then own needs. Some federal countries have then varied requirements as seen in Canada, U.S.A., Australia and also India. As such, in some countries the selection procedures for teachers' recruitment vary from state to state. In countries like U.K., France, Germany the requirements for teachers recruitments are decided as per national requirements. In India, there are many states where different languages are spoken and different religious forms, varied cultural patterns are found. Also, there exist varied climatic conditions, ways of living, different folk and tribal cultures. So there is need of varied educational patterns. So the educational requirements also vary to large extent which there states to have teachers of different varied abilities. So, diverse way of teacher training due to different languages, cultural patterns require specific training for appointing teachers in different educational institutions. So the appointment of teachers vary from place to place and country to country. It is also true that teachers should be recruited on merit.

IN SERVICE TEACHER TRAINING

In service training is not only necessary for the teachers, but also it is necessary for all who are doing some jobs and are in service. Govt.

officials, all ranks in the armed forces, police, home guards, N.C.C. Cadets and even technician working in workshops are required to undergo in service training for some time. It is necessary because flux takes place in all working areas. The in-service training generally innovate and motivate the workers. In teaching also due to scientific development some changes are inevitable. To meet the changing situations in teaching profession in-service training though, for a short period, is necessary. The teachers while get experience out of which some teachers get more proficient. Such experience should be shaped by the fellow teachers. Therefore, it is necessary to arrange some extension service programmes, through seminars, conferences, workshop, either in the autumn break or in summer holidays. The department of education should arrange such extension service programmes. The teachers should be paid some conveyance allowance. In service extension programme for teacher there may be a broader system of communication, whereby all those involved in educational activities—like school teachers, college lectures and technical teacher are benefited. In service teacher training all teachers, demonstrators, research workers laboratory attendants, library attendants, art teachers, craft teacher and all specialists in education should be involved. This type of programme establishes rapport amongst teachers and other educational staff, which increases sound educational environment, which increases epistemacy in teachers and students. So, it is necessary to arrange in-service programmes at all levels.

USE OF LEARNING MATERIAL IN IN-SERVICE TRAINING

1. Learning material plays a vital role in in-service teacher training programme. In such material printed materials like news paper cuttings, school journals, educational edition of some news paper, magazines news letters, articles written by prominent education's pictures of some prominent institutions, educational historical abstracts, bibliographies, educational indexes and lists of some reference books may be useful. These can encourage the teachers for reading. And reading will enhance the knowledge of the teachers. Learning material can be termed first media.

2. Secondly, lectures, facing to instructions and discussions, presentation of case studies and personal experiences and some stimulating materials like use of T.V., Close circuit, T.V., Films, Strips, Slides and special audio-visual aids made by the teachers with the help of the students if presented in in-service teacher training extension service can be very useful.
3. Other multi-media approaches like discussion on T.V. and on close current T.V. with in the school compound can be useful.
4. Encouragement to know, the realism through talks in morning assemblies, encouragement to the formation of teacher bodies which could foster a spirit of self leaning and also for the betterment of teachers. The teacher bodies should also try to make the teachers proficient in teaching through seminars or meetings.
5. The school councils should be set up for the curriculum development. These councils should apprise the teachers about the national culture and also should educate them about enculturation, acculturation and about the necessity of national culture development.
6. All schools should be covered by in-service training, programmes. There should not be any discrimination against any school. The state government and department of education should look into this matter seriously.
7. Every school should be provided an in-service-cum-exhibition room for the teachers. The teacher's role should be of an organizer and manager of learning rather than a solo-performer on the class rooms teaching stage and doing his teaching duty only as a mere formality. The gap between the teacher, students and administrators should be bridged.

For the future development in teacher training education a lot is required to be done. The teacher training institutes must introspect into their functioning. These must innovate to meet teachers of these institute, who are teachers of teachers, to introspect in themselves for the betterment of the teachers who are builders of the nation. These institutes must provide new developments in the field of educational technology. These institutes must provide new programmes in the field of education which could prepare the teachers for enculturating the students by igniting moral, social, co-operative and epistemic values in the students. The spirit of sharing, brotherhood, tolerance and unity are necessary for the national unity. These can be developed by the teacher. And in-service training programmes can help in this regard a lot.

5

Teacher Education in India

These day teacher education prevalent in India was first started and developed in England from the monitorial system. Prior to this no such system existed in India. During the Vedic age, the teacher was a Guru in India. He was well educated, dedicated and devoted to 'Vidyadan' (विध्यादान) knowledge donation through 'sikhsan (शिक्षण)—teaching'. First of all Dr. Andrew Bell (most probably a Christian Missionary) while he was in Madras (1789-1796) thought of starting monitorial system in Madras Presidency. The monitorial system was a kind of mutual instruction system. A senior student, who used to help the teacher in controlling the class room discipline and also to help the teacher in class room teaching, was also to be involved in teaching by the teacher in class room teaching. This system was considered congenial and economical. Later on, this system came to be known as "Madras System of Education". Dr. Andrew Bell apprised the English Government in England about its introduction in Madras, and received recognition and support for a while there. Similar system of 'monitor education' was independently worked out in England by Joseph Lancastee. In due course of time it was changed in England.

In other parts of India too, the monitorial system was tried on Madras Monitorial teacher pattern. In due course of time it was replaced by pupil—teacher system. In Bombay Native Education system was established in 1820. In 1833, it was recommended that "intelligent natives' should be trained in Lancasterian system of teaching" with a view to introduce the system in schools of certain districts in which they were to be appointed as superintendents. The Vernacular schools came into being in 1826 when 24 teachers were trained in Native Schools of Native Educative Society.

Thomas Munto the Governor of Madras Presidency held that no progress could be made in the province "without a body of better instructed teachers", and, "establishment of a central school for training teachers was necessary"

In Bengal the Calcutta school society was established in 1819 A.D., aimed at giving education to people for educating teachers. The Board of Directors of East India Company approved it. They said, "training of class teachers was essential for extension of improved education to a portion of native Indians. In this way an English pattern of education was first introduced. It was the beginning of education, as well as teacher education. It can broadly be said that a satisfactory advance was made in the field of teacher education which continued to the middle of 19th century.

WOOD DISPATCH 1854

Wood Dispatch 1854 was an important landmark in the history of education in modern India. Important features of the Wood Despatch are (1) Among the important things the wood despatch was, that if made a provision of qualified Teacher's "Senior Training School", for providing teachers (2) Training School" for training primary school teachers. (3) Adoption of Pupil-Teacher training pattern. It was adopted earlier in England (4) Selection of pupil teachers and stipend to be given to them was to be decided by the school head masters (5) Wood Despatch's another recommendation was that the pupil teachers were to be engaged in schools as pupil teachers and, after successful completion of training at school, the pupil teachers were to be given employment and engaged in school as pupil teachers, and after successful completion were awarded certificate (6) Woods Despatch stressed the need of carrying out the system in India—both in Govt. Schools and in aided schools.

Following this, there was marked increase in teacher training colleges and in normal schools by 1850 in Madras Presidency at Madras, Cheyur, Vellor, Bangalore, and Ellore.

In Bombay Presidency, Eriskin, the first Director of Public Instructions recommended that selected youths in each presidency, in every Taluka should be apprenticed as pupil teachers for 3 years on stipend rising from Rs. 3 to Rs. 5 per month to select school master in neighbourhood schools, and on successful passing of their apprenticeship, they should be sent for further course of instruction on stipend of Rs. 6 per month.

By 1858 there were four normal schools in Bombay Presidency located at Poona, Ahmedabad, Dharwar and Karanchi. In Bengal too, there were four normal schools for training of Vernacular teachers training upto 1857 at Hoogly, Dacca, Gauhati and Calcutta. In Central provinces, the establishment of the institution of Normal school was some what delayed. though the provinces had taken some steps in this direction. By 1860, the then North West Frontier provinces which included the big parts of Northern India had only four normal schools at Agra, Banaras, Meerut and Amroha. By 1865 there wee seven Normal schools in Punjab. By 1862-63 there were nine Normal Schools in Central Provinces. By 1882, the year in which Indian Education began its work, there was a gradual development in the field of teacher education, due to the development of education. Between 1854 to 1882 there had been a steep development in the field of teacher training and many normal schools for teachers training were established. But still the arrangements for secondary schools teachers training were far from satisfactory. By 1882 there were two teachers training institutes for training secondary school teachers for the whole India, one at Madras (1856) and one at Lahore (1880) now in Pakistan. Subjects for teacher training was a matter of controversy for the Indian Education Commission. Some believed that to further study of subjects should be given priority as this would enhance the knowledge of the teachers. It was also considered necessary for increasing the volume of teaching methodology. The others believed, rather advocated, for principle of teaching and teaching methods. These should be given priority in teacher training institutes. The Indian Education Commission favoured the view and recommended in its report (1884) that: (1) there should be examination in teaching principles. It should be a condition for employment for a teacher, (2) the graduates should go for shorter course of teacher training, (3) there should be an initial appointment subject for the enhancement of knowledge and proficiency and finally (4) the commission recommended that permanent posts should be given to those who could spare time and money for further study.

By 1902 there were only six teacher training colleges for secondary teachers located at (1) Saidapet, (2) Rajmundri,

(3) Kursong, (4) Allahabad, (5) Lahore (now in Pakistan) and (6) Jabalpur. Bombay had no such institution till 1902. It was in 1904, the Government of Bombay Presidency, in its resolution on Indian Employment had recommended the examination system of secondary education, teacher training facility in the Bombay Presidency Province, where it did not exist.

The resolution referred to above was noted with satisfaction that the institutions of normal schools for primary school teachers, which was recommended by Woods Despatch in 1854, had been generally carried out through out the Country Also steps were being taken to provide courses in teacher training institutes especially suited for teachers in rural schools. Such courses it was believed would help to ignite the interest of the teachers in studying things and they would be able to connect their teaching with these objects in teaching. The children will also be familiar with the objects and will be motivated to learn. In other words it was the beginning of using teaching aids in teaching covertly, not knowing their importance.

The period of 1904-21 witnessed a craze for the availability of facilities for secondary school teachers. The number of teacher training colleges rose from six to thirteen during this period. This advance was due to large number of Government resolutions on educational polity in 1913, which stated that, "eventually under modern system of education no teacher should be allowed to teach without a certificate, that is, he should be qualified to teach. Few reforms, according to this resolution were more urgently needed then, extension and improvement of training of teachers, for both primary and secondary schools in al subjects; including in the case of then later schools established for teaching science and oriental subjects taken by students. The report of the Calcutta University Commission published in 1919 reiterated the need of substantially increasing out put of trained teachers, and it suggested the creation of the departments of education in the Universities of Dacca and Calcutta.

In 1929, the Hartog Committee was established, which gave special attention to the problems of primary school education, and made some important recommendations in respect of primary school teachers, as under:

1. Steps should be taken to raise the general standard of primary teachers,

2. Courses of training of teachers should be made sufficiently viable,
3. The efficiency of the primary schools should be enhanced,
4. Normal school established for training of primary school teachers should be adequately staffed,
5. There should be frequent refresher courses for the primary school teachers,
6. There should be periodic conferences for updating the progress of primary education,
7. There should be a permanent in-service training arrangement for the primary school teachers.

So that the quality of primary school teaching be improved and the children he better educated. Due to these recommendations several changes were made in the curriculum of teacher training education, so that effective co-ordination may also take place between the concerned people, and educational programme could be effectively implemented. Such attempts were also made in other provinces.

An educational development was direct outcome of the national freedom movement. And it was Basic Education. The Basic Education was the direct result of Swadeshi Movement of the Congress Party, pioneered by the father of the nation, Late Shri M.K. Gandhi. The main aim of the Basic education was (1) to co-relate any one of the craft of the locality to other areas, so as to bring toward self-sufficiency, (2) to educate all children upto the age of 14, (3) to meet the expenses of the school as salary of the teachers, if not full partially, (4) to create a sense of cohesion, co-operation, sociability, morality and social homogeneity, and (5) and to restore the hoary past of Indian art and Crafts which was dismantled by alien rulers for creating markets in India for their goods. As such, the adoption of Basic Education required special Basic School Teacher Training institutes as the agenda of these was quite different to other schools, and British type Normal School were considered inadequate to train the Basic School teachers. During the period of dyarchy under the Govt. of India Act 1935, many Basic Teachers Training Normal Schools wee established throughout the country. And model Basic Teacher Training Institutes, like Patna Basic Education Teachers Training Institute were established at the head quarters of the provinces. As such these training institutes replaced the traditional normal schools. The importance of the traditional normal schools also faded. As the Basic education did not touch the stage beyond fourteen years of age, the teacher training Colleges remained unaffected. But the fate of Basic education was sealed by the westernized national leaders, just after the death of its founder, the father of the nation Late Shri M.K. Gandhi.

Inspite of the development referred to above and the mid of 20th century, it would not be wrong to say that our infra-structure of teacher training till that time was inadequate, unrealistic to our social needs and was alien in nature. Our constitution came into existence on 26th January 1950, had set the goals for compulsory education for all children in the age groups of 6 to 14 years within ten years after the imposition of the constitution we could not achieve this till to day. Many blame the government for not providing sufficient funds for this purpose but the truth is that there had been little co-ordination between the Government bodies and some voluntary organizations which could have contributed for the achievement of this noble cause. Another reason might he non-cooperation of the parents for not sending their children to primary schools. Demographic explosion might be another reason. Third reason might be the mentality of labour class for involving their children in child labour for earning money. If the goals set by our Constitution builders are to be achieved we would have to develop a mental set for achieving this. All should contribute in this feat. For this we would require more funds for more primary schools and teachers. Then only compulsory primary education can be enforced.

There has also been lack of co-ordination, which characterizes the works of different grades of teachers' training institutions i.e. primary, middle secondary and senior secondary and also nursery schools education. These has also no laisson or co-ordination of any sort among the various teacher training institution working at different places or different levels. These institutions tend to work in isolation oblivious of their local common problems and objectives. These inadequacies provided major problems in the implementation of new plans of educational reconstruction, that were, and still are being undertaken in various states. Even at any single level, there has been a lack of strange initiative of creation for novel community, education communality common purpose and co-ordination among teacher training institutions in different parts of the country.

Take for example, at the post graduate level of teacher training education there had been, and still there is no difference, in the nature of theoretical courses prescribed by teachers training colleges at B.T. stage (also B.Ed. L.T. and diploma in Education) in some universities. But there had been, and still appears, a wide difference in its kind and extent of practical training in various teachers training conducted in various training colleges, Dr. Radhakrishnan Commission had made a positive reference to such divergences from university to university and the candidates for B.Ed and M.Ed degrees. Some Universities award M.Ed. degrees on presentation of thesis as well as written examination while some universities award M.Ed. degrees on the basis of written examination only. It is hoped that, now after independence these fundamental difference well soon be eradicated. The conferences of teachers training colleges in India, in the mid fifteen of 20th-century, had set the ball rolling in this direction. It is for the different universities in the country to take up and implement the recommendation of the conference in this direction.

Another field, in which greater interest and greater efforts are needed, lies in affecting better co-ordination between the teacher training institutions on one hand, and the schools for which they prepare teachers on the other. At present, there is a very little co-ordination between these institutions. Many school principals do not allow practice teaching in their schools. And it is also noticed many of them are very discourteous to teachers of training college and staff while they approach them for such a favour. They forget that some time back they had also gone for practice teaching in some school. Dr. S. Radhakrishnan Commission had visualized this difficulty of teacher training institutes were facing at that time. The Government while awarding recognition to the schools should make it a conditions. The schools feel that their regular teachers would go out of teaching if practice teaching is allowed. Prof. Stephen M. Corey had suggested that practice teaching would help in 'action research'. He had suggested that while he was doing (Action Research) on school functioning under U.S.A.I.D. in early sixties of 20th centuries. He had done research on 'School in Action' while he was at Central Institute of Education, Delhi sponsored by U.S.A.I.D. As such school research is important. The school teachers' associations should also take a note of it. Along with their duties and rights, the teacher must consider the well being of their students also. As such school research is important. The school teachers' associations should also take a note of it. Along with their duties and rights the teacher must consider the well being of their students also. As such, the school teachers should have a collaboration with teachers training colleges. And such an effort should be throughout India. Late Maulana Abul Kalam Azad freedom fighter and first Minister of Education, Govt. of India had conceived this idea first. He had thought of changing the alien pattern of education to national educational system. He had set up Central Institute of Education on December 19th, 1948. The institute (C.I.E.) did a lot of pioneering work in this regard. It is still doing a lot, but not with same zeal as was done by the former Principals—Late Prof. A.N. Basu, Late Prof. E.A. Pires and Late Prof. P.K. Roy. It may be due to C.I.E.'s transfer from Govt. of India to first to N.C.E.R.T. and later on to Delhi University. It may be due to sliding work. Culture which happens due to flux in administrative working. There should be a mechanism to reform this situation.

During the seventies and eighties of 20th century, the new development in the field Teacher Education had emerged. It was commercialization. Some universities opened teacher training commercial outlets. Such commercialized teacher training out-lets had neither teaching faculties required for proper teaching and giving theoretical knowledge nor any arrangement for practical work such a practice teaching, making of teaching aids nor any input for classroom research work as doing case studies etc. They conducted the B.Ed. course through correspondence course. As such, the teachers were produced in thousands and lacs. The products of these institutes were appointed at the cost of meritous students who had done B.Ed. from the teacher training institute of national repute like C.I.E., B.H.U., Jamia Millia Islamia, Institutes of Education run by the N.C.E.R.T. and Aligarh Muslim University. Naturally this affected the school teaching, as many of the products of these commercialized teacher training Institutes were not even aware about the utility of black board. The government took note of this commercialization and an organization called "National Council for Teacher Education (N.C.T.E.) was set up by Govt. of India, which did a wonderful job and derecognized all such Commercial Teacher's Training Colleges.

If we summarize, we will find that in first phase of teacher training a good number Basic teacher training colleges were set up. And teacher training appreciably increased in early 20th century. In some states like Punjab due to increase in the teachers training college and because of inadequacy of teaching staff and shortage of equipments, lack of library facilities the standard of the college remained low for some period. Also the condition was worse in many Art and Science Colleges which were permitted to open the teachers training colleges due to lack of facilities.

During the 20th Century another development had been an increase in the provision for training of teachers in subjects like economic, commerce and home science in addition to general subjects. But the training of art teachers and Craft teacher is still lacking. But it is observed that provision for training in teaching methodologies in many subjects is still insufficient and inadequate, and the quality of teaching in schools still requires some improvement.

During the sixties of 20th century another commendable useful development had the assumption of responsibility for in-service training for the teachers. Ministry of Education Government of India, Ford Foundation of U.S.A. provided funds and equipments through U.S.A.I.D. By 1958, 23 colleges in India were doing the sale in-service training through seminars, workshops, demonstrations, melas, world conferences, publications, visits of some dignitaries and film shows. Central Institute of Education was on topmost list in this regard. It had a full-fledged ex-services department which used to arranged regular in service teacher, training even world education conferences used to lake place. The writer remembers such world education conference held in Oct-Nov. 1962 in which educationists from whole world except China took part. Central aid was available for such programmes.

A conference of BT and B Ed. Collage held in Bangalore which had reviewed the then existing teacher training programme. The conference held that the teacher training is a key for the development of all round education. The member of conference opined that he quality of the teachers depend on:

1. The innate aptitude of the pupils and teacher's teaching,
2. Right understanding of the pupils by the teacher while teaching,

3. Insight and dedication regarding teaching profession by the teacher,
4. Interest of the teacher towards knowledge gaining,
5. Clerity of the ideas of both the pupils the teacher
6. The teacher training institutions should explore and infuse all these.

There is another idea is that the teacher can teach by experience and there is no need for teacher training.

This is a dangerous idea, because a set of experience can not develop without training. As such, a sound mind can not be developed, which is essential for thinking, reasoning, analyzing, comprehending and learning. And mental health of the student can not be developed without infusing a spirit of thinking and reasoning without which students' personality can not be developed. This is why educationists recommend two way process of communication in teaching.

The future of teachers training now seems to be bright as the National Council of Teacher Education has totally removed the commercialization from teacher Training which had threatened the ingenuity and sincerity of teacher education. Still the no work culture, where it exists, is threatening the life of teacher education. Therefore, it is necessary to remove this virus from teacher training institutes. The teacher should be apprised about the verstability of teacher education. He should know about the teaching profession, its ethics and Indian past history of the teacher. The society should also give due respect to the teacher. This can only be done by the reversal of hedonism to simple living high thinking in the society.

6

The Teacher

"गुरु गोविन्द दोनों खड़े काके लागू पाँव।
बलहारी गुरु आपनो जिन गोविन्द दियो दिखाये।।"
गुरु बिन जग अंधारा। संत कबीर

—संत कबीर

"The teacher and Almighty both are standing to whom should I bow, thanks to the teacher who enabled me to see the Lord".

"There is darkness without Guru (teacher)."

—Sant Kabir

The individuality of the teacher has many faceds. From the emergence of human beings and consequent evolution of human society in the world, teacher has ever been a constructive upbringer of the young. The man has ever been educating the youngs to lead a good socio-economic life and create cultures and civilizations. It is the teacher who has been doing this role. He has always been respected in the society by all.

The teacher has ever been doing noble work in the society by upbringing the youngers—educating them in all aspects of life, that is, in social moralization, enculturation, in gaining skills for earning live-hood. So the teaching profession was considered a noble profession in olden times. In olden times, the teacher was a religions preacher, he never desired material gains, so he was non-inclinative too. Being sympathetic to his disciples, he had sympathetic love to them, so had a close rapport with them. In reciprocation, the students also always respected their teacher considered with unique and equate him with their father. The teacher was respected by all including the ruler or the king of the country in all societies. As such, the teacher has always been a specific functionary in educating and up-bringing the youngsters.

Education of the young existed in al times in all societies. And the teacher has ever been a main functionary in this pursuit. Now, because of scientific revolution and consequent industrial development, urbanization, decrease in child mortality due to health care and also emergence of democratic political structure, education of the young got a boost. The demographic explosion has also changed the social scenario of the world. Every body has right to education. So number of the educational institutions, like schools, technical institutions and universities, has enormously increased. This required a large number of teachers. So the scope of teaching profession has also enormously increased. When there is an expansion in any sphere of social activity, it entails a flux in its working standard so there is a fear of falling down of standards. So fear of fall in the standards of teaching profession can not be ruled out. So there appeared a lot of changes in teaching profession. Now teaching methodologies, techniques, various ways of presentation, use of teaching aids have also emerged. But due to over loaded curriculum and process of formal cducation teaching profession became mechanized and purpose of teaching became more of passing of information, not taking out knowledge. In older time, especially in India taking out of knowledge was done through Vad-Vivad. Clergy was prominent teaching profession, and conservative method based on verbal communication was the only method, but it entailed a deep personal interaction which is necessary for education. Now due to the development of science and technology new methods of progressive teaching have emerged. So it is necessary to make the future teachers aware about all perspectives of teaching profession. Therefore during the course of teacher training, the teacher is to be made aware about all pros and cones of the teaching profession.

If we peep into the etymology of the word 'teach' we feel that it has many, wide and varied meanings which indicate that teaching, which is done by the teacher, has also wide and varied spectrum. The word 'teach' has been derived from the Anglo-Sexon word 'teccon' which means—'to teach', 'to instruct', 'to point out', 'to guide', 'to train', 'to tell', 'to show' and 'to punish and to command', and 'also to demonstrate', 'to do preaching', 'to act' as a 'mystic gospel' etc. etc. The Sanskrit word 'Sikhs' (शिक्ष) means 'a process of upbringing' and 'Siksha' (शिक्षा) is 'upbringing'. The Sanskrit word 'Vidh' (विद्य) means a method of self-learning and 'Vidya' (विद्या) means self-learning which is tantamount to English word 'Education'. And this is done through the process of teaching which is done by the teacher. As such, who teaches is a teacher. The teacher is an expert and passes on his acquired knowledge to the students. The teacher applies different teaching methods and techniques for educating the youngs—in other words using his/her acquired knowledge in the form of information, to motivate the students to learn themselves. Telling, narrating, showing, instructing, training, demonstrating, questioning and guiding are the methods a teacher uses while he/she teaches. And above all these, innovating, motivating, sympathising for self-learning, establishing rapport with the students and praising or encouraging the students are necessary tools of teaching. These can make the teaching a success and concert it into education.

In the present socio-economic, cultural and political scenario of the society the teacher's job has become very complex. The members of the society are generally engrilled by hedonism, xenophilism, meglomaniaism and acculturarism, which have badly affected the younger generation, so the teaching has become very complex and an arduous job. It needs a thorough study of prevalent socio-economic,. cultural, political and theological conditions of the society, and also the visualization of the present and past systems of teaching in the society.

In the older days the teacher, who was given the teaching job was a pivot in the society for the social development. He was a preacher first and a teacher later. In old Indian Brahmanical system of education, carried on in and Ashrams and Gurukulas, only preachers of religion, morality, and sociability were preferred to teach. Their days used to start with preaching, meditation and thereby initiating the young students in religion, sociability and telling then about 'dharma', 'adharma', 'netika' and 'anetika', 'naya' and 'anaya' and thereby preparing the youngster for leading to make the whole society as a sane society. These social concepts were explicitly elucidated through teaching. The teaching was based on exposition of nature to the students (छात्रों), through Vad-vivad and samvad (debates and symposiums). This process used to give the students a chance to think, to reason, analyse, comprehend and finally to learn, or to motivate the students for self-learning. Such type of education was purely based on conservative methods of teaching and was purely for the preparation for life making a person for sane social life while living in granthashrama.

The teacher was called 'Guru' which means heavy. The student was called a 'shishya'—a learner one who used to acquire knowledge under the guidance of the Guru. The 'Shishya' was not only supposed to be obedient, cordial, intimate, punctual but one who was to be believer in blood relationship nature. The relationship between the Guru and Shishya used to be of father and son relationship, not only while living Gurukula but throughout life. In Gurukulas the life of the Student was shaped as per requirements of the nation. This is why Gurukulas were called forming houses, as Takshila (now in Pakistan) was named, and it was famous. The Gurus used to ignite an unique life pattern. 'Early to bed and early' to rise was the base of life building. After natural calls the students use to take bath and thereafter, they had to do *pooja*, meditation and yoga and, thereafter help in the ashram activities as catering of cows. The Rishis used to live in dense jungles, they also used to teach the students and give religious sermons. The Gurukulas were also situated in jungles on river banks. The way of living in Gurukulas was very simple. Gurukulas kitchens were supported by the society. On the whole the teaching aim of Gurukula', education was to inculcate the religious tenets, morality, sociality and ethical codes in students.

In Buddhist monasteries in India and abroad in Muslim *Madarasa* in middle east and in Christian church schools the education was imparted on the same lines as was done in India. The preacher-cum-teacher was proficient in religious preaching, having deep knowledge of religious literature and scriptures, language and social institutions. His teaching was co-relative. He had always soft ear and heart to words the students. The teacher has very little desire and wants. He used to have food along with the students. As such the teacher was not inclinative at all. The teaching was considered a sacred and pious job, as the teacher considered teaching his dharma to pass on knowledge to next generation and motivate the students for self-learning.

In olden days the aim of education was to establish a stable, sane co-operative and honest atmosphere in the society which was only possible when the future guardians might be honest, corruption free and diligent citizens. It is also noticed that the

Gurukulas used to admit the students from both rich and poor families but only from 'divijas' that too 'Brahmans' and 'Kshtryas'. Ujjaini Gurukula was one such example where Shri Krishna (Yadav Rajput) and poor Sudama Brahman's boy studied together under Guru Maharshi Sandipti at Ujjaini. Likewise, in Maharshi Vashist's Ashram King Dasarath's Sons—Ram, Lakshman, Bharat and Shatrughan had to renounce the royal family status for getting education. In Gurukulas instructions were given in tap-Sadhna, i.e., austerity, Lokardhna (public welfare) and Vashistha Vayahara (good manner lines). The another aim of Gurukulas was spreading education. Gurukula of Maharishi Vedpuri at Vedpuri, Gurukula of Maharshi Bhardwaj at Prayag, Gurukula Sudarshana of Swami Vishwamitra were the examples, where the educational aim was 'Loksiksha' that is education for the masses. The imagination of 'Ram Rajya' was given at Sudhashrama of Maharishi Vishwamitra.

In due course of time many of Gurukulas got wide spread recognition at national and international level. Nalanda (Rajgiri), Vikaram Shila (Bhagalpur) in Bihar, Vallabhi in Kathiawad and Taxila (now in N.W.F. Pakistan) Gandar were such universities where students used to flock from far of places like China, Thailand, Indonesia, Kandhara and Greece for studying Indian religion, religious literature and Indian culture. These Vishwa Vidyalaya (Gurukulas) had produced teacher like Chankaya who had imagined greater India. Nalanda had teachers like Kumaril Bhatt on whose lines Shankacharya laid a strong foundation of Indian religious monotheism and of splendid Indian Culture. Many thinkers from eastern Europe Countries came to Taxila to know about the Indian Culture and religion. It is from Taxila the Greeks get the idea of immortality of soul. Teachers from these Universities also travelled to far distant countries like China, Thailand, Vietnam, Indonesia and Shri Lanka etc. etc. Ujjaini, Kanchipuram, Amaravati, Auditpura were the Gurukula, where the teaching aim was to educate the pupil and make them cultured and socialised. Gurukula 'Aryanaka prampra' (making aryans) consolidated the Indian culture and religion which fostered morality, sociability and brotherhood inspite of rigid caste structure. Main stalwarts were the teachers of the Gurukulas and Rishi Asharmas.

Every religious place, and tirthsthals like 'Badrinath', Kedarnath, Rishikesh, Gangotri, Yamunotri, Haridwar, Mathura, Prayag, Varanasi, Patliputra, Ujjain, and Puri etc. etc. were the places where Maharshis and Rishis used to travel along with their disciples and used to give Praverehans (discourses) to the people during their stay at these tirthsthals. As such people in the vicinity of tirthsthalas were largely benefited. These gurukulas and religious matters like Nalanda were functioning like open Universities where any body from India and abroad could get admission and get education by interacting by the teachers.

In recent times, Gurukul Kangri Haridwar (UA), Gurkul Narsen Distt. Muzzaffer Nagar (U.P.) and many Gurukulas at other places as Shanti Niketan (Bengal) established by Guru Rabindra Nath Tagore and Rishi Valley Schools established by Shri J. Krishna Murthy for the revital of Indian old culture and stopping cultural diffusion and acculturation. The teachers of these institutions tried to retrieve back the honour and prestige of the teaching profession. Still these institutions are doing good jobs.

Hereclitus said that every thing is in flux. Society also changes with the passage of time. Our society became modern due to westernization and consequent industrialization and urbanization. Not only Indian society but all societies changed due to fast strides of communication, better travel facilities. All world societies are coming closer to each other. So our educational systems have also changed. Our present system of education is also an alien system of education. So the roles of the teachers have also changed. The teacher is a permanent functionary of the educational institute; his role is formal which yields formality in the process of education. The teachers role in olden days was to look to common enterprise of the society and not of students alone. Now the teacher is to devote to complete prescribed subjects as per school curriculum and prepare the students for examination. The state is to provide funds. It has little to do regarding enculturation, whereas in old Indian system of education enculturation was the main aim. Now the state has total control over the educational infra-structure, not only in India but in the whole world, with an aim to provide same education to all students irrespective of their individual differences, in all subjects, is not logical. In other words it is like mass production of epistemacy on the pattern of consumer goods. And this mass operation is like an operation of a die machine producing nuts and bolts. In the words of late Shri R.N. Tagore our educational is operating like a production unit of a factory. The teacher has no option but to follow what is desired by the state.

So, the present teacher is a tool in the hands of the educational administrators for achieving stipulated and designed desired ends of the state. No doubt the state desires to give maximum information and knowledge equally to all younger generation of the state irrespective of their taste and abilities. But, in many case the state rulers want to pass on their ideology on the youngsters. Every teacher is supposed to be proficient atleast in two subjects. The state and its educational bureaucrats and democrat decide what to teach? How to teach? and when to teach? How much content of the course is be taught? The teacher has no say in this regard and he has to follow the instructions. The teacher has to teach a prescribed content of the subjects with in a specified time that is, with in one academic season which generally starts from first week of July and ends in the last week of March every year. And at the end of the session the students are examined at annual examination, are certified and are promoted to next higher classes. This is necessary because our system of formal education gives top priority to the examination results as to face the existing blatant competition in the society.

Our teacher has to observe some formalities for teaching. He/she is required to be a class room teacher of a particular class. He/she has to maintain a teaching record, and prepare unit and daily teaching lesson plans for the lessons to be taught. A teacher in a school has to take six periods approximately every day. Besides this, the teacher is to do some writing work or office work as maintenance of class room records, checking of exercise books and preparation for period and annual and half yearly examinations. All this takes a lot of time. The preparation of first unit plan and, later on lesson plans for number of lesson to be taught is an arduous job. So the teacher in school has to work in a mechanical way. Such was not the ease in older days. This is why, the teacher in older days was able to keep a close rapport with his students, through Vad-Vivad and Samvad (debates and seminars). The present teacher is also supposed to enculturate the students. But it can not be possible in an atmosphere of cumbersome load of teaching. Take for example lesson planning. It is not any easy job. The teacher is supposed to decide the subject content first semisterwise in unit plans and, then termwise unit plan is to be divided in daily lesson plans. The lesson planning is to have a strategic way or plan, how to proceed. It should have (*a*) how much subject is to be taught in one period (*b*) how to proceed? (*c*) What teaching aids are to be used. (*d*) the main emphasis is to be laid on the evolvement of the students to make elicitations as much possible can be, (*e*) use of black board and finally, (*f*) recapitulation to be done. And if necessary some home work should be given to the students. Generally, the academic year is divided in three terms (*a*) first July to September, (*b*) second October to December and (*c*) the third from January to March. April is reserved for examinations and for fresh admission. Usually teaching in schools takes its full form in July. While planning a lesson a teacher is also supposed to indicate the topic to be taught in the class, age group of the students, period number and time, general and specific objectives of teaching the particular topic. Also the teacher is supposed to mention the method of teaching to be applied, the procedure of introduction of the topic—either by referring to previous knowledge or pointing out or relating to particular problem or problems prevalent in the society. Since the teacher is supposed to adopt a progressive method of teaching, he or she will have to mention the particular teaching method of teaching and use of related teaching aids. The teacher is not supposed to be a mere informer or narrator. Teaching and Educations are entirely two different concepts. The teaching should be used as a tool for education. The aim of teaching should he that the students may be encouraged to learn themselves. As such, the whole process of teaching should be based on interaction between the teacher and taughts. In Other words the teaching should always entail two way communication between the teacher and the students. Inter-action can contributes to self-education. So the whole planning of teaching should be aimed on self-education of the students. So questioning and thereby clinching of information should he written on chalkboard. The teacher should encourage the students to respond. This can only be possible if there exists a friendly atmosphere in the class room. Questioning, and in term, cross-question and thereby reinformation and recapitulation should always entail the lesson development.

Doing all this is not an easy job for a teacher, in a situation when a teacher is bound to teach at least six periods every day, out of eight periods. Generally, it is also noticed that the chalkboards are so defective on which he teacher can not write. Other teaching aids are also not available in majority of the schools. In such a such a situation how can a teacher follow the progressive method of teaching. So the teacher is bound to depend on verbal one way communication and full fill the teaching requirements of taking six periods every day. In such a situation the teaching becomes a boring and tiresome job. And main aim of true educating the students is not achieved. The annual results of the students do not come as are expected and teacher is unnecessarily blamed for this.

In some schools the number of teachers is less. It is because of centralized system of governance of the schools. In such a situation, the teaching load on teachers of such school is burden some. It become more difficult when some teachers go on leave. Some teachers avoid such extra-teaching on some pretexts, as they are not proficient in that particular subject. In a situation the arrangements periods are forced on some co-operative teachers which become tiresome for them. In such situation the teaching become a new formality. In some schools there are teachers who are incompetent being products of the so called commercial teaching institutes. They are like some unskilled craft, physical and yoga teachers. Such teachers come through reserved or preferential quota. Services of such teachers remain more or less unulitized or semilitized and they as pass their time either in doing some other work or pleasing the authorities. Such a dys-functioning elements, affect the working of other teachers also. As a result the teaching at the school as whole is badly affected and standards of the school teaching go down. Such preferential teachers badly affect the teaching in industrial schools, because they lack required skills. Since they get certificate they get employment in schools. As such, it would be better if teachers are appointed on merits.

There are various categories of schools and other educational institutions. Different categories of schools are like, 'Creches, day care schools, kindergarten schools, Nursery schools, primary schools, middle schools, secondary schools, senior secondary schools and industrial training schools. For all these schools different categories of teacher are also required. These teachers need different kinds of varied teacher training. In addition to these schools there are colleges, higher institutions and universities which also do teaching and educating. There are industrial training institutes, polytechnics Engineering colleges, Regional Institute of Technologies. Indian Institute of technologies and university and also research institutes. The teacher are also equal for such institute;

but these teachers are not required professional training. For colleges, the University Grants Commission has laid down a text called NAT which is compulsory for all requirement of such teachers.

Nomenclature of the teachers of these different institutions, schools, colleges and university also vary. These teachers are designated as per schools and institutes. They are called as—Creche teachers, Nursery School teachers, primary school teacher, middle school teacher, secondary school teachers—as T.G.T. and P.G.T.S., instructors, lectures Asst. Professors, Asocial Professors (in I.I.Ts). Lectures Readers and Professors in the university. Creche teacher perform motherly roles. The Nursery school teacher generally play with the children. And other teacher teach in school and train teachers the youngs in 3Rs. These youngs are further taught in secondary schools colleges and university at advance level. So the teachers at all levels perform their assigned roles sincerely.

If measured in terms of numbers teaching is the worlds' biggest profession. In early 1980 it was estimated that there were 30,000,000 teachers through out the world. Now due to demographic explosion are expansion of democratic rights in the world we see an immense explosion in the educational world. we can presume that number might have crossed the figure of 40,000,000. Though roles and functions of the teachers differ from country to country. Variations are also generally found with in the country.

Because, the nature of the activities that constitute teaching depends on the age of students being taught, and subject content to be taught. The role of the teachers widely differ, so also there is categorization. The teacher categories in 1980 had appropriate ratio of 57 per cent at secondary (including primary and middle schools) level and at senior secondary level and, 9 per cent at university level including technical institutes. These proportion differed from country to country.

As regards the status of the teacher, in the society, the teaching is still considered a respectful profession. But due to materialistic and hedonistic atmosphere prevalent in a rich section of the society the teacher does not enjoy the status to which he deserves. Also a credential of teachers status depends upon his/her educational qualifications, training, sincerity to words the students, and application of innovatory techniques in teaching, rapport with the students. Mostly the teachers are well qualified. But the teacher are not well paid. There are little chances of promotion for the teachers. Main cause of disregard of the teacher in the society is materialism. Because of moral degradation and corruption many become rich with in a short period in the society. They start to consider the teacher purchasable. The examination based formal education has added fire to this problem. The neorich class engage teachers as tutors of their children. Doing tuitions always entails contempt on the personality of teacher, which many teachers do to meet their house hold expenses. Girl teachers are always favoured by males as their life partners because they earn. For a better social status for the teacher, the society should think deeply and, should create a congenial atmosphere in the society for that. The teacher should also peep into the past history of teaching profession and should earnestly follow the teacher's professional ethics.

7
Teaching Profession

For effective teaching, knowledge of some of its sociological cultural, axiological as well as epistemological aspects in historical perspective are necessary, so as to understand its professional imperatives. Let us, first understand its etymological as well as epistemological aspects, so as, to know its professional bearings. The word 'teach' is a derivation from the Anglo-Saxon word 'taccon' which means—'to impart', 'to instruct', to train'. So teaching is an act of instructing or imparting knowledge to a person who is unaware about it. Also its equivalent Greek word 'dicknilin' also means to 'impart' to demonstrate and to give instructions for doing a business, 'to preach', 'to act' to punish as a minister gospel etc. The Sanskrit word 'Siksh' means to bring up and the Sanskrit word 'Vidha' means a process of learning which is tantamount to English word 'education'. Thus, the act of teaching, which is done by the teacher, entails a process of self-learning by the taughts. The word 'prafession' is a derivation from the Greek word 'profession' which has its roots in Latin word 'profitere' meaning 'to profess' to lay down, 'to claim' something new, 'an opening for new knowledge'. Both the words—teaching and profession have epistemological bearings in their own their boundaries. Teaching is done by a knowledgeable person to younger generation. So teaching and education are two side of an epistemic coin and are two different activities. A youth or a person who is unaware about something, is generally informed about that thing by a knowledgeable person. If the youth or person is innovated and motivated to think, reason about the information he can comprehend and learn which becomes his education. Teaching by giving mere information is insufficient for educating a person. It should always entail an educational process. This is what the modern progressive methods of teaching require.

The teaching profession is as old as the evolution of the human society, culture and civilization. Not only man, being a rational being, but other animals, birds, beasts and insects have always been trying to teach their offsprings. In the beginning oral teaching was a common feature. Parents, grand parents and other elderly men, women used to teach their youngsters by telling about the family as well as social life. They used to narrate some stories of animals, beasts, birds and insects about morality, fraternity and about their social life. These stories were used from Jatkas'. This was to emphasise how these are important for human life and how these can lead human beings far saneful living. The oral system of teaching continued in primitive age. When man learned speaking and developed writing the human experiences are recorded and passed on to the younger generation, finally a solid system of education came into being. Indian old system of education was developed this way.

The British people imposed their western type of formal education on Indians in forties of the nineteenth century. The aim of this type of education was to produce loyal, cheap government employees for the then British Government in India. This alien system of education out-tracked the old indigenous system—the Gurukula system and non-formal education which were aimed at the bring sociability, economic self-sufficiency and homogenity economic self-sufficiency and homogenity in Indian society. The formal system of education turned the old system of education totally topsy-turocy. So the non-formal educational old teaching system has totally changed. The alien formal system of education has totally changed the earlier Indian system of education, that is, Gurukula system and non-formal system and Madarasa system, which had teaching professional ethics. The mode of Indian teaching profession changed to commercial from axiological and teleological. Social harmony was converted to cut-throat competition and social disharmony. The Britishers set up industries which required workforce. So the formal education system created a social infra-structure on the western model. The aim of education remained limited only to 3Rs. Important educational aims like enculturation have been totally ignored. With the result acculturation took place of enculturation. The English rulers established, new educational infra-structure keeping in view their covert aims. Educational infra-structure was called Departments of Public instructions which were to be ruled by the Directors of Public Instructions in all provinces. One Director of Public instruction, who was posted at Lahore (now in Pakistan) had bitterly criticised the imposition of formal system of education and had praised the Indian non-formal system of education saying that this would damage the Indian culture. The introduction of formal education totally changed the Indian educational scenario. The Education which was based on teaching ethics and aimed at enculturation has totally gone. As such the role of the teacher became vocational in place of professional.

As such roots of teaching in every society are very deep and have some professional norms. Men/women have always been aspiring to prepare their offspring by training and educating them for good living in the society. The joint family system, in the past used to teach and to educate the youngs first demonstrating and talking which was to be imitated by the youngers. The family used to follow an axiological code while teaching the youngs. The grand-parents and elderly men and women used to play a prominent role in teaching the younger generation. Main agenda of teaching used to be, to generate basic tenets of character building and enculturation through ushering them into religious activities and thereby creating axiological norms, which ought to infuse a spirit of honesty, integrity, sharing and co-operative living. The main aim of initiating the youngster in moral truthful and religious activities was to prepare them for leading a saneful, social, truthful, corruption free life in the society. The joint family system, which is now crumbling, used to play a key role in imparting this type of ideal education. The Indian institution of joint family was a boon for Indian society. The intoxication of material greed, which has been inculcated in Indian social life due to cultural diffusion and consequent acculturation has not only damaged the Indian institute of joint family system but made the people very greedy and has totally mitigated the Indian teaching professional ethics. The Indians now are continuously killing the joint family system, while some western countries like USA are aspiring for joint family system of Indian type. A few years ago the America first lady Hillary Clinton had pleaded for a joint family system of Indian pattern in USA Indian joint family system was best teaching and educating institution, which used to teach its children using a teaching professional ethics. This system has been crumbled down due to westernization, urbanization, modernization, industrialization and aculturation. This trend is like adulteration of food stuffs and edible oils which finally results in devastation and deaths Human self-centredness, greed and corruption, which were effectively checked by professionally imparted familial education through in-built system of teaching and educating the youngs, now has spread its wings to crumble the joint family system by dividing into nuclear families. The new social change has robbed us of our age old social values which were imparted by familial education in professional ways. We have lost our antique methods of character building good behaviour, some social traits, customs, morality, cultural heritage and non-competitive self-sufficient economy which had roots in our age old familial professional system of education. This was done by the joint families through sound familial education. Now in the modern materialistic age it is very difficult for the teacher to achieve all these aims.

Now the wife and husband both are in material rat-race for acquiring materialist and hedonistic materials as much as possible. They both go for jobs and drops their kids at the mercy of creches for day care. Now-a-days running creches is a big business especially in metropoloses like Delhi, Mumbai, Chennai, and Kolkata. Creches are run even by rich ladies who employ ladies as teachers and they do provide space of creches. Now-a-days, generally, husband and wife live in nuclear family, and they do not have time to devote for familial education of their children. As such, the young children are deprived of their familial education. And grand parents also do not want to do this as they also live separately from their sons and daughter-in-law.

In olden times in India, through familial education, the parents wanted to further educate their children ontology, epistemology, axiology, metaphysics and grammar. They used to send their male children to Gurukulas. Generally Gurukulas used to admit the children of two upper varnas Brahmans and Kshtriyas. The children of other two Varnas Vaishyas and Sudras used to get education of their family occupation in non-formal way, as occupations were done castewise. Particular castes used to do particular trades. As such, neither there was need for out teacher, nor for a technical institution for training in particular trades. The parents were the teachers, as well as the preparators for jobs, as they used to train their offsprings in family trades hereditically.

In Gurukulas the teacher were preachers of religion. The Maharishis, Rishis and Munis were experts in ontology, astrology, mathematics, sanskrit, axiology and metaphysics. To pursue these disciplines throughout their lives was their life motto. They were self-appointed teachers as they were dedicated to epistemacy, sincerity for spreading of epistemacy to the younger generation and used to offer their services in Gurukula for teaching without any material gains. They were all educated and proficient in the subjects, they were going to teach. They were very sincere to their disciples. They were called Gurus—the auspicious and pious real teachers who used to observe professional ethical code. These students—the disciples were called then shisyas' who also used to observe a code of conduct of 'shisyas'. Many famous Guru like 'Ved Vyasa', Vishwamitra, Bhargawa, Droanacharya, Shukracharya, Acharya Chankaya and Shankaracharya etc. etc. are still on our lips. The state had no control over Gurukulas, and likewise later on Muslim Madarasas. These institutions were supported by the society alone. They rulers were allowed to contribute but they did not have any say in the administration of the Gurukulas. The Dharamacharyas upgraded Gurus, used to manage the Gurukulas with the assistance of other Gurus. Epistemacy, specificity in one area, simplicity, high thinking, and sincerity to words the students was their professional ethics. And these were the ethos found in all Gurukulas and ashram. A Gurukulas was like a family—an abode of Gurus and Shishyas. The Gurus were like parents and Shishyas were like children at the Gurukulas family. The Gurus used to deal with the conscious being, working for the righteous upbringing of Shishyas. There were series of group discussion which were called Vad-Vivad. Also when large number of participants used to take part in discussions, this was called 'samvad'. These were the common features in Gurukula Education. Thus the teachers (Gurus) were not mere informers but they were real educators. Their clients that is Shishyas, were not ignorant clients, like the clients of a doctor, lawyer and clergyman. The teacher (Guru) at Gurukula was a true professionist. Similar was the position of Christian Priest teachers at churches and Maulvi teachers at Muslim Madarasas. Gurukul Kangri Haridwar (U.A.) and Darul alum at Deoband, Distt Saharanpur (U.P.) are still examples of the professionist education in India.

If we look to Helenistic culture we find that were two kind of teachers—Sophists teachers and philosopher teachers. Sophists—like Epicures, Democrats, Protagores and Ananagores were the travelling teachers. They used to charge from their disciples for their subsistence. Our contemporary teachers can be equated with the sophists of Greece. On the other hand there were philosopher teachers like—Thales, Permendes Hippocrates, Socrates, Crito, Hereclitus, Plato, Isocrates and Aristotle who hailed from rich families. Their were epistemic, proficient, sincere to their disciples and non-inclinative. They can be equated with the Gurus of Indian Gurukulas. The spread of knowledge, promotion of philosophy, ontology, justice and law, axiology, teleology and metaphysics was the aim of their life. They discussed epistemological problems like opposites, atoms, planetary, system of law, medicine, art and craft, education beauty, soul, sociability and good government. They always encouraged their disciples to think, reason, analyze, discuss and proficiate on these issues.

In Buddhist monasteries and *mathas* in India, in confusicious centres in China and Sufi centres in some Islamic countries, the teaching was done which led to education. The teachers were there, proficient, sincere and non-inclinative like old Indian teachers, the Gurus at Gurukulas. They used to maintain teaching professional ethics. Teaching in technical trades were given in technical guilds in Europe unlike India. Skills in trades like carpentry, blacksmithy, tinsmithy coppersmithy etc. etc. were imparted by journey men at the guilds. The guild master used to be an expert in these trades. Besides, this he was a teacher in all these technical trades. He usually did not charge anything for pupils' training. The guilds were training-cum-production centres. The pupils basically used to go for an apprenticeship. They used to stay at the guild for specified time and work for the guild incharge.

In olden times, generally teachers used to follow professional ethics throughout the world. Be it a guild, or a church school or an Islamic Madarasa or a Gurukula, the teachers used to follow the professional ethics which entailed proficiency sincerity and non-inclinativeness. On the other hand neither a capitalist nor a soldier, nor a bureaucratic or businessmen never followed a professional code of conduct. All of them worked, and still work, to earn money not only for their subsistence but for hedonism and xenophilism. Their working was considered vocationalism. Now, the entire teaching community wherever they are working, share the critical elements of bureaucratic working. The teacher should have (*a*) a specialized knowledge of the subject he or she is going to teach (*b*) a formal training in teaching theory and processes (*c*) he or she must have a certifying degree for teaching, (*d*) the teacher should have a set of standard of performance in the teaching profession—as intellectual, practical and ethical. All these are defined, and inforced by a body of teaching community.

Before 20th century, teaching young children and even adolescents could hardly been called a profession anywhere in the World. It was instead an art or craft in which the young entrants—men/women hold most of the teaching positions. They used to teach the youngs and adolescents generally through verbal communication. The teachers are considered knowledgeable. They learn the art of teaching by observing, imitating their own teachers. Only University professors and few teachers of elite secondary schools teachers have the merit of being called members of the teaching profession in the sense of definition of the term profession. Even to day, in most of the countries there is no clear demarcation about the teachers, as to whom the title of profession can be adorned. Therefore, it will be useful to consider the following parameters for deciding the term profession. (1) What should be the status of profession?, (2) What kind of work or works related obligations a profession should entail? and (3) how should it be organized?

Sociologists say that a "profession is relationship between an expert and an ignorant client. There are three parameter necessary for a professionist (1) a professionist should be an expert in his/her field of work. He or she should always continuously add to his/her knowledge. He/she should be epistemic, that is, should not be satisfied with the boundaries of his/her acquired knowledge, (2) A professionist must always be sincere to his ignorant clients and (3) professionist should never be inclinative. In the olden days only three professions were recognized by the sociologists and other thinkers (1) doctor—a doctor always deals an ignorant patient. Sometimes the illness of the ignorant patient is so deep, it becomes very different for the doctor to diagnose it. Therefore, it is very necessary for a doctor to be epistemic and enquiring. (2) The doctor is supposed to give full attention to his ailing patient, even at the cost of his/her comfort and finally (3) the doctor should be non-inclinative. He should not aspire anything from his ignorant ill client. Now the situation has gone topsy-turvy, doctors sometimes are so greedy that they ignore the interests of their ignorant clients. For the sincerity the doctors take Hippocratic after completing the medical course (MBBS). But, it is doubtful whether all doctors know what does actually profession mean? Like, allopathic doctors the vaids are also required to take 'charak oath'. The vaids are also supposed to be epistamice, sincere to his patients and non-inclinative. In the writers village, there was a famous vaid late Pt. Chinta Ram Sharma. He has passed five year course of 'Vaidacharya' from Govt. Ayurvedic College, Suttar Mandi Lahore (now in Pakistan). After doing this Vaidic course when he returned to his Village he decided to follow "Charak Oath" strictly and decided not to charge any thing from the village patients. He used to get up early in the morning and after doing his prayer, he used to visit patients in all four Mohallas of the village. Generally all patients he used to attend, used to be healthy very soon. Few villagers asked him Panditji "why you did not charge', and reply was that he did so under 'Charak Oath'. Finally the villager decided and advised the people to throw some amount in his 'Baithak' through window. Adherence to charak oath and sincerity to his patients made him a famous vaid of Punjab and Uttar Pradesh. Many Rajas and Nawabs used to be cured by him. He used to follow the same principle with Rajas and Nawabs, who used to drop some money in his back bag. Likewise. There was a Muslim Rajput of village 'Sikrodha'. He used to entertain Sadhus going from Shakumbra Devi (शाकुम्बरा देवी) temple to Haridawar. One day a Sadhu was impressed by his hospitability, and took the Muslim Rajput in adjoining hill. He apprised this Muslim Rajput about a herb which was to be used for snake bite and said that herb would be effective if he would be sincere to snake bite persons and would be non-inclinative. The Rajput Muslim buyed a horse, and after getting information he used to cure snake bite patients. He had become famous in district Saharanpur, U.P.

Like doctors or medical profession a lawyer's or legal profession is considered a profession. A lawyer is supposed to follow the professional ethos like a doctor. But, now-a-days medical profession as well as legal profession have become inclinative professions. And people know to what extent these two professionists are gripped in greed. The third profession is clergy.

In the olden days, in all religious the priests used to follow the professional ethics and they used to guide the people about spirituality, truthfulness and about all ontological and axiological issues. Now-a-days, it is seen that the pujaris, Maulvis and Priests have become tantriks and earn money. Their tantras harms many people.

Now, the boundaries of profession have extended and many vocations like engineering, education claim that these are professions, because the followers of these profession try, the epistemacy and are sincere. But these are not non-inclinative. Also many service occupation like barbers, sweepers etc. claim that there work areas are their professions. Such assumption is wrong.

Some sociologists and thinkers doubt whether the teaching can be considered a profession. They argue that the present teaching neither has the required credential of a profession as most the teachers are not non-inclinature. They say that the present teachers is at lower level and in most cases at the university level also the teachers do not fulfill the requirements for being called a professionist. Many of the primary school teachers in rural areas mostly devote to their home work in the morning. They till their lands, feed then cattles and then come to the primary school for taking rest. Also many of the teachers in middle, secondary and senior secondary schools do not upbring themselves, which could get the status of teaching profession. They lack proficiency and sincerity. Similar is the case at university level. Many university lecturers lack proficiency, sincerity and epistemacy, so they do not deserve to be called professionists. It is also noticed that many of the teachers lack sincerity to their clients, that is students. As a matter of fact teachers' job is more difficult than a doctor or a lawyer. A teachers client is not an ignorant client like that of a doctor, or a lawyer or a priests' client. A teacher's client is an intelligent and diligent client, his handling is much more difficult than a client of a doctor or a lawyer. The teacher's client is a conscious being. He is eager for self learning. But in many cases the teachers hardly care about do their clients and teach them formally by passing information. The teachers should innovate and motivate the students for self-learning, which can be done by igniting thinking, reasoning and comprehending in them. Undue work-load on teachers may be one reason for this negligence in teaching. Another reason may be hedonistic ostensity found in the society. The teacher also wants to earn money for becoming hedonistic and xenoplastic. This trend affects the sincerity of the teacher. This raises a question mark on the sincerity of the teacher. Many teachers do side business covertly. The situation in rural school is more bad. For the teachers teaching is an additional business because they devote to their home work. This is why the younger generation in rural areas remain backward. The teachers do not have any time for adding to their knowledge. There are hardly school attend libraries. Only guide books are advised for preparation of the annual examination.

The condition at the higher level is also not good. Rather it is worse. Observance of hartals and strikes is a common feature in some universities. The university teachers unions have only the priority to force the teachers go on strike for the material gains. This unions do not have any place for inservice teacher training for motivating the teachers to motivate the students to be epitemic, and encourage the university teachers to follow the profession ethics.

As a matter of fact that teaching profession which was considered a noble profession in the olden days has now became a commercial and mechanical profession. It only devotes, to the examination good results securing highest marks. Teaching profession is hardly seen. Good teaching can not be done unless the teachers know sincerely and fully about professional ethics, culture, sociability and national economy, sanity and enculturation.

8

Professional Requirements of the Teacher

For doing or learning any work some process and rules are to be adopted. It can not be denied that all animals including human beings try to learn themselves. But it is seen that human beings when guided and helped, learn quickly. Such help first start from home. Thereafter the youngers are guided and helped to learn in the school. So, it would not be wrong to say that the teacher is an agent of social change. He is the moulder of the personalities of the youngers. He is the builder of the nation, as it is who teaches the younger generation. As such, generally the quality of education depends upon the quality of the teacher. So, the quality of the society depends upon the quality of the teacher. If the teacher is not good how can there be a good social change and good social atmosphere. And in other words we can say that social improvement is impossible without a good teacher.

Every person can never be competent in all social activities. So every teacher can never be a competent teacher. In olden times there were born teachers, who were proficient and competent to impart knowledge to the students and encourage them for self-learning. These teachers were prominent epistemic scholars. They were dedicated to social cause. They used to apprise the students about the Indian cultural traditions, religion, axiology, sociability, thereby they used to enculturate the youngers.

As the time passed and due to the demographic explosion, the teaching avenues expanded, and the demand of the teachers also increased manifold. When expansion in sphere of any activity increases, it also always entails distortion in the quality. Increase in educational activities also increased the demand of the teachers.

Educational activities also became formal. The concept of form or formal always entails a notional formality which always entails fall in standard. In such a situation the responsibility of the teacher training institutions becomes complex. But when the number of teacher training institutes increases, the performance quality of these institutes also falls. Now, there are so many teacher training institutes in the country. And four or five years back there was a spate in such institution due to B.Ed. correspondence course started by many universities. The National Council of Teacher Education has put a halt on such courses. Still there are so many teacher training Institutes in the country which are not well equipped. And products of these institutes, and also of the erstwhile correspondence course institutes, generally are not fully aware about the basic teaching skills and related theories, leaving apart about the teaching profession and its professional ethics. Many of the teachers trained by such institutes which are not fully aware about the genesis of chalkboard and its proper use. Many teacher training institutes have become outdated. These do not have sufficient staff and necessary infra-structure. These institutes run on outdated curriculum. The products of such teacher training institutes are generally ignorant about their professional requirements and teaching professional ethics. As such, such teachers apply informative teaching technique. As such, the teachers always apply transmit what they had learned. They do not apply any innovative approach in teaching. The advancement of science and technology has become a challenge for the teachers. Therefore, the teacher has to be smart by updating his knowledge and teaching skills.

Herbert Spencer said that the main purpose of the teacher is "the formation of character especially in the early stages of youngsters' lives, so that the child's mind could be rational. He many think, rationalize and, react in a creative way. This makes the teachers' role more significant and profound. This aim can be achieved only if the teacher is committed to logical teaching and devoted to teaching professional ethics for the individual development of the child. Though the pay-packets of the teachers are comparatively low than the employees of other organizations. Yet teaching and educating of the youngers is relatively very important for the national development. So, before teaching there should be proper planning, how to teach and what to teach? And what process, methods and norms are to be applied while teaching? How the subject matter is to be taught, and what teaching aids are to be used. For all these teacher should plan and, this plan should be recorded in lesson planning book. Above all, the teacher should be able to tape the curiosity of the children. For this the teacher should have a soft heart towards the children and should establish a good rapport with them.

In comparision to Government school teachers, the Public school teachers devote some extra time. They help children through school extra co-curricular activities which help in enculturation and cultural development. Such activities should also be arranged in government and government aided schools. Such activities are also necessary because it breaks the academic boredom of the students and motivate them to creative work and social environment.

Teaching has been noble profession throughout the ages. Still it is an ideal profession. The teachers are assigned the noble teaching add education work which help in bringing up our future guardians. They should be assigned the job of enculturation of the students. In comparison to other vocations the teachers are well paid. They have conformable working hours. They pass on their time amongst educated colleagues.

The clients of the teacher, that is, pupils, are intelligent clients, unlike the ignorant clients of the doctors, lawyers and clergymen. As, a doctor, or a lawyer or a clergyman are bound to look after his/her clients. So the teacher as bound to look after his/her clients.

A doctor is bound to follow the professional ethics and code of conduct under the Hippocratic oath he had taken at the time of taking his/her M.B.B.S. degree similarly a lawyer follows code of conduct while defending his clients. So also the clergyman and a vaid follow coxes of professional ethics. So it is imperative that the teacher should also follow a professional ethics and code of conduct.

Guru Rabindra Nath Tagore rightly said that "a teacher should function like a burning lamp, which burn itself and enlighten others". Therefore, a teacher should always try teach his/her students for enlightening them. So a teacher should always enhance his knowledge. He/She like the doctor and the lawyer is also bound to update his/her knowledge and increase his/her proficiency in educating his/her clients, that is the school children. This can be done if the teacher up builds his/her teaching techniques keeping in view the modern pedagogic norms and also applying these techniques having in mind the teaching professional ethics. This is necessary for the lives of the future guardian of the nations, who are entrusted to his/her care. This depends on his/her knowledge of the teaching subjects and skills of communication. The teacher should he modest, patient, tolerant and kind to his/her clients or students. Then only the teacher can come to the rescue of his/her students and help them in educating themselves. If a teacher really wants to be a real professionist, there should he an enhancement in his subject knowledge, general knowledge, sincerity to his/her clients, that is, students and, he/she should perform his/her duty without an inclination, which can help him/her to be so. As a doctor or a lawyer takes care his clients through his personal involvement and due care. A teacher should also personally involve himself/herself for the well being of the students.

It can be done through listening of students problems patiently. A sympathetic teacher can create confidence and build up rapport between him/her and the students. For a teacher it is much more important than a doctor or a lawyer because his/her company with the students is constant and remains for a longer period of his/her life. Whereas the company of the doctor or lawyer remains for a short period till his client remains in touch till the problem of the client is soloed. Moreover, such clients are basically ignorant of their problems. They always depended upon their expert advice. On the other hand the student, the client of the teacher is never an ignorant client. He/she is an active explorer of knowledge by himself/herself. He/she is a contributor of knowledge and also a supporter and helper of the teacher. As such, a sympathetic attitude of the teacher is much more important than a doctor of lawyer because a teacher is required to create confidence in his/her clients. This is essential in modern times. When families are mostly nuclear and both the parents go outside home for doing jobs leaving their wards at the mercy of day care creches. In such a situation it is necessary for enculturation also. A continuous permanent cordial rapport between the teacher and taughts most important in the present materialistic and hedometic socio-economic conditions. In other words "Guru—Shishya Prampra" (deep cordial relations between the teacher and the taughts) of the type of old Gurukula education system of old perennial Indian Ancient Brahamanical education is to be revived. In Indian education main aim of education in olden times was to prepare the youngs to face the life situations. The life of a man/woman was divided into four stages, Brahancharyashian, Grahsthashram, Banprasthaitram and Sanyarhasham. The main aim of the duration was to make a man/ woman a moral being. A student was to live in Gurukulasharm far from his parents house. The Gurukula was situated in the lap of nature, in jungle on a river bank. The daily life of the student was regulated so the he was evacuated from the material life. The student used to get up very early in the morning, and after routine natural performance he was required to do yoga, participate in yajna and then start his regular educational duties. It was a complete inbuilt system of education for generating rational habits, traits, traditions and for co-operative living. such an education was aimed at enculturation. This was possible because the Vedic teacher was true professional. His proficiency in the subject, sincerity to his disciples and non-inclinativeness were ways of his life.

Not only the old Indian teacher was having all necessary qualities of a professional teachers, all teachers in Muslim Madarasa and the teacher of Christian missionary schools were true professional teachers. Their non-inclinative attitude, proficiency in the subject knowledge and deep sincerity for the pupils were of high standard. It is the Christian Missionary school teachers to whom the credit goes for developing the modern methods of teaching and enlarging the base of self education.

So, it is very necessary for the teacher to be a true proficient in subject knowledge, and a professionist instead of mere occupationist. As a patient prefers to be treated by an expert and sympathetic physician, rather than by an unskilled, unknowledgeable medical practitioner, a student always wants to be taught by a proficient, kind and sympathetic teacher. Therefore, kindness sympathy, patience to listen, tolerance, even ready to reject egoism are the pre qualities, in addition to profound subject knowledge, which make a teacher a true professional. Therefore, there is a need of a code of teaching ethics in the teaching world. It should be adopted by all schools. The institutions like National Council for Teacher Education, National Council of Educational Research and Training, University Grants Commission and All India Council for Technical Education should take initiative in this regard. A code of ethics in all teaching, training and teaching cum research institute should be adopted right from the beginning.

Teachers and Teacher body should also pay utmost respect to such a code of professional ethics.

Ours is a secular state. Our teacher should create an atmosphere of morality based on religious tolerance. The teacher should be fair, kind sympathetic and co-operative. Kindness, sympathetic attitude, inventive gestures, establishment of good rapport with the pupils and play of parental role should be the instincts of the character of a teacher. Above all the teacher should be innovative, diligent sincere non-megalomaniac while performing his/her duties. A teacher should abide to teaching ethics at any cost. The teaching is a noble profession. The present materialistic accultured socio-economic atmosphere has brought down the status of the teacher to the lowest ebb. The teaching is considered a vocation. The teacher by adopting and practicing the code of teaching profession can restore the prestige of teaching profession enjoyed by the ancient teachers (Gurus) who had taught in Gurukulas. For attaining this end a lot of sacrifice is needed, for which intelligence, an urge for epistemacy and diligence are required. Where is a will there is way. If a person work hard every thing is possible. Improvement in teaching would bring good sparkling results in our social structure. It will bring peace amity co-operation in the society. And the teacher will have credit for the social change which is a necessity of the day.

So, it can be concluded, that the teaching which is done by the teacher, is an august job. This can only be possible if a teacher develops a habit of reading and habit of writing, experimenting, analyzing first himself and then innovate and motivate the students. In addition to this the teacher must know pedagogic norms modern teaching techniques and also must fellow teaching professional ethics. This is necessary for upbringing the younger generation who are our future guardians and are also the guards of the nations. This depends upon the ability and sensibility of the teacher. If the teacher is not sensitive to words his responsibility, these aims can not be achieved. Sensibility in the teacher, towards responsibility can only be aroused through a deep sense of professionality. Therefore, the teacher must be proficient in the subject he/she is going to teach. In addition to this he/she should never be satisfied with his/her acquired knowledge and should always try to learn and acquire more and more knowledge. The teacher must be proficient in communication skills. He/she should be human, kind and sociable. He/she should always argument these qualities. The teacher, be man or women, should have a good character. He/she should be sober, patient, tolerant. He/she always behave with students, and his colleagues nicely. He/she must be able to establish good relations and rapport with the students and renounce maglomaiaty. It is observed that many teachers are unable to know the names of all students and, they handle the students like raw-material, like an artizen handles raw material for manufacturing usable items. As such, the teacher should keep all teaching professional requirements in mind and follow these requirements earnestly, then only proper education can be possible.

9

Profession

There exists a group of professions in every society. It is not a new social phenomenon. Since, the rise of the societies the groups of professions always existed. Many thinkers have tried to define and classify professions. Durkhiem called profession a social fact—a social phenomenon. According to T.H. Marshal a profession is a relationship between an ignorant client and an expert practitioner. An expert professionist uses his expert tested knowledge and skills to benefit his ignorant client. He has a sense of specific function towards his ignorant client. The ignorant client has a trust and deep dependence and absolute faith on the advice or service tendered or to be tendered to him by they expert practitioner. As such a profession always entails specificity in the field of working of the professionist. Sincerity to the ignorant client is one of the most important factor of working of the professionist. Another important factor is non-inclinativeness of the professionist. A professionist should not expect any thing for the services he is going to discharge or render to the ignorant client. In other words a professionist should not be inclinative at all.

Traditionally the concept of profession was limited to (*a*) medical man, (*b*) a lawyer and (*c*) a clergyman—the Priest or Pujari or a Maulvi. Specificity requires the following qualities which enable a professionist to function and discharge his/her duties very sensibility. He/she should be well educated. The base of his/her education should be so wide and strong that he/ she should be capable of thinking, reasoning, analyzing, comprehending, and should be competent to arrive at a reasonably acceptable solutions. Further, his/her educational and epistemic base should be so wide and strong that he/she may do some research and find out new things. A professionist's education should also entail a training in the areas in which he/she wants discharge expert service, and wants to become an expert. Wide understanding of the discipline in which a professionist wants to work is a must. Without necessary experience and proficiency a profession can never be possible. Above all there should be an urge to gather or collect more and more knowledge in the area of functioning of a professionist. Many professionists generally try to collect more knowledge. They collect material such as books, generals etc. and arrange it in their libraries.

The second important criteria for a professionist is his sincerity to his ignorant client. This is mandatory for a professionist. If a professionist who is also an expert in the area of his/her profession is not sincere his client/clients and merely functioning for earning money, he or she can never be termed as a professionist. Like the doctor, lawyer and clergy man if an artist creates something to earn money, he can never be termed as an artist, he/she merely will be a craftsman or artizen.

In the olden times the term profession was a sacred phenomenon. The medical man used to attend the ill at any time or for a longer time. He never demanded money for his services. He used to carry out treatment and give medicines till the recovery of his patients. In the area of the writer, he witnessed a person—a Muslim Rajput, living in village 'Sikrodha' at the foot hills of Shivalik hills. Of course, he was a Muslim (Hindu converted to Islam during Aurangzeb's period), he was very kind, hospitable and helping. During the months of 'Srawan' he used to collect food items from the villagers and used to arrange, food, kitchens for Hindu 'Tirth Yatris' going to Haridwar, for 'Ganga Snan' after paying tributes to Sakumbhra Devi. The Sadhus used to take food from the 'Sadavart' ashram of village Sikrodha (Saharanpur) and used to go to Haridwar. One day a sadhu was very much impressed by the Charitable work of the Muslim Rajput, the took this Rajput to jungle and apprised him of a herb which could be used in snake bite. But the Sadhu told him to utilize the herb only with sincerity and without inclination. The Muslim Rajput purchased a horse and whenever he was informed about the snake bite, he used to go there and cure the patient. Till the patient is fully cured he did not even take water and smoke Hukah. He never bothered about the beasts and spate water at Solani river. This was his sincerity he had pledged before the Sadhu. Mostly all of his snake bite clients used to recover. This was because of his sincerity and non-inclinationess. This is one example there are so many example of this sort.

In the village of the writer (Vill. Bhalaswa Gaj District Haridwar, U.A.) there was a vaid Pandit Chinta Ram Vats. He had done five years course from the Govt. Ayurvedic College, Suttar Mandi, Lahore (now in Pakistan). After the Ayurvedic Course completion (BAMS), he was administered 'Charak' oath to be sincere to his patients and non-inclinative to words them. After the completion of his course be decided not to charge anything from the patients of his village. He also decided to attend the ill patients at his own in four Mahallas of the village. He used to get up early in the morning and after during puja and meditation, he used to visit all patients at his own. To whom he used to attend used to be cured. If a villager used to give him some money, he used to refuse. The villagers were amazed to see his proficiency, sincerity and non-inclinativeness. They also thought how the vaidji would afford this non-inclinativeness for a longer time. The village elders like Late Baba Mansinghji and Mukhia Late Shri Harbans Singh advised the villagers to throw some coins, Athani, Chavani, or Rupee in his baithak through window. This gave financial support to vaidji. He became a famous vaid of the area and some rich people like Rajas and Nawabs used to invite him for the treatments of their near ones. He also followed the same practice and used not to demand any fee. And the people used to drop some coins in his back bag. This is an unique example of sincerity and non-inclinativeness. Now what medical men do every body knows. They try to make money even from poor ignorant clients.

Similarly lawyers and clergymen, in olden times, used to follow professioned ethics strictly. The lawyer was considered the promogulator of justice. He used to defend the helpless ignorant person who was prey of crime and was denied justice in the society. The lawyer used to fight his case in the court of law sincerely without any inclination. Such practice was in use in Greece and in Roman Empire. It was the will of client as to how much he could give him. The lawyer used to wear a black apron while he was defending his ignorant client. The apron did not have front pockets. It had only one pocket at the back of the apron in which his client used to drop a coin or coins after he got relief in the court, that is justice was done to him. Likewise Temple pujari or church priest or Maulvi of the mosque used to render free service to their clients. Now-a-day the legal profession has become a hi-fi inclinative profession. The lawyer makes a contract with his client in advance. Every body knows what is the condition of legal profession these days. But it can not be denied that the lawyers are still epistemic and are very eager to collect the law related materials. This is why the lawyers have their own libraries. This is not the case of priests. Their knowledge generally is only limited to performance of rituals. Sometime, many of them do fraud with their clients by involving them in tantrik practices. As such, it would not be wrong to assume that the earlier famous professions—the medical, legal and clergy are no more professions in real sense. These are vocations. In the field of educations a few senior teachers who are called professors are still doing research work and are following the norms of professions. They try to find new areas of their discipline. They enhance their knowledge. They are sincere to then students and do work without inclination. But in the educational fields too there are some professors who are not actually aware about the etymology of the profession.

Not only the recognized professionals but many criminals like dacoits partly used to observe some elements of professional ethics, like sincerity to some fair sex, weak and poor persons. For example 'Sultana Dakoo' (dacoit) operative in early 20th century in districts of Bijnore and Saharanpur, U.P. had soft heart for ladies and poor persons. He used to loot the rich exploitative person, and distribute the loot amongst poor persons. When he used to enter the house of a rich person for looting him, he used to direct his fellow men not to touch any lady and harass her. Once 'Sultana' was proceeding from Shivalik hills to village 'kotta' to loot one of the richest person Late Lala Asharam. When he along with his fellows passing through "Chaura" village Dist. Saharanpur, U.P., he noticed some lady was weeping. He asked his second in second Shri Pitamber to stop and find out who was weeping. Pitamber found an aged Brahman widow was weeping. He entered in her house and enquired why she was weeping. The lady told him that she was a widow and had three daughters. Her husband had died recently. She was harassed by some people as her daughter was of marriageable age. She told to Sultana that she was afraid of molestation of her daughters by young boys. He told the widow that she was his sister from that day. He announced that any body who would misbehave with her and her daughters would be killed by him. He further advised the lady to arrange the marriage of her elder daughter and he would come to perform *Bhat* (donations by brother in the marriage) on the occasion of marriage. Marriage was arranged soon. And inspite of the close watch of the police under the directions of Mr. Young, Director General of Police, U.P., Sultana came and did the *Bhat* ceremony. Also earlier on the day he had interrogated the widow he had given her one thousand rupees. This was example of professional courage. And what has not been happening with the ladies? Rape of young ladies has become a common feature.

These examples of professionalism are not new. There were many examples of medical men, lawyers and of priests who were not inclinative at all. In olden times, this tradition was followed by Hippocrates. He was a renounced Greek medical practitioner. He used to keep with him his disciples while attending the patents and used to train them in non-formal way. Specificity, sincerity and non-inclinativeness were the roots of his profession. And he directed his disciples to follow these principles while doing medical practice. And when his disciples used to take up medical profession as an independent work, they used to take a professional oath. This medical career oath, which is called 'Hippocratic oath taken by all medical men'. The medical principles based on 'Hippocratic oath' are adopted throughout the world as professional ethics. Since Ayurveda is older than Allopathy, the 'charak oath' is older than Hippocratic oath. This Hippocratic oath is necessary for all medical graduates, which is given at the time of convocation arranged for medical graduates. Hippocratic professional oath is taken by all medical men. White dress is prescribed by all medical men. Besides, this epistemacy, sincerity and non-inclinativeness are the basic requirements of medical profession.

Since the evolution of life on the earth and emergence of social institutions, it has been noticed that the stronger has always been the exploiter of the weaker. And the demand for justice for the weaker has always been noticed. A weak has never been able to defend himself. He always depended on other person. In the beginning cases of exploitation were heard locally by the social bodies like panchayats. With the passage of time the rulers appointed the authorities like Judges, Qaizis and Nayalayas to hear the grievance of the exploitees. The sympathisers came forward to help the aggrieved ones by pleading their cases free of cost. And in due course of time the legal profession emerged. The main aim of the legal profession was to give relief to the sufferers providing them social justice through the institution of the court. They did not demand any remuneration for the legal services they rendered to the poor and weak.

Also, many thinkers like Socrates, Plato, Crito, Iscrotes discussed the injustice in Greece and Plato compiled these discussion in a dialogue called Justice in which professional codes have also been mentioned.

Clergymen of the world, be in east, middle east, China, India or West had always dwelt upon metaphysical questions, like the existence of God, the immortality of soul, the mortality of all living beings, planetary system and the place of earth in it. They had always been trying to mould a person as a sane human being. The man has been rewarded by the nature with unique biological structure, that is, with a head having bigger brain with a capacity to think, reason and comprehend. The man has also flexible hands and erect posture. As such, the man can think reason and plan for the future. Due to greed the man is also exploitative. He can also exploit the natural resources for his own benefit. Man is rational being than other animals. But man is greedy, hedonistic, xenophilic and maglomaniac. So, the man/woman always tries to exploit others. These all creates serious social problems. The clergymen, right from the beginning, be it of, any religion in any part of the world had always been trying to educate the people about the menace of the greed. They had been making the people aware, in the world, about their real position. They had been socializing the people through religious discourses and telling them about axiological norms. The Indian religious teachers were the super most in this regard. They used to make the people aware about 'Dharma', 'Adharma', 'Satya, Astaya, Ahimsa and Hinsa', Swarath-Parmarth and 'Samveda and Asamveda'. India produced a hoast of 'Dharam Gurus' like Shankaracharya, Vashistha, Rishis, Ved Vyas, Bhardwaja, Dayanand Saraswati and Swami Vivekananda. They were called Acharyas. They were teachers of highest order who maintained teaching ethics, which also contained proficiency, sincerity to disciples and renouncement from the material gains. India produced many Rishis, Munis who not only taught in Gurukulas and Ashram but also contributed to Indian religious literature and scriptures like Vedas, Upnishads, Brahmans Aryanakas. The old Indian Brahmanical education system was a hoast of producing such enlightened thinkers and teachers. These old Indian teachers were true professionists who used to observe the professional ethics. The old Indian Brahmanical system of education was designed to prepare a person to live in the society amicably harmoniously. And this was done by the teaches by inculcating a spirit of sociability, sanity, harmony, spirituality, co-operation sharing, we feeling, equality and brotherhood.

The Hindu (Vedic) religion was very tolerant. The offshoots of Hindu religion like Buddhism have the same characteristic Buddhism spread in many Asian Countries, like China, Japan, Thailand, Cambodia, Korea, Vietnam and Shri Lanka due to the epistemacy and proficiency of Buddhist Dharam Guru and by evading enforceable religious (conversion). Once a Dharam guru always a Dharam Guru, was their religious philosophy. These Dharam guru (clergy men) always maintained a professional ethics and professionalism, and did teaching through out their lives. They always lived to increase their specificity by continued study of metaphysical and social problem. They had always sympathetic attitudes towards the problem of their disciples. Thus they always had a close rapport with their students. They never charged for the religious and social sermons they used to deliver. Rather they used to do so as an act of charity. They depended on food cooked in Gurukula kitchens out of the food items begged by their disciples. As such, their life was very simple, honest, epistemic, philosophic and professionistic. Their main of life was simple living and thinking. Materialism, Hedonism, Xenophlism, consumerism and meglomaniasm had no place in their lives. A renounced life—Vanpratha ashram, was their aim of life. Greed had not touched them. They depended on the society for their survival for which they used to strive for epistemaly for proficiating. Proficiating is a derivation from the Greek Word 'professio' which means to find out and develop new things out of which the concept of 'Profession' has emerged. The term is different and is superior than the term vocation. It is therefore, necessary to know how a profession is different from a vocation.

10

Profession and Vocation

The terms—profession and vocation, though look identical, but have different meanings, applications and purposes. Main purpose of the term profession, should be and really ought to be, not merely to proffeciate new knowledge but also to pass on this knowledge to young minds and motivate them to adhere to its specificity. The proficiator of new knowledge should also continue to add specificity, deep sincerity towards the clients without desire for gratification or material gains. Without these conditions a profession can never be possible.

Initially the profession in India was a kind of triangle of specificity, sincerity to the client and renounciation to the material gains or non-inclinativeness. In other words the profession was based on philosophy, religion, public service without any inclination. On the other hand its matching triangle in the west consisted of social justice, law and religion. This also entailed specificity, sincerity, and non-inclinativeness. This is why in the west a lawyer a medical man. and clergyman were given the status of professional or professionist and a code of professional ethics was scribed. Hippocratic ethics code far medical man was prescribed to achieve this end in Greece. In the east, in which India had a prominent place in olden days the Rishis and Munis being religious proficients and epistemics were of high class teachers who observed the professional ethics very sincerely. In china, similar was the condition. There were religious epistemologists. In the west, in countries like Greece, there were philosophers and teachers who had involved themselves in religious epistemology for a same social order without any maternal gains. Socrates, Plato, Isocrates, Crito, Hereclitus, Hippocrates, Aristotle and Parmendes were famous amongst them. They were given the sacred status of the professionals. As such, adherence to the system of religion entailed education in olden times in the east as well as in the west.

The situation remained the same till the materialistic upsurge did not take place. Due to religious orthodoxy, religious reformative movements in the world emerged. In the east religious movements, like Arya Samaj movement, were totally against the religious orthodoxy. But in the west religious movements like Protestant movement of the Christians did not go much against the religious orthodoxy, though it changed the social, economic systems. Their religious beacons like St. Calvin propounded a theory which made man totally materialistic. This changed the old manufacturing infra-structure system which was to get their men trained as skilled artisan through guilds remained no more. New spirit of natural resources exploitation for materialistic purposes made the man purely hedonistic. And this wave made the man purely consumeristic, ostantenous, hedonistic, xenophilic and maglomanious. Like Carvac's call "Eat and be merry", "Earn more enjoy more" became the cry of the present age. Daily prayers changed into weekly prayers or prayer service. The classical professionals or professionists could not escape from social change. It was true according to Hereclitus who said that every thing and every situation is bound to change. Also, according to man's nature such change was enviable.

Thus change of human spiritual temper to materialistic one was no surprise. Man has been continuously utilizing the natural resources for his better living. In the beginning he tried to protect his body from seasonal heat and cold with the leaves of the trees and skin of the animals. He used to make huts out of grass and tree branches and barks. With the passage of time the man made new discoveries, developed tools and acquired skills to make things for his use. As such, the man always tried to add to his comfort. And bit by bit the production culture developed which boosted materialism and capitalism. Due to this development, man moved man from huts to mansions. He added more discoveries which required skilled hands. As such more vocations and trades also came into being.

The Indian social situation was bit different regarding trade and vocations. Indian social stratification was, and still is caste based—Brahmans, Kshtryas, Vaishas and Sudras. Certain castes were and still are designated for their particular vocations. As such, vocations and related vocational training continued and are still continuing on hereditary basis. In other words vocations are still followed heredilically or by birth. A carpenter used to train his son along with him. Likewise a blacksmith and other tradesmen do so. As such, there was no competition in the field of vocations. Also, there was no need of vocational teachers.

The word 'vocation' is a derivation of Latin word occupatio—meaning the act of occupying a skill or trade for a tenure of period for earning livelihood. In other words it was an state of a condition which keep a person engaged himself or herself for sufficient time to earn livelihood. A word having similar meaning as that of occupation, is vocations. The word 'vocation' is French word which is a derivation Latin words 'vocalio', 'Voco' and 'vocation' meaning a call or a designation to a particular type of work or professional call or an occupation. So sometimes there is a confusion about the exact real meaning of these words. However, this can not be denied that three words, though overlapping on each other, have different conceptual meanings. The profession is that which entails proficiency sincerity and non-inclination. It is considered superior out of all these there. Vocation is a call or an assigned job. It has similar meaning as that of occupation means a business or an engagement of one's time, a calling or trade. So in the modern sense the universal meaning of the term occupation denotes a trade or business which demands a particular specialization and related skills. As such specialized training, experience and knowledge in a particular area of occupation is necessary for some work. Such knowledge may be theoretically and practically gained. In many cases it is testified and certified. In case a person wants to be a mechanic in instrumentation or in handling electrical appliances or in cabinet making or in other technical work he will have to undergo a training in a recognized industrial institute. Whereas, when adherence to system of vocationalization was on caste lines no such training and certification was needed. Institutionalized vocational training has become a necessity because of industrialization and thereby liberalization of doing any occupation by any body. Vocation, mostly all occupations, excepting business follow some norms of occupational and occupational ethics. But in business due to greed such occupational ethics is missing in many cases.

Now many vocation like engineering like fabrication and bureaucracy require specific knowledge and these vocations also entail sincerity faithfulness but non-inclinativeness is generally missing, therefore status of profession is missing to these areas of work. Persons do aspire to take up such occupation. They seek admissions in prestigious institutions. After doing the specified training the persons are tested and certified. After this they carry on these occupations throughout area lines for earning their livelihood. There are still many occupations such as barber, waterman etc. which are carried on hereditary lines. Besides many anti-social elements like burglars, pickpockets, dacoity and robbery who do these anti-social occupations. In many occupations sincerity is lacking but inclinativeness is dominating. Also there are vocations which deals with raw-materials only. A carpenter handles the timber. A blacksmith handles the iron. A tin smith or copper smith handles metal sheets, and always bend these sheets and galvanize these sheets. All these materials are unconscious. A conscious ignorant client can only be made aware and not unconscious. As such, those who deal with the unconscious materials can never be considered professionals or professionists.

Therefore an occupation or vocation can not be considered a profession. But there are many occupationists and vocationalists who claim that they are professionals or professionists even. Their work areas lack professional requirements. A business man can never he a professional or a professionist. So all those who do not deal with the conscious clients can never be called professionals or professionists.

But there is a changed situation now in this regard. Now the extended glamorous form of vocations or occupations, because of their specificity due to advanced technical knowledge, occupationists or vocationalists generally acquire specialized theoretical and practical training in an institute which is certified after due examination by a recognized authority. But even after doing this they erode professional status. The occupational glamour basically has emerged in high grade occupations like Engineering, Soft engineering, Communication, Computer and other engineering inventions which increased innovative technical activities and added a lot in the field of occupations. These occupations have left behind the professions. The occupations are remunerative. As such, the classical professionals or professionists have drifted from the path of their professional ethics. The inclinative attitude has become paramount these days. So the material gains are always given top priority. The doctors, lawyers and clergy men who were once strict followers of professional ethics and were used to be teachers in the past, are loosing their face day by day. The honour and creditability they were enjoying in the past is not there now.

Now the extended all forms of professions are of strategic occupations. Because there occupations are back bone of the socio-economic structure of the society. These also require specialized knowledge and skills. Engineering is one of such occupation, some are more advanced than those profession. Those extended applied occupationists, and even sometimes even some fabricators and service people engaged in maintenance and distribution system prove themselves more dedicated and more useful to the society. Their claim to profession can not and should not be ignored, as they often exemplify themselves better than those professors, who once appointed or promoted remain professionist at the receiving end. It is also doubted that whether a few of them even are aware about the term profession. As such present characteristics of professions have most strategic importance in all modern developed and developing societies. These applied professions or occupations enhances the mushrooms of industries which make social mobility and stability possible. Standards of living of the peoples go up as most of the consumer goods become available. And this happens due to these applied occupations. National security can only be possible through these applied occupations. These applied occupationists or vocationalists, who claim to be professionists are generally more dedicated to the national cause than the so-called classical professionists.

Interpretations by some sociologists regarding the concept of 'Profession have also supported the claim of the engineers, other applied occupationists, fabricators, artists and some highly skilled artisans for being considering them as professionists. Durkheim termed profession as a social fact. Max Weber said that the term 'profession' is the cogping of the cultural system of the society. Talcott Parsons said that there are elements which make a profession. These are (1) intellectual training and discipline, (2) relationship between the individual discipline and society has to be institutionalized. It should be covered by research and social research and finally (3) there should be ramification after institutionalizing in two categories (*a*) Primary category which should cover cultural elements of the society through, arts, morality and code of conduct and (*b*) by application of profession for the benefit of the society through professions like civil engineering mechanical engineering, electric engineering medicine and low.

There should not be any cultural boundary between intellectuals, official bureaucracy, and applied professions as existed in the past, more in India and in rest of the world. In the middle ages the clergy tried to monopolize their cultural interests in the world especially in India by applying the Rishi Manu's, Concept of Varna system. In the west during Renaissances secular intellectualism emerged which led to the professionalization based on professional competition. Personality of the "rule of the thumb" was curbed. Before Renaissance only professional role was conferred to clergy. Other vocations were given pastoral roles. The teacher used to come under this category. The doctor and the lawyer were given the status of professionists because of their dedication to the area of their work, service to the ignorant poor client. Legitimization of the authority of the clergy in the west played a vital role in recognizing the clergy as a profession. Art and sculpture helped the clergy men by doing some artistic expressions for the religion which also helped the clergy. Music also helped the clergy. The museums got courts patronage. But the artist who helped in enculturation and having the tenets of a professionists, was not given this patronage. This was the common feature through out the world. Handworkers are always denied their due status. In the modern age the intellectuals are committed to political problems, leaving aside their academic responsibilities. They always keep themselves busy in making differentiation, institutionalization covering with economics, marketing publication and restoring self patronage. This group through different from clergy try to be so, being an elite class. It is because of this group the academic profession came into being. Yet the status of professionist can not be conferred to any body. A business, a politician robber or a dacoit (even he is kind to weak and a women) a barber, or a carpenter or a blacksmith who deal with unconscious materials can never be granted the status of professionists.

In the past our clergy man was a devoted spiritualist and was an devoted teacher. He was also following professional codes. As such he was a true professionist. But in the present materialistic age of hob-knob, the teachers' claim for the status of professionist needs a through investigation. One of major objection, for not granting the status of professionist to teacher is that the clients of the teacher are not ignorant clients but rather are conscious clients is not valid. To handle the conscious clients is a challenging job which the teacher does. The teacher should be eager to be epistemic and should add his knowledge. The teacher should also be sincere to his disciples and should not be inclinative at all. He should not do tuitions.

11

The School

Etymologically the word 'school' is derivation of the Latin word 'schols' which means 'a leisure discussion', 'a philosophical thought', 'a place in which persons are instructed in species of learning, 'an educational or technical establishment where higher learning is achieved through instruction', followers of teachers are those who hold common social, economic, religious doctrines as Socratic School, Platonic school, Vedic religious schools like Vashnavites, Shankerites, Arya Samajis, Radha Swamies, Nirankaris etc., etc. and also painting schools like Italian school of painters, Indian Schools of paintings—like Bengali school, Madhubani School, Pahari school and Rajasthan school etc. etc.

The contemporary institution of school, in the field of education, aims at formal education. In addition to formal education, there are two other systems of education, which are called informal education and non-formal education. The genesis of the term 'school' in the context of 'formal education' can the traced back to the days of industrial revolution which took place in England, when the capitalist infra-structure tried to industrialize and exploit the natural resources for the human use. Necessity is the mother of invention. Man invented many new things and developed new tools to exploit and harness national resources to meet their material requirements, by capturing world markets, especially the markets of the colonies of the imperialists.

In this pursuit of industrialization the capitalists of the west invested their money for acquiring machinery tools, capital goods and raw materials. They also attracted the artizens working in their own craft guilds under the expert craft—journey men. The number of artizen craftsman was not sufficient to cope the requirements of the new emerging industries. Also some managerial and office assistance was felt by there industrialists to man these new emerging industries. To meet this requirement these entrepreneurs thought the new hands who could be engaged in their industries. So they started the institution of schools, industrial schools, for giving them formal education in 3Rs. as well as in specific training in trades, to person they required for their industries. The trades were like carpentry, blacksmithy fitting, fabrication and tinsmithy. In due course of time due to intensification of industries, which required a big trained labour force, separate schools of 3Rs. were established. As such, the institution of school first came into being in England and letter on in other European countries, which in the long run became an universal phenomenon for giving formal education to the youngsters. But in India and in some other east Asian countries a type of formal education was already in existence. It was imparted, to some extent in Gurukul Ashrams and in Buddhist monasteries. While in search of markets for selling their products as consumer goods in the world, these capitalist—industrialist countries captured some countries and made these their colonies. Where, in due course of time, these capitalist countries tried. to impose their culture also through acculturation. These countries imposed sound elements of their social structure, social values, ways of living and cultural traits. These countries used their system of education as a tool for achieving all these. In India, on the advice of Lord Macauley, the British government imposed their system of formal education in 1833 to annihilate the renowned and famous culture. And for the implementing this the scheme of formal education, the institution of 'school' came into being.

In order to exploit and harness the natural resources of the captured countries, the imperialist capitalist countries also, always tried to exploit the human resources of these countries. For this end these countries tried to change the social structure of the captured countries. They did this in the garb of modernization and development. Their alternative reform movements in their colonies or occupied countries were aimed at to destroy the indigenous social systems or cultures in the third world through cultural diffusion in the first instance, and thereafter alluring to their culture. This way these countries made the subjects of their colonies loyal to them. All sectors of these countries—such as human resources environmental system such as family system, community and educational system were affected. And the formal system of education, which was imparted through the institution of school, was considered best tool for bringing this flux.

In the beginning, the covert aim of the colonizers by providing formal education, was to make the subjects of the colonies loyal to them. They also needed a loyal workforce, because to bring the servants from England was not economical. To achieve this end Lord Macauley thought to acculturate the top section of the Indian society, that is higher castes 'divijas' and kill their culture slowly. For this the system of formal education was imposed on Indians, which was implemented through the schools. The scheme of Lord Macauley worked as slow poison and bit by bit the Indian culture was killed. And now Lord Macauley might be eating Indian sweets like Indian milk cake in his grave. As the science, technology and industrialization took a speedy pace, the formal education also grew and became increasingly differentiated. So the institute of school became prominent and got increasingly state protection and validity.

Earlier, in India, the education was not a state responsibility. It was an enterprise of the society, be it managed by a Dharamsangthan or by church or mosque. Legal validity given to the school by the state made the school drifted from the society. The society lost its say with regard to education of their children. The school management went to the bureaucrats who decided what to teach and what not to teach? The school activities like curriculum construction became the domain and monopoly of very few. Even the teachers of the school have no say in this activity. Whereas in old Indian education system it was the teacher (Guru) who used to decide what to teach? The Guru used to prepare his disciples to face life situations, and adjust themselves in the social milieu after the learning it in Gurukulas. The present system of formal education, which is imparted in schools, has no basic foundation of education. The main reason for this is schools are isolated from the society even though these are by public money under Government control. The present institution of schools is tool in the hands bureaucrats and few elites.

Most of the colonies of the western imperialists became independent one after another. But the institution of school imposed b the alien imperialists, remained intact doing the same job as it was doing covertly for the foreign rulers. The present rulers looked to earlier foreign rulers as their torch bearers and beacon light. They thought to deliver the goods and relieve India from poverty and economic backwardness. Human psyche of greed and availing of employment opportunities made the society to accept it, ignoring the need of nationality, national culture, morality and sociability. People also thought that the modern system of formal education can only deliver the goods and relieve them from poverty and economic backwardness.

As such, the third world visualized the deliverance from the age old poverty through the institution of the 'school'. They thought it can be achieved through industrialization and modernization which can bring economic growth and entail social change. So the socio-economic structure introduced by the colonizers remained intact as it was introduced. Old Indian indigenous way of harmonious living based on self-sufficiency, and which was core foundation of rural economy, started further crumbling. In the past Indian Cottage industries had a glorious hoary background of Indian economy. It became part of heterogeneous feudal economy which is based on centralized capitalistic urban economy. Old Indian system of Gurukul and Madarasa system more or less crumbled due to formal education school system. Schools and University got preference, products of these institutes, which are produced in the manner the nuts and bolts are produced in a factory. In the present system of formal education, imparted at the schools and universities neither there is a consideration for individual differences nor for enculturation. Our cottage industries which had a hoary past have completely vanished away due to formal education. Teachers primary roles like the preparation of the students for life by making them aware about the environment cultural development, sociability, mutual adjustment, axiology and moral values have totally disappeared. There is a cut throat competition in the society due to present system of education. Due to westernized echoes of industrial development for the eradication of the poverty, the school ignited a spirit of self centeredness which also resulted in dire competition in every sphere of human life. And the old concept of homogenous living disappeared. Joint family system has been crumbled.

Therefore, it can be safety said that the institution of school could not provide education for life, which was done by old Indian Vedic education. The present school can only prepare the youth for the annual examination. The best student is one who could secure highest marks in the examinations and compete in the society. The parents, the community the school, the media try to give up beat to this trend, as we notice in newspapers daily. As such, the school cold only prepare our youths, who aspire only, for government jobs and nothing else. The school system has also routed our famous. Indian non-formal system of education. There is no place in school curriculum for axiology, sociability, character building and enculturation. So called public schools openly acculturate our youths to western culture. And parents tolerate this. Cultural diffusion is not bad but it should to be at the cost of our national culture. The age old religious teachings and traditions of character building in exiological syndrome and morality based social ethics are generally ignored for good examination results. The so-called secularism also boosted this trend. Age old social value system which was handed over to us by our elders has totally disappeared. Dysfunctioning of joint family system also encouraged this phenomenon. New value system—money, money has strongly set in our hearts. Therefore, to achieve only material gains has become the prime value of human life. And school is considered the prime base for achieving this end. Self centerlines, isolation non-sociability among neighbours which result in alienation is the rule of day in the modern society. Now society as a 'whole' is quite indifferent to true and real education? Respect for the elders, sympathy to weak and women, feelings of sharing and co-operation are no more. Joint family system is breaking and going weaker every day for which the adoption of western value system, which includes the present school system and indifference. Our elites towards all there problems are responsible, and not only school teacher and school.

Organizational, professions and pedagogical roles of our educational system, of which the school is the edifice are totally alien and, do not serve our educational needs required for our social needs. It could only create an euphoria of modernization. Modernization in which we believe is tantamount to initiation of westernization. It aims at the renouncement of our old values, beliefs, traditions, cultural traits and age old social and cultural values. In other words it is nothing but adoption of a heterogeneous social system based on feudalistic social structure and renouncing our age old homogenous social system. It negates our age old social values and culture given to us by our ancestors. The present school education fails to enculturate our youths, rather than it acculturate them and, it creates a class system in our caste based society.

Lord Macauley, who had conceived the idea of 'formal education schools' while introducing new type of English formal education for Indians, not only had in his mind to prepare clerks for the East India Company British government instead maliciously killing of Indian culture and cottage industries and trade. His conception of achieving these two goals has been so successful that his soul might be enjoying in his grave. We have lost our dress, food habits, speech, custom, cultural traits and what not. This can not he denied that we have been immensely benefited too. Knowing and speaking English could unite us and we could achieve our independence but a heavy cost. Our country was divided. But a nation which looses its culture looses every thing. Our political leaders and educationists could never visualize this fact. The emergence of a special kind of elite class which also remains doomed in maglomanity also encouraged the formal education based school system. Because it provided them, their wards good job opportunities. Those who know and speak the mother tongue do not get a chance to speak on educational matters. So the educational administration of school system became the monopoly of English speaking elite class. It is this class invented the Public schools system which created a special English speaking rich class. It is these schools, which have openly commercialized the education and promoted acculturation openly. English speaking products of these schools consider themselves superior than the masses. Bulk of bureaucrats, administration and army officers come from this class to govern the rest of the majority. It is this class which fosters English education and adopts western culture styles to reap the fruits of employment and power. These Public schools fostered ugly competition in every sphere of human life.

The present formal education in technical trade skills provided by special trade institutes like I.T.Is. which replaced the age old non-formal system of education. The non-formal system of education used to prepare a person for a station of life. Earlier the non-formal education was hereditically transmitted on caste lines. It used to generate a permanent of way of social stratification in the society. Through non-formal education a man used to be more skilled than the present training in industrial schools. Through non-formal hereditary training a man used to go through a wide spectrum of learning trade, that is, he had an opportunity to visualize a lot of raw-materials and variety of tool. The industrial schools can not provide such experience with in a short period of time. Through caste based non-formally trained artizens still have deep roots in Indian society. Due to industrialization caste based vocations lost their eminence, with the result non-formal education system faded away, as the artizen who do not have paper qualification, are not considered for technical jobs. Only those who have certificates from I.T.Is. are considered for technical jobs. As such some of the vocational castes have been totally wiped out of their vocational roles, resulting unemployment and migration to city slums for doing some petty jobs for earning their livelihood for survival.

The politicians through reaped a rich harvest from the age old caste structure in winning elections and capturing power, totally ignored the social transition of caste system. Though some castes are still doing some wonderful works but their merit of vocation is ignored. Still their children remain backward. They do not get a chance to go to school. These artizen castes remain backward in the society. As only the certification from the schools, like industrial schools, art schools, polytechnics pay dividend, not ability and skills. As such, hereditary skilled artizens remained generally unemployed. Consequently production at national level in production units falls. Also work culture get fumbled. Those who are not skilled workers exist due to buttering. So this fact can not be denied that institution of 'school' which is alien is responsible for it.

In olden days the scheme of socialization was so designed that from the birth of the child there used to be many ceremonies performed, which are still observed such as 'drasto-uthan' (द्रष्टोत्थान), unyan (उन्यान), grahpavesh (गृह प्रवेश), Dikshuttasve (दीक्षात्सव) and grahsthashama parv (गृहस्थाश्रम पर्व). Through these ceremonies or Samkaras have special way of social mobilization were initiated. Now, there is no place for religious teaching at home and in school. The home atmosphere is totally hedonistic. 'Earn through out week go to the temple once a weak' like protestant Christians do. Religious prayers are totally banned in schools because of secularism. There is no place to learn about religious education which is necessary for enculturating and imbibing moral values and character building. The tragic result is what we often read in newspapers that mother-in-law got murdered her daughter-in-law for dowry, son murdered the father for property, and crimes like chain pulling, loot, burglary, bribery and encroachment of public places have become common feature in the society. Not in only big metropolis like Delhi and Mumbai but in small towns like Ghaziabad are becoming the dens of criminals. As such, the crime index is raising every day. Before, independence there was no fear while walking in the night in both rural and urban areas. Only one had to fear of the beasts like wolf etc. Now beasts and wolves are found no more but human wolves are found in abundance. One can not walk after sunset in both rural and urban areas. Urban areas like Delhi have become the dens of criminals like rapist, burglars and dacoits. It because of our imported alien formal system of education in which axiology has no place. And the schools are blamed for it.

Generally our youth, aspire for white collar jobs. For this end they run for university degrees. After getting the degree they knock many doors for employment. Very few get job as there is a cut throat competition. Nor they develop abilities and skills and also attitudes to work with their parents on farm, and shops. The concept of sanskritization is another factor to promote this condition. From the very beginning due to varna system, the hand worker has ever been looked with contempt by higher castes which promoted sanskritization. The unemployed youth find it easy to do crimes to meet their expenses. The result is the emergence of a criminal society.

The greatest tragedy in our society is that even after more than fifty years of our independence from foreign rulers our politicians, bureaucrats and educationists are still immune to the present state of our school education system, and are still glued to alien one. They cemented the new innovative education scheme like Basic Education along with the cremation with the dead body of the father of the Mahatma Gandhi. It would not be wrong to assume that of course the institution of the school has been very helpful in educating the youngers. But the core issues of national education like employment social development and enculturation remain to be attended. The concerned authorities should look to these issues also.

12

Formal Education

Etymologically, the meaning of the word 'Formal Education', is giving a form or shape to education, according to the prescribed norms by the society or by the state. The word 'form' is a derivation from the French word 'Forme' meaning shape and manner and Latin word 'Forma' meaning 'shape', 'extreme appearance of a body', 'a phenomena', 'to give shape', 'to mould' and 'to do make up'. It can be said that 'Formal Education' is a process of providing a shape to an educational infra-structure of a country to achieve socio-economic and cultural ends. According to Platonic conception education is a self-discovery or upliftment of hidden potentialities of a man/women and, thereby enrichment of knowledge, truth, beauty and goodness. According to Durkheim it is an influence exercised by adults and, as a result of it arising out certain physical, mental intellectual and moral states which are demanded by the society. Max Weber says that society is an area of competition, conflicts and struggles, the education prepares a man/woman to develop all these. Karl Marx considered education to combat all these. Karl Mannihum thought that education is the only possible measure through which social up-bringing is possible, through the development of social institutions. Other sociologists considered education as a process of social up-bringing. These views of the modern sociologists and educationists are more or less matching with the conviction of Gurus (teachers) of old Gurukulas. They say that education is a way to prepare the child to live in the society according to some social norms. The functionalists consider education as care taker and dispenser of cultural resources of the society. The culture can be revised, raised and enriched through formal education. The main aim of the present form of formal education is to equip the youngsters with the knowledge of 3Rs which are considered necessary for socialisation and social control. Formal education is expected to do it systematically and explicitly. The joint families and community were doing and accomplishing social aims in a differentiated manner before the society become complex. Due to the slippage of educational and cultural functions of primary educational agencies like family and community and also emergence of machine-age the institution of school came into existence and formal education came into being. Before industrialization the education was transmitted to the youngers by the social institutions like family community in informal and non-formal ways of educating. Informal education was received by the youngs by observing and imitating the elders and peer group members. It is a kind of associated learning. Non-formal way of education was given through continuous, association with the parents and imitating their activities while they were doing some work. As a matter of fact the child starts getting non-formal education from the parents and elders from the very beginning at an early stage life. The non-formal education is more substantial and concrete than the formal education. Skills acquired through this method are permanent and continue life long. Also through informal education the youngsters get some knowledge which is not obtained from parents and elders as some information can not passed to them. And it is peer group which educate them informally.

If we further peep into and, look to its perspectivity we find that the word 'Formality' has emerged out of the work 'Form' means an action that has been done for a mere obligation, having no intense desire to do for a result. Likewise the 'Formal education' which is being imparted in school entails a kind of formality which is done as a mere obligation to ward off the responsibility of the teacher for imparting 3Rs to the young generation. It does not entail the aim of making our youngsters aware about morality, sociability, norms and traits of character building and cultural development. The importance is given to the study of subjects for the preparation of annual examination. Whereas the non-formal education imparted by family members and informal education given by the peer group entails these qualities because of instinctive character of these.

RISE OF FORMAL EDUCATION

Years ago Auguste Comte said that "the old society is dying and new society is emerging". Before this utterance the education was given in informal way through familial method of education. In many pre-literate tribal societies, an age group used to undergo and, still undergoes tuitions in religious beliefs and practices through symbolism under the care of a specially selected adult who had/has proficiency in henotheistic religious practices. Likewise the youths used to acquire skills in many activities from their parents in non-formal way. Also for acquiring or learning skills activities which were different from their parental activities the youths used to acquire proficiency from other skilled persons, too in non-formal way.

Already mentioned, in India going to Asharams, situated in jungles generally on river banks was also a kind of formal education. First step towards formal education was going for apprenticeship in craft guilds and remaining with the guild masters or journeymen for a specified period. This practice was prevalent in Europe. Secondly due to the invention of machines and development industries, first in England and later on in Europe, there arose a necessity of persons proficient in different skills like acquaintance in workshop practices etc. So schools for imparting these skills were established, where elementary education was imparted and knowledge of 3Rs was given. Initially these schools were set up by businessmen for their children. Later on there arose a need for vocational schools, common schools and basic schools which were later on called grammar schools.

In olden times the academics like Academy of Plato in Greece, schools of higher learning in India, which were called 'vidyapeeths' like Taxila, Nalanda, Ujjaini and many other such Vidyapeeths in India, show that there existed some sort of formal education in Greece, India, China and at some places in Europe too. Also some sort of extra schools, like Padha (पाद्या) schools in India were teaching in Mundi Hindi (मुन्डी हिन्दी), Madarasas in Muslim community used to give instruction in religion to make the youngster aware about the teaching of 'Holy Quran' and Hadees and in church schools the youngs were taught 3Rs and Holy Bible. Such schools existed in al societies. The full development of Formal educational set up came into being, rather boosted, after the development of writing. First of all in the beginning it was the monopoly of priestly class, upper class and upper castes. The priesthood promoted the diversified schools for their children. The lower classes and castes were not having any opportunity to such schools, which were established by the priests for imparting education in Formal way. Another reason might be the men in position to command and rule always tried to keep away the lower class/castes men who were weak and powerless did not have the facilities for their development. In Greece, the society was diversified in four categories—the nobles warriors, philosopher/teachers and artizens. The nobles and warrior were considered superior to other two classes. In India also the society was divided on varna system. Only Brahmans and kshtriyas were having upper hand in the society. The other two varunas were exploited by the upper varunas. There are still ignored. In Greece the craftsmen met the same fate. In Europe the society was stratified in feudalistic manner which was based on exploitation of poor by the rich. So the feudal class in Europe always enjoyed the fruits of formal education denying it to the serfs.

In pre industrial days schools were widespread in china and in less elaborated form in India and in many parts of the Islamic world. The Western world was not having such school. The reason might be climatic conditions of the world. So the formal education in western countries came into being after industrialization and expansion of their trade in eastern Asian countries. There are evidences even in primitive societies, where techniques existed, having schools to keep records and chronicles for correspondence. This helped these societies to enculturate youngs.

Initiative first came from craftsmen in the development of school for formal learning of 3Rs for keeping accounts, preparing useful illustrations and drawings for preparing business catalogues and booklets for widening the scope of their crafts business. After the industrial revolution many of these crafts enlarged their establishments. And in due course of time they felt more need of skilled labours. They established schools for imparting formal education. Firstly, such schools were established and run by private establishments or organizations. These organizations developed the curriculum for imparting formal education at these schools, matching their needs. When the number of such schools increased the state extended its control over these schools. As such, the state exercised its power to influence the implementation of formal education. It influenced the industrial organization to chalk out the school curriculum as directed by state. And bit by bit the state control over the schools for carrying out the stipulated formal education increased.

Theoretically, the educational institutes like schools and universities should never be under the state control. Because, the state always imposes its will on the educational system and always tries to implement it own agenda. If the state is theocratic it would like the agenda of the formal education which could promote religious in schools and impose restriction on education of a particular section of the society. Many Muslim countries do not permit girls to attend the schools. A monarchy would like to prepare obedient and faithful citizens so that the monarchy could be protected. In such a situation the community institutions are restricted and the development of an epistemological atmosphere is limited or marred, and, individual freedom is restricted. In an autocracy it becomes paramount to create a situation which always keeps in mind the interest of those who are in power. On the other hand, in a democracy the freedom of speech, freedom to the press and equal opportunities for all become the agenda of formal education, which meets certain common necessities like a national culture, morality and sociability etc. So providing equal opportunities for all becomes the agenda of formal education in a democracy. This entails certain common necessities like inculcation of morality, application of knowledge for proper use, desire to socialize the youngsters, enculturation and to make them aware about political activities through extra co-curricular activities along with the formal education.

The school has its limitations for imparting extra co-curricular activities along with the formal education. In the present materialistic age hedonistic allurements are a common feature. Main aim of the formal education is securing good marks in examination, so as to face the cut throat competition in the society. The schools prepare the students only for examination. Also the students under the formal education work hard to secure highest marks in their annual examinations. Due to dire competition for getting employment in the society the parents not only desire that their wards should secure very good marks but lay emphasis for this. They do not want miss anything this regard. In order to acquire hedonistic amenities, as much as possible, they both do jobs. They are ignorant towards the real education of their children. Present system of formal education is based on differentiation and competition for economic exploitation. As such, present formal education considerably is a licence for employment and not a way for the preparation for life. Many private schools, such as public schools have emerged as business organization to clinch money from the public.

On the whole it is also true that the system of formal education has helped the Indian people making them literate in large numbers. Because of this the national development could be possible. It gave equal opportunities to all irrespective of castes, creed and economic status which was denied under the earlier the Brahmanical system of education. Also, it can not be denied that the present system of formal education totally ignored cultural development and enculturation. The authorities should visualize this awkward situation and try to revive the cultural development.

13

Curriculum and the Teacher

Role of the teacher in school is always tagged with the school curriculum, pertaining to the subject contents, he or she will have to teach to the students. The teacher will have to proceed according to curriculum. The teacher should not only be aware about the curriculum but he/she should be involved in framing curriculum. As such, the teacher should be involved in the meetings and conferences held for curriculum construction.

ETYMOLOGICAL INTERPRETATION AND DEFINITION

The word curriculum is a derivation from the Latin word 'curricula' meaning 'a running', 'a race'. In educational context the term 'curriculum' refers to a specified course of study at a school or college or technical institution or university etc. Theoretically and more in practice, the term curriculum is used to mean to plan and execute the students total systemic of learning activities at the school or at the institutes of higher learning through the planned experiences that take place at the school or institute of higher learning. School is an agency which provide such initial learning, through planned teaching activities, to the younger generation. So, through curriculum, the school, teacher tries to infuse the general awareness in the students which finally lead them to gain experience. The teacher makes them aware about the world, flora and fauna, about the vicinity in which the students live, about the physical things and about the prominent culture of the society which they are required to adopt through the process of enculturation. As such, the teacher in the school has an ardons responsibility to perform in making the future guardians of the nation, the responsible, sane future citizens. The teacher makes them competent to earn their livelihood and live a responsible, rational, sane and peaceful life. In other words, it is the teacher who is the builder of the life of the future guardians and the nation.

In the modern sense of the term curriculum, through curriculum the teacher is supposed to build the total structure of ideas and an activity process in the students. It is done by the teacher through a planned action plan which usually promotes a spirit of thinking in the students, which results in elicitations. Such activities meet the desired educational aims and meet the needs of the students and achieve the desired national educational aims. The curriculum consists the means and ways of instructional process to be used by the teacher in the school to provide opportunities for the students for self-learning through experience and reasoning leading the students to the desired learning outcomes. And for achieving this end, it is necessary to provide some logical solid means of instructions, during the course of teaching, which may include, teaching, class studies, guidance and counselling and extra-co-curricular activities programmes and also community and familial services. Under these activities come school camps, excursions, common community programmes such as celebrations of some functions as Diwali, Christmas and Id functions. The community programme may also be like folk arts.

Curriculum as defined in 'Spens Report 1938 England', in strict sense, is a statement of courses of study or teaching or instruction, all experiences which a pupil acquires under the guidance of a teacher in a school or in an educational institution. So the curriculum is a planned scheme or chalked out programme of directed learning by the students at a school or at an educational institute which occurs in the four walls of an educational institute; and a group of students irrespective of their tastes and individual differences share it. Directed learning is a training whereby a pupil has to learn which is considered desirable for him. And such a learning is imparted by the teacher in a pre-planned way in the school or in an educational institution.

WIDE AND VARIED VIEW OF CURRICULUM

Some people use the term 'curriculum' to refer to the content what is taught by the teacher in school. Others argue that teaching and learning is a complex method which comprises varied techniques which are imbibed in curriculum. While some say that the curriculum is the moulder of all beliefs, values and social understandings which are passed on to the students by a teacher is an educational institution in formal way. This can not be achieved through informal way of teaching. But these values can be generated implicitly by the educational institutions through some institutional informal cultural programmes which can motivate the students to develop some good socio-cultural habits. The students learns unconsciously through such programmes, which can be arranged through extra-co-curricular cultural programmes. Such programmes can enculturate the students in real sense. Also the students can develop habits of regularity, punctuality, diligence, work habits, honesty cohesiveness in the group, co-operative we-feeling, sharing, motivation and deference to the authority.

As such 'curriculum' is a path or road through which a students covers his journey of study to achieve a desirable goal and attain a viable destination. It is deliberate road map of educational process whereby a student or students are supposed to attain the desirable goals. And the educational institutes try to achieve the desirable educational aims. For achieving the desirable aims and objectives, the educationists prepare the appropriate courses of study, underlying the subject contents to be covered with in the specified time, by applying appropriate teaching methods, communication media and method of assessment. This is all embodied in curriculum. The schools and other educational institutes implement the curriculum in order to achieve the desired educational aims.

GENESIS OF THE CURRICULUM

For looking to the genesis of the term curriculum in school education and in higher education one has to trace the steps which led to the emergence of formal education. Before the industrialization, education of the child was the responsibility of the parents and of the society. The state had no control. The children of the well to do families used to employ the teachers. The teacher used to come to the house of the child and teach him all subjects. The sophists used to do the same in Greece. Also in India, there were some distant teaching institutes like Gurukulas wherein the children of two upper castes Brahmans and Kshtriyas were only admitted. The working class and artizens used to train their children in non-formal way. The education was aimed to enculturate the youngs and inculcate in them a spirit of dedication, responsibility, competency, sociability and morality. With the emergence of industrialization such traditional systems and ways of education became redundant as it could not provide sufficient trained skilled hands to manage the industries. So the responsibility of educating the youngers was shifted from parents to the institution of 'school' where a group pupils could learn collectively. This also relieved the parents of familial education and gave them chances to work in factories and earn money. The intensive industrialization which entailed modernization and urbanization, necessitated skilled hand workers with specializations. So one teacher concept, which was earlier found, became redundant and ineffective. So the school became a social necessity a prominent prime agency for teaching the younger and preparing then for proficiency. And for this, a system of epistemic assessment called examination was also introduced. So at school instead of one teacher many teachers were/are required who could teach specific subjects for generating the specific epistemacy in the students. After passing the examination and certification thereto, the students could he qualified to find jobs according to the owners of the industries. As such, to cope up the varied industrial requirements, different courses like humanities, languages, mathematics, orthographic drawing and science subjects like physics etc. and for these a planned teaching structure of school education was to be designed, which was named as curriculum.

CURRICULUM BUILDING

Auguste Comte anticipated, when he invented the new term 'sociology' in humanities, "old society is dying and new society is emerging". He had anticipated and suggested new science of society to deal with new emerging social problem, as the industrialization has brought many surging problems about which the child is to be made aware of. Since this awareness is to be given by the school also. The school has to build up programme of instruction accordingly. The school has to discharge most of the familial educative functions. It is supposed to make the students aware about epistemological, ontological, social and axiological problems and to educate them about these. Earlier, such knowledge was transmitted by the family. The earlier school were established by affluent families. What teacher used to teach the pupil used to accept that. The modern school has wide and different roles to play. There are many subject specialist teachers who specialize the child in various fields. The pupil is living in scientific materialistic world where he gets information from many sources. The man has also become hedonistic. In such a situation the curriculum construction is an ardous job. By 1900 A.D. the curriculum development for primary schools and even for secondary schools was not a difficult job. With the development of industrialization the wings of the school curriculum also spread widely but slowly. Thinkers like Froebel, Pestalozzi, J.J. Rousseau, Madam Montessori and Margret Macmillan influenced the pedagogic thinking, and, change in curriculum construction appeared. In England, until Headow Report (1726) school education only meant Grammar schools, which was purely academic, theoretical and was dominated by external examination. Only intelligent children of the affluent families could avail it.

The broadened term of curriculum emerged due to many aspects of blind industrialization and its consequent influences. The educationists felt that the child is a total process and not only a mental process which implies that the school should have a relevant programme for the development of the whole child rather than a mere class room teaching. People generally learn more through perception, thinking reasoning and participation rather than passive hearing and listening. The children are the epitomes of adults of whom they have all qualities. Therefore, they can also learn by the assimilation of the subject. As long as, assign-study-receive was an accepted formula for the greater part of child's development, the curriculum could be conceived of the course of those subjects that were lined up for the students to take up. But as soon as they theory of mental discipline began to be realized in practice, the curriculum, as a broad total programme of activities, that were considered to survive the child was conceived, which was to be implemented by the school. To provide the wide and varied activities, outside the school/class, which have been till recently given in the school activities are called extra-curricular activities. These became necessary for the whole education of the child. These activities though considered secondary are necessary to ward off academic boredom of the students and, are also necessary for enculturation.

But still the emphasis is laid on academic subjects; the extra-co-curricular actives are only so arranged in schools that these do not hamper the scholastic activities or studies of the students, so that the performance of the students in examinations is not affected. So the subject approach was dominant in the past, and is still dominant in school studies. As such, the school curriculum is still planned mechanically by a selected group of people in order to prepare the students as mono-moulds for passing the examination in hi-fi way, killing their interests and initiatives, keeping the students continuously away from their interest, individual interests, from nature, social milieu and even away from then own parents. Only master strategists plan the school curriculum at the behest of those who are in power. The media has highlighted this aspects off and on. No flexibility or shifting approaches are seen in our curriculum building procedure. Not only the teachers but the headmasters and principals of the schools are kept at bay from the curriculum construction.

The curriculum should not only be a frame work of courses and subject content. Other activities which are going to unfold many useful experiences to the students and may enrich their personalities should be included in school curriculum. These activities should be decided in advance before the school reopens and the teachers start inter-acting with the students. Since the teacher is the main functionary of school education, he or she should be involved in the preparation of school curriculum. Of course every teacher can not be involved but there should be a way out to obtain the teacher's views for curriculum construction. Every thing is in flux, so also social phenomena is changing continuously. So why not the school curriculum should also be changed or modified accordingly.

One of the most gloring fallacy in curriculum construction is that the educators are prone to statistical goals. They ignore the students', peoples' and social interests. They always plan curriculum for common life, for common good, general training for general citizenship for which the scale of success is hi-fi success in examination results. But the individual differences in students are totally ignored. Also for reaching social consequences as the annihilation of doing hand work or manual work are not all anticipated. Due to this, it has been observed that many parents, especially mothers kill the work habits in their children for good examination results. Individual differences among students, their future social life, sociability, morality and enculturation are totally ignored by the parents and the school.

While planning the school curriculum, the school teachers, prominent intellectuals and even some experienced citizens should not only be consulted but should be involved in curriculum construction. The curriculum should not be prepared in camera. There should be a continuous research in this regard, as suggested by Prof. Stephan Corey in his book 'Action Research'. The curriculum is generally planned for general education which is experienced by the whole group. So it should be a plan of training for the whole life. The education should examine the educational goals very carefully. The general subjects and specialized subjects should also be distinguished very carefully giving attention to necessary steps to be taken.

Various committees and commissions on curriculum building were established in United Kingdom of which educational pattern the formal education, which we are following, have cautioned about the curriculum construction.

Headow and Spens Reports and Education Act, United Kingdom (1944) established education an activity for all but with the monotonous curriculum. Newsome Report U.K. (1963) highlighted the then features of school curriculum in U.K. It said that "the present form curriculum does not create, interest in the students. Also United Kingdom Headmaster report 1961 suggested that the School Headmaster should also be involved in curriculum construction. There should be a provision for the inclusion of creative arts in school curriculum. Also, there should be sufficient scope for curriculum enrichment. This can be done if new innovation in teaching methods, new teaching aids and fresh content are introduced and sincerely used.

CURRICULUM PLANNING

Edward A. King has rightly said that:

(*i*) Curriculum is an instrumentality for translating our hopes for materializing child education into a concrete reality.

(ii) An appropriate and sound curriculum is necessary for eliminating a gap between mechanical and social progress.
(iii) A sound and logical curriculum is necessary for helping an individual being to achieve a greater success in a living society.
(iv) An appropriate curriculum construction is necessary for creating a sane democratic society.
(v) The curriculum should be so formed that the pupils may be able to understand the social problems.
(vi) The curriculum should reflect the measures necessary for establishing permanent peace and harmony in the society.

As such for curriculum planning there should be a continuous permanent study and research body so as to achieve the long time social goals.

IDENTIFIABLE ASPECTS OF CURRICULUM

(i) Identifying social and national objectives.
(ii) Developing the school programme keeping in view these objectives.
(iii) Developing teaching and learning structure accordingly.
(iv) The curriculum should lay stress on elicitations for which bi-polar teaching process in essential.
(v) Identifying the aspects which would unfold the students personality and enrich it.

FOLLOWING SHOULD PARTICIPATE IN CURRICULUM PLANNING

(i) State wide leadership groups,
(ii) Local leadership groups,
(iii) Principals and Headmasters of the schools,
(iv) Class room teacher,
(v) Representatives of General Public,
(vi) Representatives of the learners that is students.

It is also true that all of them can not be involved in the curriculum planning forums. There should be some way to obtain their views.

FOLLOWING SHOULD BE THE BASES OF CURRICULUM CONSTRUCTION

(*i*) Social milieu which should highlighten the social, philosophical issues including ethical and moral problems.

(*ii*) Culture of the country, for these there should be a provision for enculturation.

(*iii*) Economy, chances of employment and thereby social mobility.

(*iv*) National Objectives of Education, which should highlighten rational integrity.

(*v*) Psychological aspects of learning such as mental health and individual differences of the students.

(*vi*) Sociological bearings of the society entailed by mechanization, industrialization, modernization, urbanization which have made the society totally hedonistic. All these entailed blind craze for money, corruption and made the man more greedy.

(*vii*) Caste, creed and class structure in the society which brought exploitation in the society and made the man self-centred.

(*viii*) Steps to make the students creature by introducing creative arts activities. These are necessary for the enculturation of the students.

(*ix*) And specifying the role of the school and teachers for achieving these ends.

FOLLOWING SHOULD BE THE INSTRUCTIONAL FIELDS IN CURRICULUM

(*i*) Core subjects like mother tongue humanities. Social studies, Mathematics, Physics, Chemistry, Biology, Botany, Orthographic drawing and one or two foreign languages.

(*ii*) Some subsidiary subjects can also be included.

(*iii*) Extra co-curricular Activities, art and games must get a positive place in the school curriculum.

Taking these aspects into consideration the curriculum should be planned. There should be a core committee which should review the existing curriculum. This committee should have a rapport with the teachers, headmasters and principals of the school and after getting their views, it should suggest ways and means for the improvement of the school curriculum. The core committee should also keep in mind the social needs.

14

Examination System and the Teacher

Human beings are trained and educated for saneful living. For the human advancement the human beings are motivated and encouraged to do activities which shall prove useful for them in future. And education is one of the such prime activity. Also they are discouraged to do such activities which are harmful to them. This procedure starts from the very beginning. Education is the beacon light for human progress. And from the very beginning the human beings have been educating their offsprings—first through familial education system and later on through the educational institutions. For the promotion of human useful activities, it is necessary to judge the individuals for doing appropriate activities according to his/her ability, because individual differences is a common feature in human society. In the field of education, judgement of human abilities and achievements is very necessary. Because, it is an instrument which makes the future guardians successful in life. Therefore, in education examination system is an instrument which makes the pupils successful in life. As such, regular proper judgment of pupils' abilities and performances is very necessary. The modern system of education, which has been designed to impart education in formal way to all students, irrespective of their interests and capacity has devised a stable system of evaluation, assessment and examination, so as to promote the students to next class and carry out their studies satisfactorily. And at the final stage of the school education the students are examined by an authorized examining body like Central Board of Secondary Education, Delhi and Board of High School and Intermediate Education, U.P. These boards certify the successful students in their final examinations. The teachers at all levels play a prominent role in carrying out examination system.

If etymologically viewed, the concept of evaluation is the development of the word 'value' which is derivation of the Latin word 'Valere' meaning worth. The word 'valuation' means to find out numerical validity of a thing or an appropriate appraisal of a state of affair. As such, the word evaluation means an act of finding the worth of a thing or an action. Likewise the word, 'assess' is a derivation from the Latin word 'assideo', meaning set beside and find out the value. The word 'examine' is a derivation from the Latin word 'examines' meaning to assess, 'to bring out', 'to observe carefully', 'to look into', 'to question', 'to consider all aspects', 'to question an accused or a witness in judicial enquiry, and 'to enquire or assess educational achievement'. As such, the act of examining is called examination. The examinee is also a derivation from the Latin word 'examinashon' one who is examined.

The genesis of the words 'evaluation' and 'examination' centres around, as already mentioned on all human activities. Every action is always entailed by a reaction. Most common characteristics applicable to all human being is to access their actions and find out the results. With various needs or objectives in our minds we desire to know the validity of our activities and for that these activities are assessed. If the results are favourable we continue the activities, otherwise either we reformulate the activities or drop the activities being unfavourable or harmful. Since the dawn of the society the man has ever been basing his activities on this premise. A farmer tills the hand saws the seed with a hope that result will be a good crop. An engineer plans and execute a road bridge hoping that it well facilitate easy traffic. A cabinet maker designs pieces of furniture and fabricate these with a hope that it will be used by the people and he will earn the money. Likewise all human activities are done hoping good results. These activities are continuously examined and, if results are satisfactory these activities are continued. If the results are not satisfactory and, are unfavourable the activity either are reformed or stopped. All human activities always entail good or bad results. All human enquiries led to the development sociological and philosophical thoughts. Thinkers have been continuously contributing in all fields from the times immensonal.

Teaching still is, and has ever been a foremost human activity, done on mass scale by the teacher with certain stipulated aims and objectives also with certain stipulated gains and results which are ascertained through evaluation assessment and examination, system, which are conducted on certain principles. Firstly, we have certain principles basing on certain objectives in mind which motivates to do certain activities for certain ends. Secondly the activities are continuously assessed for the degree of success one obtains. Thirdly, the pace of improvement occurs in the process of activity as a result of assessment and examination.

The process of teaching is a specialized activity. The teaching is an activity involving simultaneous performances of three tasks (*a*) maintaining the class room environment, alive (*b*) providing and maintaining learning experiences appropriate to the changing needs of the individual pupil and (*c*) implementing the experiences in which the teacher has to be an active participant. For the convenience, the first task is referred to as 'environment maintenance', the second is managing learning and the third is providing an impetus for self being. The teacher always deals with conscious material. His clients are not ignorant clients, but are conscious beings. He/She moulds the pupils giving a shape of good from in their mental, spiritual, moral, physical and in aesthetic capabilities. For doing all this the teacher has to do a lot of activities. These activities can be tantamount to the activities of an artist, and to some extent to the activities of an artizen, a technician or an engineer or a doctor. The aims and objectives of education are many as (*a*) mental development (*b*) physical development (*c*) emotional development (*d*) academic development (*e*) spiritual development (*f*) cultural development (*g*) aesthetic development and social development. And the teacher is expected to do all these and evaluate the students achievements. Now-a-days, the schools are expected to provide compulsory instructional type of activities and that too are not carried on properly in many cases. The reason for this gap is that, the objectives of education are wrongly conceived to be "only instructions in subjects and prepare the students for the final examination to enable the pupils to get the certificate", as the present educational structure centres around the examination results. With this aim other main objectives of education side tracked and are usually forgotten. The parents also wish to see the better examination results of their wards. Always the fear of examination results generally looms large in the minds of the teachers the pupils and the parents. Sometimes, the teachers are penalized for the results not being good. Many parents are also disheartened on poor results of their wards. For all this teachers are not at all responsible because they are not the policy makers. They have to obey the commands. This current phenomena of education has made it a Community's Commodity and Public schools reaps a good harvest being the giver of good examination results. Many educationist feel, that the examination system under which the student community assessed is often defective as (*a*) many question papers set are of sub-standards level, (*b*) examination are only held in selected studies, (*c*) cases of cheating are often noticed—such as leakage of a papers, side tracking of good qualified examiners at the behest of interested persons (*d*) important other areas of education as character building, moralization, socialization and enculturation are totally ignored and finally (*e*) structure—like teachers, headmasters, principals and policy makers are generally ignored. They are generality left out of the evaluation process, even in their specific areas. Sometimes, subjectivity is observed in examination system.

But this is also true, that without evolution, assessment and examination the quality of teaching can not be improved. According to Toreston Hussein the quality of teaching in school, depends upon its effectiveness, which could be known on the availability of accurate, detailed objectives of evaluating of teaching. According to him focus should be given on evaluation of teaching rather than on teachers. The teacher should use interactive teaching, which bad to self-teaching.

So a comprehensive criterion is to be development for evaluating. A criticism is an aspect or a dimension of a desired quality to be evaluated or to be assessed. Such or criteria should be empowered to check the arbitrary evolutionary steps, generally are noticed in many cases. Evaluation in education is a method of judging educational achievements desirable as per stipulated educational objectives. So the criterion of evolution of teaching and, resulted education, should be based upon four distinct type of achievements (*a*) teaching is resetting of academic gains (*b*) the behaviour of the teacher while teaching (*c*) learning behaviour of the pupils that is being inculcated through teaching (*d*) experience, knowledge and shills, in the total epistimacy gained by the pupil during teaching. The behaviour of the teacher employed while teaching, should be observed informally using some kind of rating scales by the headmasters and principals. Usually, what generally happens that only pupils are evaluated or assessed and not the teachers. If a teacher is not doing his duty seriously, there is, no criteria to evaluate his/her performance. Similarly, if a teacher is committed and devoted to his/her duties, and the teacher is not rewarded and his/her efforts go unnoticed. Public also desire to know about the examination results of their words and their ears remain deaf towards the diligence of the teachers.

Performance of the first three tasks requires that the teacher should use bi-polar method of communication during the course at teaching. He should try to innovate the students to response. Therefore She/He should use introductory narration which should follow experience. For experience he should use, teaching aids which should follow questioning and discussions. This principle may be the quality of good teaching which may bring good examination results. All knowledge orientations depends upon teachers efforts. The purpose of teaching, is of course, is to produce pupils learning, Therefore, it seem perfectly logical to evaluate the teaching on the basis of its out come. Since the function of the teacher, in production of learning, is to provide experience to the pupils and likely results of learning, therefore, it seems, logical to evaluate teaching on the basis of pupil's, aptitude behaviour efforts and also the teacher's contribution in classroom teaching. Therefore, the teacher's behaviour, needs to be observed.

EVALUATION

To evaluate is to ascertain the value of a process or action. Thus educational evaluation involves the passing of judgement on the degree of worthwhileness of teaching process or providing learning experiences. Evaluation involves purposive assessment of behaviour caused by the teaching tasks. Performance assessment involves three steps, all are essential

(*a*) Standard sets of tasks,

- (*i*) The candidate, that is, the pupils must demonstrate the possession of ability or quality, so as the ability to demonstrate when required,
- (*ii*) There should be a mechanism of discrimination between candidates about their ability and appropriate of performance.

(*iii*) The task set for the evaluation of candidate must be equal (same paper, same projects for all)

(*b*) Outcome of the test must be recorded.

(*c*) There should be a set standard for scoring.

(*d*) To elicit a relevant teaching behaviour should adopted by the teacher.

(*e*) The tasks for the pupils likely to perform must be defined.

LAYING OUT A BASIS OF SCORING

The scoring task should be specified so as find out the changes occurred in pupils mind. There should be equivalent tasks for internal assessment. Random procedure should be used for. this. It should be done through obtaining records of pupil's learning, rating scales adopted by the teacher; and systemic observation of the pupils by the teacher. Ralph-Tyler (1950) who is considered father of educational evaluation, assessment and measurement, said that there should be something common in educational testing, though these are not the same. None of these is synonymous. These three areas of application are considered in reverse, though these are continuous in nature. Whereas examination is taken once or twice in an academic year.

MEASUREMENT

Measurement assigns a numerical quantity to instruments like spectrometer, electrometer, hydrometer, thermometer, vernier calliper, measuring tape, micrometer and stop watch. These can be used to determine height, length race, time and temperature so on and so forth. Many intellectual and other related capacities or other qualities of interest or standards are measured directly or indirectly. Thus educational measurements are logically designed and used to measure such dimensions such as level of intelligence, ability by applying a given principles in a variety of situations. Measurement is rarely carried out for its own sake. It may be more regarded as necessary for doing research also. Through it is also included in assessment and evaluation. It is considered mini-science of physiological measurement special intelligent testing tests and special testing apparatuses are designed and used.

B.H. Choppires has described the difficult approaches to mental measurement and some of their properties. A number of psychometric concepts are relevant for the use of the tests, used for evaluation. These are such as—item analysis and objective tests. Reliability of tests results are validity, guessing, inferring, correction and confidence matching. Assessment is also used for application to general people. It is used for grading (formally and non-formally) examining, certifying and for social categorization. Through measurement of students achievement on a particular course may be examined. When such an assessment or evaluation is carried out in wider area at the end of the term or session it is termed as an examination. Through out the world education system find it appropriate to find out and record the students achievements in grades or class or category. Also besides annual examination, half yearly and quarterly examination are held. Such an assessment is based on formal evidence of ability. It can be said that the examination procedures in all educational procedures in the world is an universal common feature, though different examination system have their own merits too. The educational evaluation in all education structures is used to refer to programme, such as co-curricular activities, extra-curricular activities which entail cultural programme for enculturating the pupils, organizational variables, sports events and for social and research work.

If we took to the sociological aspects of evaluation and examination, we come to the conclusion that this system does more harm than benefit to the society. It breads competitions of social, moral and cultural values in the pupil. Whereas, in non-formal system of education there was no place for evaluation and examination. Inspite of this the products of non-formal education used to acquire strategic skills in their hereditary occupations. Now, pupils, parents, teacher educational institutions and educational administration and the society as a whole are mad after the examination results. Other prime educational objective such as enculturation and personal development are totally ignored for the sake of examination results. Also sometimes the validity of examination is found under the cloud of doubts. Every type of examination which was considered prominent in yester-years and, is still in practice to some extent, it is observed, it fails to test the pupils ability. Objective type test papers are difficult to be prepared.

So their reliability is doubtful. Only very few intelligent students fair well in objective type tests, which are very common feature these day for all recruitments. Whether the existing examination system serves our present day needs or whether it requires a change are the upper most questions, to day, in the minds of educationists who are responsible for the improvement of education in our country; and also for these whose children are studying in educational institutions. Prof. N. Hassan said that the existing system of examination began to bring negative results. University Commission (1948-1950) headed by Prof. S. Radhakrishnan described it as an evil. Secondary Education Commission headed by Dr. Mudaliar described it as a dead weight on our educational structure. Education Commission beaded by Dr. D.S. Kothari described it as defective system and suggested drastic reforms. Consequently, Central Board of Secondary Education tried to introduce some reforms in examination system. Oxford University, U.K. had introduced internal examination only in 1958 with an idea that it would motivate the students and the teachers but this did not happen. Gunnar Myrdal in his book "Challenges of World Poverty" described the 'examination system' as a legacy of colonial rule. Charles Colton said, "To-day the examination are formidable, even the best prepared may be greatest fool who may ask more than the wisest person who can answer well". The present examination system can only benefit those who can afford to get their children prepared for examination; and those who can not afford it are not benefited. The examination system has proved very very harmful for those who learn non-formally and become skilled workers, because they do not get employment due to lack of certification.

Therefore, there is an urgent need for examination reforms. There is a need to review the whole system of examination. To start with, some steps should be taken with regard to paper setting such as (*a*) orientation and training for the paper setters, (*b*) the system of essay type of question paper should be replaced by appropriate balanced paper setting system (*c*) there should be a logical internal option system for the students, (*d*) there is need to inculcate ethical code for examiners, teachers and students, (*e*) habit of selective study in students can only be eliminated when examination system is broad based, (*f*) there should be a device for checking cheating like copying in examination and also impersonation, (*g*) covert influencing the examination bodies for side tracking qualified honest and neutral examiners, (*h*) there should be a system to awaken consciousness in students so that they may avoid doing or getting tuitions and rely on self study, and even doing self-assessment, (*i*) there should be a qualitative certification in place of quantitative certification, (*j*) there should be a quality based employment in place of quantity based employment in Government Departments and in Govt. run workshops. Unfair means applied in these processes should be strictly checked.

In place of annual examination, it would be better if periodical internal assessment system be introduced. The teachers body of the educational institute like teachers council should look to the internal prescribed assessment and, not the individual teachers assessment. This should be a continuous internal assessment system. It should function objectively without bias. This will invoke study habits in the students. There are educational institutes in the country like I.I.Ts., C.I.E., Delhi, Aligarh Muslim University, Jamia Millia Islamia, Delhi and many other universities which have been adopting this system.

Finally, it would not be wrong to say that the teacher has to play a vital role to play in evaluation assessment and examination system. Still, there is a need of improvement in examination system. It will take time to materialize it. For the sake of national development it has to be done. The teacher being builder of the nation should contribute in this. The educators should also recognize the versatility of the teacher in this regard.

15

Teacher Training

In the past there was a saying that "the teacher is born and not trained". As such, in olden days the teachers were not professionally trained, as now-a-days they are trained. Teachers in the past were sincere, earnest and had inner consciousness and desire for teaching. It was also believed that Vidya Dan (विद्यादान)—knowledge donation is the best donation'. Therefore in olden days, in India 'Vidya Dan(विद्यादान)—Knowledge donation was considered most sacred and auspicious social contribution. Therefore, in olden days in India all epistemic persons used to do teaching as their life long profession. They needed not any training in teaching. They used to do life long teaching without any material gains or inclination. They used to follow the teaching professional codes and ethics—(*a*) they always used to add to their knowledge, (*b*) they were very sincere to their disciplines. They had always parental relationship with the students. They used to treat them as their own sons, and (*c*) they were always non-inclinative. The teachers in olden times were called Gurus, and the students were called (छात्र) Chatras. The chatras used to respect their Guru tantament to their fathers. There were no teacher training institutes as existed these days. Also education was imparted in Gurukulas situated in jungles at the river banks, far away from the students' homes.

Also education was bifurcated into Gurukula education which was for the two varnas Brahmans and Kshtryas. The Gurukulas education was formal education to some extent. Rest of the population used to get non-formal education. The youngers used to go for apprenticeship with their elders for learning their family occupations. As such, their elders used to be their teachers who also did not need any training. This system of continued till the alien type of formal education got total acceptance in Indian society in thirties of the 20th century.

With the passage of time some factors like sociological, economical, political and theological changed. Due to increase in human population there has been a demographic explosion not only in India but in the whole world. This entailed many changes which required many things. The necessities for many things developed science and technology. Consequently there has been industrial development which entailed urbanization, modernization and sanskritization. All these boosted educational development not only India but in the whole world. The trade and industries required many expert hands for which education was necessary. Therefore steps were taken to educate all children. The formal education system came into being. Schools were established. All this required many teachers. The earlier concept of 'Gyan Dan' (ज्ञानदान) became redunt, and the teaching became a source of white coloured jobs. Many young men desired to take up teaching as a honourable vocation for earning livelihood. As such teaching became a honourable profession.

For preparing suitable teachers many teacher training institutes like 'normal schools' emerged during the British period. Later on, after number of teacher training institutes increased. These institutes used to train teachers of various levels as—nursery school teachers, primary school teachers, secondary school teachers, senior secondary school teachers and technical training institutes teachers. Since the teachers are considered the moulders of the new generation hailing from different social, economic and cultural backgrounds, it became necessary to apprise the teacher trainees about all philosophical, sociological, psychological and historical aspects of education. As such, it became necessary for the teacher trainees to know about (*a*) philosophy of education, (*b*) psychology of education, (*c*) historical aspects of education, (*d*) methodologies of teaching used in education and (*e*) certain specific areas of education. All these come under the theoretical arena of education.

Only theory does not yield any good practical results. All theoretical knowledge always entail practical activities also, because it is doing which sustains the human life. So also, philosophical knowledge in teaching profession makes the logical teaching possible. Teaching also requires practices as (*a*) Practice Teaching, (*b*) use of Audio Visual Aids and (*c*) Doing extra curricular or co-curricular. So while training teachers, the pupil teachers should be apprised about all educational, philosophical and psychological theories. They should be given training in teaching aspects as mentioned above. The teacher training institutes generally give practice teaching training and ignore other aspects of practical training. All fields of practical training should be given appropriate attention. As such, during the course of teacher training following pedagogic areas should be covered earnestly.

EDUCATIONAL THEORY

The following areas should be covered under the Educational Theory—

Educational theory in teacher training either it is of graduate level (B.Ed.) or under graduate level (C.T. or JBT or Diploma in Teaching) should be covered in five theory papers:

Philosophy of Education

From the very beginning many thinkers have been presenting various philosophical views. Some presented Idealistic views. Some presented rationalistic views. On the basis of such philosophic views various social structures have emerged in the world. On the basis social structures education system emerged out of the philosophies of the respective societies. Since the teacher is supposed to mould the future guardians, he also must be made aware about the basis of social and philosophical roots of the society in which he/she is going to mould the future guardians. Also, he/she should also generate thinking, reasoning in the pupils. Under the philosophy of education the pupil teacher should be made aware about the philosophies of Hegel (Idealist), Rene Descartes (rationalist). John Locke (empiricist), John Dewy (Pragmatist) and also about Indian thinkers like J. Krishnamurti, Vivekanand, Rabindra Nath Tagore and M.K. Gandhi. Pupil teacher should be made aware about the Indian social structure and culture. And also about the knowledge of genesis of education.

Psychology of Education

Psychology of education is very important for educating the youngers. Psychology is a wide discipline. Under the education some important topics of the psychology about which the teacher trainee should be taught are (*a*) human behaviour, personality, development, (*b*) psychological theories of learning, catharsis, finding out the students I.Q. and doing some action researches, while teaching, like preparing case studies etc. etc.

History of Education

Every aspect of society has a historical background. Until and unless one knows about the past events, he/she can not proceed amicably. It is therefore necessary to know about educational history of the country in which one is living. For the teacher the knowledge of the educational history is very important. Because without the historical knowledge of education the teacher can not proceed on right teaching track. If we look to our past educational history. Indian Brahmanical Gurukula education was an ideal system of education for life building, socialization and enculturation. But it was only for two upper varnas. Even the ladies of these upper varnas were barred of it. Likewise the history of education makes aware about the imposition of alien formal system of education on Indians which killed our culture. The teacher trainee must be aware about all of the historical aspects. Then only the teacher can proceed well.

Special Educational Areas

The modern scientific period has put forward many problems before the man. For facing these problem there is a need for special knowledge educational aspects as (*a*) Educational and Vocational guidance, (*b*) Basic Education, (*c*) Audio Visual Education, (*d*) Art Education, (*e*) Physical Education, (*f*) History of Education, (*g*) Women education, (*h*) Library Education etc. etc. Some students have special choice in this regard. Each should choose one paper out of these.

Methodology of Teaching

Knowledge of methodologies of teaching is very important for the teacher. The teacher's client is student who is a conscious being. He/she has some inner potentialities and taking out of these potentialities is called 'education'. As a spade is used for digging out some underground hidden property, the teacher is supposed to use appropriate teaching methods to take out the potentials of the students. These methods may include, narration about the topic to be taught, questioning, bio-polar communication, use of teaching aids, recording of elicitations on the block board. For all this, the teacher has to do lesson planning and proceed accordingly. The pupil teacher will have to teach two subjects in school. So he/she should be trained to teach these two subjects. This training and its allied or related activities are practical training for which the pupil teacher trainee should be carefully trained. As such, practical training of the teacher trainee should be done correctly and carefully.

THE PRACTICAL TRAINING OF TEACHER

Teacher training is a professional course like other professional courses, as engineering, medicine, Art and Crafts which need a regular practical training without which person can not be proficient in has/her area of action. Therefore, there is a need for adequate practical training for the teacher also in practice teaching and related activities, while he/she is being trained for the teachers job.

University Education Commission noted that one of the major deficiency in our training programme is inadequacy of practical training given to the pupil teachers. Very little time is given to it. Also, whatsoever practical training is given, is given too little weightage. There are so many areas which need adequate practical training, in teacher training, are not at all thought in many teacher training institutions. With the result, the condition of teaching in many schools, which employ such practically untrained teachers becomes more worse. So in addition to practice teaching, all sorts of practical activities should be compulsorily undertaken by the teacher training institutes for the teacher trainees.

What is required is that there should be sufficient opportunities for the pupil teachers for doing multiple tasks of practical nature which are necessary for the enculturation of the students, while they would go for teaching. The practical training should not be merely restricted to practice teaching. In practice teaching there can be training of fellow teachers of tne school in which the practice teaching is carried out. During the course of practice teaching pupil teachers should be trained in preparing the lesson plan. The concept of lesson planning has emerged out of the term planning. First of all the concept of planning emerged in Soviet Union of USSR, when after dethrowing the czars. The communist government prepared first five year plan for the economic and military development. Thereafter the concept of planning become a worldwide phenomenon. As the pupil teachers are trained to teach two subject in the school. They should be trained in making lesson plans for these two subjects. There is a specified performa of the lesson plan. The main features of the lesson planning are lesson planning are: Lesson no., topic to be developed during the course teaching period no, time, class, objective of teaching, teaching aids which are to be used and methodology of teaching is to be employed. Methodology should be based with an introduction of the topic he is going to develop. He/she should start with an elicilative narration which could create an eagerness in the minds of the students to learn. And this should follow with questioning and counter questioning. For the development of the lesson blackboard work should be done. Also elicited points should be written on the blackboard. And finally there should be recapitulation through questioning. And if necessary home work should be given to the students.

The supervisor, who is supervising teacher trainees should have a close watch on the practice teaching of the pupil teachers. He should see whether the pupil teachers are properly guided by subject lectures. Whether their lesson plans prepared are guided by subject lectures. Whether their lesson plans have been properly checked. Whether the pupil teachers are using teaching aids properly. The Visual Aids lecturer should also guide the students for preparing the teaching aids. There should also be criticism, observation of the lesson development atleast one in each subject daily. The pupil teachers are generally trained in two teaching subjects, so there should be one criticism lesson daily which should be observed by all pupil teachers. The school authorities, where the practice teaching is being conducted, should earnestly co-operate with the practice teaching supervisor and with the teacher trainees. They should make arrangements for conducting experiments. They should allow the teacher trainees to use the library and visual aids lab, if there is any. They should help the teacher trainees to prepare projects for using in the practice teaching in hierustic method. The teacher trainees should do it atleast once a week. If it is not possible atleast once a month and should encourage the pupil teacher to become good school teacher in future by adopting diligent way of working. The principal of the school should invite the pupil teachers to witness the school co-curricular activities on special occasions. If the pupil teachers are interested they should be allowed to use the school playground for games and yoga. The Principal or Vice Principal should make the pupil teacher aware about the difficulties of students in the school and motivate them to help students in the school when they are appointed as teachers.

The practice teaching should be given adequate weigtage. The pupil teachers should he guided in doing lesson planning and developing it in heuristic way. The practice teaching supervisor should be also he devoted to practice teaching. He/she should be fully aware about the practice teaching operation. In teachers training colleges many practice teaching supervisors are not devoted to their duties. They go to the practice training school late and come earlier. Sometimes the practice teaching supervisors are not aware about the teaching methods and its logic, but they are deputed to the practice teaching schools. So the practice teacher supervisor must know basic rules, if not all and knowledge of few teaching subjects.

In addition to all this teacher trainees must know about the cultural programmes. The teacher training colleges where they are trained should arrange cultural programmes periodically and all pupil teachers should take part in these. The teacher training or pupils must be made aware how the school should be equipped. How the sanitary conditions should be maintained. They should know how good books should selected for the school library. They also must be trained how the subject syllabus be prepared and, how the school time table be prepared.

On of the important function of teacher is to test and examine the students periodically. Therefore, the pupil teacher while under training must learn how to test and examine the students. For doing this they must know how to prepare for the tests and examination. The must know about the categories of tools, like subjective tests or objective tests and they must learn to prepare respective papers. They should learn how to check the answer books. If the pupil teachers learn all this. During then training they shall be able to discharge all these duties after being appointed teachers in schools.

Another important factor of teachers training is extra-curricular and co-curricular activities, because without these activities, there can not be enculturation of the students in the schools. The process of encultivation, as matter of fact has been badly affected due to western cultural diffusion, and it has made us totally accultured. Earlier the encultivation process used to start from home and family. Earlier there were joint families. Now the joint family system has been eliminated by nuclear family system. Both the parents are in the rat race of money earning they do not have time to enculturate their children. And the schools are also supposed to do the enculturation of the students. This can be done by doing extra-curricular activities in the school. These programmes should be performed house wise and should be judged by an expert committee. The winning house should be honoured. This will encourage the extra-curriculum activities and thereby the students will be benefited to the maximum.

Games play an important role in the personality development. The games also come under the extra-curricular activities. If we look to the young children we find that they are very much interested in games. Every child wants to play in his peer group. But it is regretted to note there is no provision of games in teachers training colleges. If some college has a provision of games, there, the physical education teacher ignores the games activities. He shifts to other disciplines. It is because the games activities like other activities like crafts are looked upon with contempt by other teachers. And teachers, teaching games and craft adopt a sort of sanskritization attitude. The teachers of teaching games and crafts should be treated at par with other teachers at the teachers training institutes.

Another important field extra-curricular activities is hand work. Through handwork students can do creative artistic hand work and express their emotions. The hand work provides involvement out of class activities. Through this a spirit of co-operation and sharing is generated, which helps in the personality development. A spirit of socialization and sane morality development is generated. It increases aestheticity in the students. So, training in hand work like painting, craftwork sculpture, making of mobiles, doing alpna and rangoli and also arranging display with mobiles, and posters should be given at the teachers triangle colleges. For doing, so art and craft clubs should be formed and pupil teachers should be encouraged to take part in these clubs.

Regular effective programme of using Audio-Visual in teaching is necessary for good education. There should be compulsory training in Visual Education for all B.Ed./B.T. students, and for this training, knowledge of art is necessary. Along this the use of different media for making models and diaromas is also necessary. Also for making many other teaching aids different material can be used. Visual education is necessary for teaching. So the pupil teachers should be trained in making variety of charts, maps, flash cards, model, cards, posters and scrap books and transparencies which can be used in teaching. The pupil teachers should be apprised about the preparation of chalk broad, roller chalk board and also about the importance of the use of chalk board (black board) in teaching. Also other audio-visual aids like slides, epidioscope, projectors should be used by the pupil teachers. But it is noted that many training colleges do not apprise even about the chalk board or blackboard. It is true that non-verbal communication, which is possible through visual aids, makes the analytical observation possible, and motivates the students to respond.

In the present age, scientific generalization of human development and behaviour need balancing. Therefore, the pupil teacher should be trained to analyze these aspects of the students during practice teaching. This needs some psychological equipments like I.Q. testing equipments which should be provided by the teacher training institutes to the pupil teachers. And they should by trained for using there instruments. So that, the pupil teachers may be analyze the behaviour of the students and deal them properly. In addition to this the teacher trainees should be encouraged to be innovative. They should be apprised about the importance of the teaching profession. They should be made aware about teaching professional codes and ethics.

In the olden days teachers were given due respect in the social milieu, which is not given in the present times. The main reason for this that the teachers have become inclinative. They devote their time for inclinative purposes. Many do tuitions. Many do their home work first as agriculture and give second preference to teaching. Some involve themselves in part-time business. All this hamper their teaching in schools. Such teachers should realize this drawback for the improvement of then teaching career.

Theory and practice must go hand in hand. The practice teaching should get due weightage. Atleast 25 lessons in one subject should taught during the practice teaching. And for two subjects there should be 50 lesson. Sufficient weightage should be given to internal assessment. There should internal assessment. It should be in theory papers as it is done in Central Institute of Education, Delhi as given below:

Theory 500 marks				*Practical 500 Marks*		
	Marks	*Internal assessment*	*Examination*	*All Internal Assessment*	*250 Marks*	*250 Marks*
Paper I	100	25%	75%	Practice Teaching	I Tutorials	5%
Paper II	100	25%	75%	I Subject 25% 125 marks	II Psychology Practicals	4%
Paper III	100	25%	75%	II Subject 25% 125 marks	III Visual Education	5.5%
Paper IV (Methology)	100	30%	70%		IV School Assignment	5.5%
Paper V	100	25%	75%		V Extra curricular activities	5%
Total Marks		130	370	Total marks 250	Total Phy. Edu. Total marks 250	Total 25%

N.B. Total Internal Assessment 63 per cent. External Examination 37 per cent

Besides these there are other areas of practical training such as study of school records, knowledge about school functions such as parents day, alumni day, school evaluation system, national days, hobby club, fine art club etc. etc. The pupil should be made aware about all these. Evaluation of physical health and health care, social work and extra-curricular activities should be done by a especially appointed committee.

16

Human Attitudes, Moral Values and the Teacher

Human attitudes subscribe to morality in every society. These go hand in glove. Morality lays down certain social moral norms to be followed by the members of the society for harmonious, sane and truthful social living. This can only be achieved if the members of the society adopt proper human attitudes.

Now-a-days unprecedent social happenings, like loots, burglaries, pick-pocketings, rapes, deceivings, eve-teasings, molestings, sodomisings, dacoities, murders, kidnappings for ramsons, exploitations, hoarse trading in politics, family troubles over property matters and malfunctioning leading to dysfunctional of age-old joint families are a daily common feature in the society. Such anti-social activities are making the society like a harbours society. Daily we come to know about such anti-social activities through newspaper. Man has become an animal, there is hardly any day when there is no news of rapes, loots, murders and cheating in the society. Happenings like bride burning for lack of dowry. Child abuse, rising distance from the neighbours are common features. Newspapers deserve praise for highlightening such anti-social activities.

We make lofty claims that we have considerably gained a lot economically. But simultaneously we forget to realize that we considerably lost a lot axiologically. We feel proud to be in western cultural garb. Actually the western education and contacts, which has accultured us, has took us away what actually we were. Our way of living, that is, speaking, eating, dressing and behaving in the society have altogether changed. This is all because of acculturation which has taken place due to westernization and urbanization. Our ethical values and standard have come down to such a low level that we do not hesitate in abusing, mud slugging and killing each other in our temples of democracy like assemblies and parliament. Our standard of sociability has come down. Our ways of life, customs, traditions cultural traits have totally gone topsy-turvy. As such our social attitudes, which are the nerves of national culture have altogether changed. Materialistic and hedonistic craze may be one of the prime cause of this debacle.

The terms 'human attitude' may be described as a desire applied in one's operational behaviour towards others relating to his/her personal social actions. It reflects one's will to act and his/her personality traits. Some are very active, some are very lazy and lethargic in their lives. Some are pious and kind whereas some are very pragmatic and are only dedicated to their personal gains. Some take life very easy going and on the other hand some are dedicated to desired set of achievement, even sometimes at the cost of others. As such, human beings are very heterogenic in the field of their attitudes. Since, society is composed of human beings and function as an organic whole for keeping all members together. It is necessary that all individuals in the society should, as per well set certain social norms, function for the betterment of all. It is, therefore, necessary, as much as possible, that the human attitudes are so formed and modified that the society may proceed in harmonious way.

The human attitudes are formed by personal emotions, inheritance and by tutoring social and economic inclinations. Also the interaction with groups like social, religious, economic, political and also learnings towards those who inculcate moral values. If a person is born and brought up in a religious and moralistic atmosphere and is associated rationalistic people, he/she will certainly develop kind attitudes towards others in the society. On the other hand, if a person is associated and oriented and also innovated to an usurping zeal in his/her life, and there is no check to it by the society, such person will be greedy, egoistic, individualistic and self-oriented. He/she will not hesitate to harm others. Criminals, murderers and cheats belong to this type of category of persons. Sometimes, such persons get innovalid and motivated, and, sometimes are helped by politicians, criminals, religious fundamentalists. In olden days Spartans were such persons. Thirty years war in 543 B.C. between them and the Greeks was the result of such an attitude. We still find such groups in many societies whose life aim is to spread extremism and terrorism and harm innocent people. To spread extreme terrorism against many unknown poor and innocent-persons is their sadistic aim of life, which actually is against the tenets of their own religion. Though, such persons are alive but purity of their soul has totally gone. The present wave of extreme terrorism is they result of their sadistic attitudes. The sadistic fundamentalistic religious orders, non-ethical political set ups and materialistic greed of some persons generally generate and provoke such terroristic and criminals these days. This reminds whether the monarchies were better than the present day democracies. All this shows that morality is lacking now-a-days in the society.

If a person is brought up in a moderate tolerant religious atmosphere which considers that all are equal definitely such person will be moderate and tolerant. He/she will be kind to others. He/she will look to common cause and will not infringe upon the sights of others while harbouring for his/her own interests, betterment and welfare. The greed will not overpower such persons. On the other hand if a person is born in a hedonistic family, he/she will always try to be hedonistic, and will always try to satisfy his/-her hedonistic, xenophilic and maglomaistic appetite. Doing so, such person, more or less will be self centred greedy and indualistic. The morality will not touch such a person. He/she will not bother for others. His/her own interests will be prime. Such a social phenomena will always hamper social organic functioning of the society. The individual's desires, wishes and interests become prominent and dominant in such a situation. And the individual is never satisfied with what he/she acquires. Getting more and more becomes individual's life's motto. He never realizes that one day his end (death) will come, and will not remain here. He/she will not take any thing with him/her. He/she will go empty hands like Alexander the Great. So the individuals become for material gains which they try to gain by fair or foul means. Such an urge shapes the human emotions which generally becomes the genesis of morality. Such a tendency is found in majority of the people, excepting a few who realize the truth of their mortal existence. Because of humans animal nature majority of the people try to accumulate unlimited wealth that becomes difficult to hide. Even though many try to bide it through Banami (बेनामी) transactions. This is sign of immorality. Politicians, religious fundamentalists and mafia groups have tremendous leads in this respect, as has been observed. Human greed which is the outcome of bad human attitudes results in so many murders kidnappings, burglaries, dacoities and loots. Such criminal actives also entail other heinous crimes and rapes of minor girls, molestations of innocent women and acts like pick-pocketing etc. etc. All such crimes are the result human greed, which is the result of human excessive wishes and desires, which ultimately inculcate bad undesirable human attitudes which mitigate the human spirit of morality.

J.J. Rousseau said that the child is born free but the society makes him corrupt. According to our culture, we say one acts according to his/her sanskars or human actions which also develops human attitudes. Human 'sanskars' and 'attitudes' are transmitted by families to their children right from the beginning. Right human attitudes can make a society sane and humane. Sprawling spread of corruption is the root cause of all social evils. It can only be rooted out from the society by inculcation of right attitudes in our children. Now-a-days corruption has became a menace in the society. The society as a whole, for bringing morality, can only mould good human attitudes. Parents have to play a dominant role in this regard. If parents do not care to develop right attitudes from the very beginning, the community and the schools or other educational institutions can not do it at the later stage. So the parents should initiate the building process of right attitudes through their model life attitudes. The community and the educational institutions should enhance and perpetuate this process when the children come into their contact at a later stage. If the community can not create a congenial atmosphere for better human attitudes in its future guardians, then surety the whole society will go to barbaric stage of social degradation. If the society as a whole lays down certain social norms and create some parameters for building ideal human attitudes for universal moral upliftment, then certainly all individuals may be happy sane persons.

Heterogenity is the law of nature. All living beings—animals, rational beings (human beings) and flora and fauna are heterogeneous by nature. So the nature of every human being has its own character. Human nature of one individual can never be identical to the nature of another individual. Human attitudes mould individuals behaviour, character and personality. Some individuals are extravert by nature whereas some are very introvert. Some individuals are active in their work habits whereas some are very lethargic and lazy. On the other hand some even do not do, what they are expected to do as required according to their pay pockets. Some do not earn by doing some work. They only usurp others hard earned money. They commit heinous crimes. Some are involved in cut throat corruption. All this need morality and sanity in the society. Human attitudes which differ from person to person are determined by human nature, which can be put on the right track by social nurturing. The social nurturing is to be done by the whole society in which the teacher is one of the main functionary. In the present materialistic society teacher is expected to generate humanity and morality which seems to be impossible when the teacher is overloaded with the teaching load under the formal education. This is also true if this is not done, the society is likely to be doomed. Without morality there will be crimes on large scale and the innocent people will fall prey to the criminals. If the members of society become human and moral, the society will be an assembly of noble sane people. There will be thinkers, actors, dancers, artists, artizens, philosophers, creators and inventors in society. No body will be haunted by the fear of crimes and injustice. Such a society will be an ideal sane society. It will prosper well, so the creation of positive human attitudes for vulnerable morality is the prime need of a society these days.

The present sort of social phenomena of human attitudes basing on materialism is an universal fact and not found alone in our country. The world at large is gripped into the clutches of anti-social attitudes. A large number of thinkers through out the world have already predicted that, due to anti-social attitudes, many people in their countries, are inclined to do anti-social activities. As such many, anti-social crimes do occur. Such a situation, in various societies may become a crime ridden and socially cancerous day by day. We daily read in newspaper about many heinous crimes. Such a criminal situation may become socially cancerous one day. Also this is a matter of shame that many of our representatives sitting in our temples of democracy not only shield the criminals but also encourage them. In such a situation one section of society tries to repress the another section of the society. If this concerns social phenomenon is not checked through inculcation of night attitudes and thereby creating morality in the society, there may be a barboures jungle raj. So the inculcation of right attitudes and the development of morality is very necessary. The teacher can play a positive role in this regard, but the society should lay the foundation of it.

The present social scenario of negative human attitudes as exhibited by number of individuals in the society, has become an acute social problem. It is because of changed social materialistic, hedonistic and xenophilic atmosphere the human attitudes are changing day by day. The teacher can make the students aware about all these materialistic human tendencies and put a break on the undue social change, which is changing human values day by day. The Greek philosopher Hereclitus said that "every thing is in flux. It is a perennial process." Social change in our country has reverted our attitudes and values in wrong direction. Now this change should be reverted again in right direction. Our social traits, cultural traits, attitudes and values should be so as were in the past. It is necessary to keep the society united. If this happens, the human beings will develop right attitudes and values, which will build morality in the society wrong direction change should be reverted again in right direction. It is necessary to keep the society united. If this happens, the human beings will develop right attitudes and values, which will build morality in their society. The parameters of the human attitudes are human actions and functioning. If the human actions are carefully well nurtured and developed the society will function smoothly and will prosper. If this is not done the society well be deemed and barbarous.

How can this ardous job of inculcating good, attitudes can be achieved in human beings and development morality can be possible? It has to be a common venture of all institutions, the teacher is one member. Its initiation is to be done by the family. But old institution of joint family has crumbled down due to materialistic and hedonistic tints in our family life. These days nuclear family system is a common social feature in which husband and wife and the two children live alone. Father-in-law, mother in law also do not want to give up their independence. Therefore, the Sanskaras (initiations) which used to emerge in joint family are totally absent in nuclear families these days. Often the parents in nuclear families give too much love to their children which is poisonous. Husband and wife both generally work to meet their hedonistic needs. The children are left at the mercy of creches and day care schools. So the good attitudes which generally emerge from the family are totally absent. Nuclear families hope that the teacher will also enculturate their children which is impossible due to heavy work load of the teacher. The nuclear families have become more or less semitheistic if not atheistic. So the moral values the children used to get from the joint family are totally absent. In the past the grand parents used to be ideal familial teachers. They used to transmit healthy life attitudes and moral values in the youngsters through oral instructions, stories and tales. These are all absent.

It is necessary to inculcate healthy attitudes for generating moral values in the present conflict ridden society for harmonious social living. Our old caste ridden social stratification was considered harmonious one. Even Karl Marx praised it. It is became most of the people were (and are still) living in the villages. Mostly villagers are self-sufficient, simple, co-operative and hard working. In joint family, right from the beginning a child had to be enculcated for different social actions. The elders used to make the youngers aware about 'Dharma' (धर्म) and Adharma (अधर्म) and advise the children to do good 'Karmas' (activities). Dharmas were considered the nuculous of human attitudes. Tolerance, hospitality, co-operation and sharing were considered the basic norms of social living. Due to long foreign rule we Indians became utilitarian, materialistic, hedonistic and accultured. And due to all these a sort of Calvinistic thinking has emerged in our minds. We have become totally materialistic, self-centred and unkind to our fellow beings. As such our human attitudes have changed altogether. This has destroyed our old value system. Our sphere of life, even our prayer methods, have also changed. So, it has become inevitable that family, community and schools should do some thing to revive the human attitudes for generating morality. This could be possible, if parents, peers, the community and elders set an example before the youngers.

Human attitudes generate and mould the human behaviour and character. All this depends on human emotions, axiological and sociological norms and culture. All these are transmitted first by parents, family members, thereafter by the community and school. Because of sociological change due to materialistic atmosphere, generally, if not all, but many parents keep themselves engaged in earning for their livelihood. The joint family system which was the pivot of our educational system and used to create necessary ground to inculcate night human attitudes which were suitable for young in making youngers, moralists and true social living. So earlier foundation for creating good attitudes was based on sane personalities of the elders of joint families and of the community. This base has totally been crumbled. What was done by the elders of the family and community is expected to be done by the teachers of the schools.

Since initiations (Sanskar संस्कार) for human attitudes, social habits, good social behaviour is must, and the family is in accultured conditions, is not fully equipped to do so, the school is supposed to do this. And teacher is the main functionary of the school, this burden falls on his soldiers. But keeping in view the examination and certification system under the formal education the teacher is to do a lot in the academic field. Only better results is the only criteria of excellence in the present system of formal education. If the school does not show good examination results both the school and teachers are reprimanded by the educational authorities. Therefore, the whole scenario needs an intense examination. And the society and the education have to look whether the examination results are important at the cost of enculturation or culture building which is to be done through enculturation, is necessary. For this deep heart searching is necessary. The teacher can not do both the things alone. His teaching burden is to be modified, then he can do enculturation also.

As the school authorities and the school teachers are in dilemma how to develop good attitudes while preparing for annual examination. They also fully aware that enculturation for good attitudes which lead to good sane personality development, is necessary. If any student becomes antisocial and indulge in crimes, it is the school which is blamed by the community, society and also sometimes by the parents. No body raises or fixes a finger directly on the parents for not doing their duty. Only the school is blamed. And ultimately the schools and the teachers think of doing something in this regard. Though it is a difficult job. This can be done by organizing co-curricular activities which should be given equal weightage with curricular activities. These activities should get a place in regular morning assembly programme, periodic cultural programmes, organization of get together programmes through seminars, symposium, debates, discussions, and cultural competitions on these activities. There can also be permanent artistic displays, exhibition, and house wise competitions and class room group discussions. Some philanthropists, moralists, artists, thinkers and writers should be invited to deliver talks on sociological, philosophical talks like identity of man, mortality and immortality, morality, theism, atheism, axiology, materialism, urbanization, westernization, modernization, enculturation, acculturation, and national culture and cultural heritage. A teachers' team in the school should be formed for doing all these activities. If possible a state council of teachers should be formed to monitor these activities. Besides, this the school should organize religious functions on various festivals of all religious as Dussehra, Diwali, Holi, Janamasthmi, Id-ul fitter and Christmas festivities. This is necessary for religious tolerance and for moral building. Parent teacher association should be formed in every school. In one years there should be a function of Parents Teachers, which should called Parents Teachers day. On this occasion, a cultural programme relating to human attitudes and morality building be organized so that the parent may also know also about their responsibility regarding the development of good attitudes and morality in their wards. They should also be advised to enculturate their children.

17

Work Culture and the Teacher

Work is an activity done for a special purpose. It involves efforts and dedication and is done for specific aim and not for mere amusement. As such work may be said to be a job or business done for ones livelihood and betterment. All human beings, even animals do such an activity for their subsistence. So work is very essential for one's existence. It keeps an individual healthy and provides him means for his/her existence.

Work entails many aspects such as, aim for what one is working, that is purpose, one has in his/her mind while doing a work. What is being produced through a work, procedure and for what end? What technical skills, tools machinery time raw-material workforce and market are required? How long one is working and for what returns? How serious is one while working and with what content of sincerity? Does the work fulfil the job requirements, and job sincerity for which he/she is being paid? Is the work is done for wider interest of the society and of the nation as a whole? Is the worker getting due wages or substantially paid for doing a work.

As such, the concept of work entails many things like suitability of the work to do a particular job, tools, raw material, pay pockets seriousness to work and work agencies providing and affecting the work. Every work requires an efficient worker, tools and material. Above all this, a work needs prior planning and financial sustenance. Agencies like employer, bureaucrats, trade unions which regulate work culture. A work culture entails new ideas, urge for creativity, aestheticity, good performance as per requirement of the job or pay packets, whether the work activities are done for self interest or for common good or for national interest. Whether the work culture ethics is maintained by the worker which involves sincerity to the job for which he is paid, whether the employer is also sincere and, looks to the interests of the worker. These tings are covered by the work culture. The work culture vary from society to society. Also many work related terms like—workshop, workman, employee, employer, work load, work out put, work sincerity work chance and eliticity are there.

Largely, it is believed that the work is necessary not only for the subsistence of the worker and his family but it is inevitable for the existence, safely and security of the nation as a whole, But it is also observed that all individuals do not have similar work attitudes towards the works for which they are engaged or employed. Psychologically it is true that all individuals have individual differences. They do not have similar working attitudes and aptitudes. They differ due to their heterogeneous nature. Also climatic conditions, orthodoxy and dogmatic beliefs, class and caste hierarchy affect the work conditions and work culture. It is also true that all individuals neither can exist nor can prosper without doing work. Some are ignorant of this fact. Pedagogic conditions also affect the work temper and culture. Some country like India have sufficient work force. But due to proper work culture, these countries lag behind in their work outputs. Whereas some countries do not have sufficient work force of their own and depend on alien workforce. Some countries have skilled labour force whereas some do not have. In some countries manual workers are not treated well. Such countries fail to exploit the talent of their skilled force.

Since human nature is heterogeneous, some people are very keen to work. Whereas some are not. Gender difference also affects the outcome of work. Demographic conditions also play a vital role in work culture of a country. It is, therefore, necessary to study the all these factors which are influencing the work force of a country and to find out ways and means for developing a healthy work culture for the progress and prosperity of a nation. Then only the outputs of the products can be enhanced and a country can be on right a track for its progress and prosperity.

It is also necessary to know the term culture. The word 'culture' is a derivation from the Latin word 'Cultura'. In its intellectual and artistic sense culture is a metaphonic term analogous to the art of cultivating of the soil. It's relative term 'civilization' is a derivation from the Latin word 'Civis' which means actual living conditions of the people. The term culture also means an indirect simple control over the concept of barbarism which originally was a description of such persons or group who were generally considered irrational aliens doing unhumanistic deeds for their own self-interests against the general interests of the people affecting peace and prosperity of the society.

The analogy of cultivation of human mind to the cultivation of soil is applied to culture because the human beings live on the social and are multifaceted like soil. As for the fertility of the soil is concerned, we have to go through the phase of human activities, like tilling or ploughing sawing irrigating and manuring the soil for its cultivation and for good crops. Similar approach is to be applied for the cultivation of human potentialities for the good of the human beings and the society.

It is, therefore, very essential to apprise the individuals, especially the younger generation, about the basic traits of work culture which ultimately will lead to formation of good human habits. Basic work culture traits ultimately will lead to formation of good human habits. Basic work culture traits will entail—proper way of living which will also encourage to develop work habits, good living styles as ways of earring livelihood, eating, dressing, behaving with the fellow members in the society nicely. This can be done if one will follow well established social norms about working, behaving, developing good habits and observing cultural traditions and social norms. All this will motivate a person to be aesthetic. He will do artistic activities and, he will shun unsocialistic activities. As such the process of culture need a sound cultivation of human minds. We call it enculturation that is following one's own culture. If we ignore the traits of our own culture and follow an alien culture, this is termed as acculturation. Due to mass interaction through universal communication and consequent cultural diffusion took place in every society. India is no exception. But we should not acculturate blindly. We should only adopt good thing from the universal cultures. Enculturation is essential to retain our own culture and to bring an ideal change in human behaviour attitudes towards fellow beings and to develop good work habits. This requires a national sound code. This social code carefully be followed if a person has god habits. And if this is done encultured persons may be good workers who may be ultimately called civilized individuals.

The modern process of cultural development started in Europe in late 18th and early 19th centuries. Whereas, this process had perpetuated in India, China, Greece, and Persia thousand years back. Many of the far east countries like Indonesia, Thailand, Cambodia, Vietnam, Shri Lanka and many of the eastern countries like Malaysia, Fiji and Mauritius were benefited by the old Indian culture and also by the Chinese culture. Middle east Arabian countries were benefited by the Persian Culture. About the process of culture we find some mention in John Milton and Kants' books. It progressed in four ways, keeping in mind—

(*a*) Development of state of mind of pertaining to human attitudes conducive to moral and development.

(*b*) Human epitemacy, that is, intellectual development for proper knowing and understanding physical things, which entails reasoning and acting rationally and doing work for proper living in the society.

(*c*) Development of general arts, crafts, and skills for doing intellectual hand work. This is considered essential for human emotional development also, and development of whole way human life.

All this implies that main function of the culture is to prepare an individuals to think of new ways of life about all human beings and do proper social, economic and moral actions in the society and to develop a work culture. In other words, for culture development enculturation is necessary, which can prepare a person to do work and achieve social aims faithfully. It is culture which helps a person to develop work habits. A member can interact in the society with other members, intelligently, morally and diligently and can do work according to the needs of the society. Social structures differ from state to state and country to country. Main function of the culture according to anthropologists and sociologists is to make the individuals aware about the mechanization and do work accordingly. Though mechanization has helped the man materially to a great extent but it has harmed man emotionally, morally, aesthetically. It has harmed the creative based works like handicrafts.

The idea of revival of old values and work culture is necessary. The warding off the materialistic values generated by mechanization which emerged due to industrialization is also necessary. Mechanization made the man materialistic, self centred greedy which resulted in the fall of old social values. So modern concept of cultural revival is an effort to ward off the effects industrialization which has given boost to modernization, urbanization and acculturation. It has made man mad for hedonistic gains, consequently resulting in loss of common interest aimed at social love and affection. So revival of culture, covering work habits also, is necessary for peaceful living in the society. According to Thomas Carlyle, Samuel Tylor Coleridge (1830) and Mathew Arnold, revival of culture is an attempt to save the human beings from greed and immorality. Revival of culture is also aimed at (*a*) to enrich folk life, (*b*) renewal of old values and traditions, (*c*) to apprise and educate the youngster about the old culture and civilization. Old cultures civilizations of India, China, Greece and Persia innovated the idea of work. In other wards these cultures and civilizations had laid down a strong foundation of work culture. These cultures were more humanistic due to good work traditions. These could develop work based good social stratifications.

All aspects of culture always entails a form of work culture. If an individual does not develop good work habits he or she can not progress. It depends on a particular culture what kind of work habits it inculcates in the citizens; whether the work habits are based on dignity of labour morality, honesty sharing and humility or on self-interest. The later always drags the individual to activities like cheating, fraud, corruption, using second hand methods like avoiding working or performing according to legally assigned work and doing black marketing etc. In such a situations, like this, other individuals who are sincere in their work are badly affected, and they also start skipping their assigned works. As a result the work proficiency as a whole is also affected.

The present work culture in our country, inspite of work force, is not upto the mark as it should be. It is seen that many people employed in government departments and public understanding do not work as expected as per their positions and pay packets. After employment when they are made permanent many employees start avoiding doing the work as they should do. As such, due to lack of work performance public organizations suffer losses. In government departments tendency of skipping work by the employees is generally seen. There are good number of employees who do not work at all and totally are blind to their specified duties. They come to their departments to enjoying loitering and playing cards. Situations in educational institutes is not different. There are teachers who force the students to take tuitions from them. As such, the teaching in schools suffer. In universities there are teachers who take only one period in a week. In private sector the employer keep a vigilant eye over the work of workers. The workers do what the employer wants to get done. But in Government departments and public sector it is also seen that those who work hard also are not rewarded. As such the work culture in our country is in bad shape and needs a regeneration. Our work culture can only be improved if some serious steps are taken to improve it. This is to the done by the whole society and Government. Some steps are necessary for the revival of old values system and traditions which have been shattered due to modernization.

The teacher is a nation builder. He/she is a trend setter. He/she is a conscious being, a thinker, a rationaliser, an analyst and knowledge builder. And above all a teacher is an educator. Also a teacher is an actor, an inculcator, a civilizer and a knowledge doner. If the teacher follows those, who are inactors and victoms of not doing work and are unconscious of reality, truth and social facts can be corrected. Such persons knowing that they are proceeding a wrong path, do wrong actions (Karmas). They knowingly ignore their assigned duties for which they are being paid. They are living in lap of inaction do wrong which is tantamount of 'adharma'. During so such persons commit sins and damage the national work culture which is against the national interests. The teacher will also be guilty if he/she does not do his/her duty sincerely. Such action will harm the interests of the future guardians. If this situation is allowed to continue and workforce is allowed not to perform well, we will definitely loose our culture, education, social and moral values. It will affect our religion, political structure and we shall not be abie to do our national obligations. If this situation is allowed to continue in the long run it will become a permanent social feature. We will all become lazy lethargic and our national unity would be fragile. We should not be able to defend our nation, and in future and we shall be slave again.

The teacher should not forget that in the past the Indian teacher was an ideal teacher. He was a trend setter, a builder of the social unity, an education donor and was non-inclinative while performing his duties. The Indian teacher was a true professionist even before the western thinkers thought of the concept of 'Profession' for the medical men, lawyers and clergymen. Indians are proved of having distinguished teachers like Vishwamitra, Ved Vayasa, Sadipitti, Arya Bhatt, Dronacharya, Chanakaya and Shankracharya to whom the national interests were of utmost importance.

It is therefore, very necessary for the present teacher not forget that he/she is the successor of past Indian teacher, and enjoys similar status, and as such, similar obligations to the society. It is therefore, most important, for the contemporary Indian teacher not to fall prey to inaction and not doing their work sincerely. There are some teachers who are blind to their senses of duty, which spoils the spirit of good health national work culture.

As a matter of fact if ignorance of the inaction of the teachers goes unnoticed it is tantamount to committing a crime in the society, and those who do not take any action against defaulting teachers can also be termed as guilty and criminals. Such people being inactive not doing their assigned duties, will not only spoil and damage the national spirit of work, national interests and national work culture, the effect of their inaction will be most dangerous for the whole nation. By forgetting their pious duties they too forget their real identities.

The teacher has a great responsibility towards the pupils and the nation. He/she will have to educate, prepare, bring up and build and mould the future guardians. This should be done keeping in view the national culture. The teacher has to enculturate the pupils also. In a sense, the teacher has to be the booster of the youngsters who are future guardians. The teacher should give prime importance to his/her assigned duties in the schools. There are teachers who do teaching as a side business. It is observed that in rural areas many teachers give preference to their home work. First of all they do this and thereafter they do go to the school. They are not devoted to their assigned teaching duties in schools. Other culture building activities as extra-curricular activities do not touch them. As such, the teacher should be very sincere to his/her assigned teaching duties and its related works. In addition to this the teacher has to be very kind sympathetic and sincere to the pupils. The teacher should also know about code and professional ethics of the teaching profession. May teachers fall prey to the greed due to materialistic orientations like hedonism, xenophilism and consumerism. The teacher should realize this fact. Simple living, high thinking and also doing the assigned teaching duties sincerely should be the motto of teacher's life, as this was followed by the Indian teachers in olden times.

18

Economy Education and the Teacher

Education is a crucial type of investment for the exploitation of modern industry. In an advanced industrial society it is incredítable or most necessary that educational system should be in close relationship with industry. In a mechanical productive process, capital, bureaucratic laision for its maintenance and effective communication system are necessary for its polifrication.

Modern industrial societies are distinguished by their structure and development from others in comparable scale of complexities, institutionalizing of innovations, large scale scientific researches in service, economic growth and military growth. The occupational structures are, by and large, diversified which require high educational qualifications for employment at all levels. Therefore, education attains unprecedent economic importance as a source of technical innovations, needs for vast apparatuses, and training for occupational structure and recruitment for this. Traditional function of social differentiation and social stratification has been replaced by cut throat competition. Mass industrialization changed the status of labour, non-formally trained artizens, and education which is imparted to cater the needs for employment.

As such, education has become an investment for economy as a whole. Old educational forms have now become redundant in the face of new economy. This has also changed the role and status of the present teacher. Old educational set ups which earlier were designed to achieve socio-cultural gains are now outdated in the age of new eco-political class structure which has totally renounced all axiological norms. The Guru (ancient teacher) has now been changed to a poor teacher, who has no financial status in the society now. Man is in the rat-race of money acquisition. Due to this conflicts unsociability, frictions entailing personal jealousies, acculturation, crumbling of joint family system and producing materialistic greed are common features of modern society. Every body is endemic of hedonism, xenophism and consumerism these days. All these show that education is studied miscrospically as an industrial tool in relation to the totality of materially structured society. Less attention is paid to the fact that microscopically structured education makes a man like a machine which is not at all helpful in building an interactive, as well as sharing as well as co-operative way of human life which is essential for a sane co-operative society. The role of teacher in modern society also remains restricted upto microscopically system of teaching and not for inculcating axiological and sociological norms in the pupils and are not creating conditions for enculturaling the pupils. As such character building through good human attitudes, which are necessary for hormoneous social living and for social integration neither get any proper attention in the school nor in the home and family. The teacher is used as a tool in the modern system of educational structure and he can not do anything in this regard. As the microscopically designed principles of educational opportunity and provisions exhibit the elitist and populist theories of educational opportunities which confront each other. There is a controversy what proportion of population is benefited by the university education. At microscopic level there is parenial class struggle for education between classical and modern curricula between 'intellectual' and 'social' which entails a personality requirements for admission, and between consolidation and expansion of schools.

According to Peter F. Ducker, an abundandent and increasing supply of highly educated personals is pre-requistic for social, cultural and economic development in the world. It is necessary condition for survival. Uneducated masses are becoming an economic liability. They are considered unproductive. Therefore, all members of the society must be educated, so as to progress, to grow and to survive. There is a sudden change in the meaning of education and also for knowledge for the betterment of society. For economic growth upward mobility and for creating viable political potential, and in true sense, supply of rightly educated persons is necessary. And the role of the teacher becomes increasingly important, though seems difficult for this purpose.

There is a complete reversal of men's history with in sixty or seventy years. Until the beginning of twentieth century there were handful of educated people. It is believed and to some extent, it is also an axiomatic truth, that the man with little education will find it difficult to survive in the present modern technological age. He is likely to loose his traditional methods of earning. Due to industrialization and mechanization, all Indian cottage industries either have totally disappeared and, which are functioning in a fractured way will disappear. Tools like potter's wheel, carpenter's framed saw (फरनाई), turning wheels and blacksmiths old forging and tempering techniques are being used in fractured way and likely to disappear in near future. Not only these, with the introduction of modern computerized recording techniques and use of other software system, the man will also loose and deprived of writing and reading skills. In other words it would not be wrong to say that modern education does not encourage manual work at all which is the need of the day in view of the demographic explosive conditions in the world.

The word 'school' is the fountain—head of education. It is derived from the Greek word 'schola' meaning 'leisure'. And to support the dictum of more educated men required the gross exploitation of the procedures. The expansion of education in Athens (Greece) in Perciles times rested on slavery. The artistic and intellectual splendour of Italian Ranaissance depended on sharp debasement of economic and Social positions of peasants and artizens. Utopian scientific projects like nuclear capacity of erstwhile U.S.S.R. recently have rendered the Russian people nowhere. At home, in India, we can see the expansion of untaught institutions of higher learning and research has brought misery to down trodden and opened hedonistic avenues to whose who were rich who are becoming richer and richer.

Idealist tried to break this tendency by combining manual work with education. Though Homer had pleaded for guiding a plough in education, but the Greek oligarchy was all for class hierarchy which consisted—nobles, philosophers, soldiers and artizens, like Indian Varna hierarchy—Brahmans, Kshtryas, Vaishyas and Sudras. Jafferson's concept of higher education was for those who are deserved. At home in India wē see caste system, a hierarchical social stratification which had closed the doors of education for the weaker sections of the society. As such, the stronger has always been suppressing the weaker man for economic gains. And, always elite class has been contemplating such education which is suitable for their economic gains. The establishment of public schools is one of the example.

The scales educational expansion vary. Sixty years back, if we find, the ratio of school going children in U.S.A. it was 1:8, today it is more than 4:5 proportion of school going population. Sixty years back ratio of those engaged in hand work was 3:100. Now it is more than 18:100. Adult education is looming large. Educational explosion has been even more in earstwhile USSR. The basic literacy was confined to a small majority there. Now education is a patent force. Education is now a capital resource of economy in modern industrial society.

In Switzerland and Maxico, the secondary education is universal. Expenditure is not deferred on education. In the contemporary society productivity, which generates economy involves around the work, that requires vision, knowledge and concepts. Work is based on mind rather than on hand. In to-day society's economy, there will be over supply as well as greater demand of educated people. Educated people are the capital of a developed society. So the development of educated people is must for capital formation. Their number, quality and utilization is the most meaningful index of wealth producing capacity of a country. And in this productivity teacher plays a very vital role in educating the people.

THE IMPACT ON SOCIETY

Automation is a rapid sublimation caused by knowledge and machine. Automation lies in specific machinery, technical ideas and skills. Automation should be exposed through formal education to the age group of 12-16 years. leasing on expectations to work and to do manual related jobs. Our future work force should have the capacity to accept what they can properly do and apply their knowledge. Those who do not have capacity to do the complicated jobs should be prepared for skilled jobs. For them assigning a training is necessary. Fallacy lies, that we try to make every job to be done by every body. Every job can not be done by all. Individual difference must be taken into consideration while assigning the jobs. Each person has specific abilities, potentialities capacities, this fact should not be ignored. In the initial stage, while the futures workers are in school the teacher can work as a guide. But this can only be done if the teacher is made aware about the vocational education, guidance during the course of teacher training. Such a teacher can check the students about their unrealizable hopes.

The educational revolution has had an equal impact on work economy, international trade having an epigenic impact (to take for upward mobility) on economic competition. The educational development above all has become a central problem of the poor countries. Many poor countries spend large amount on education. In USA one fifth of their young do not complete high school education. The most of the parents desire that their wards should complete University education, irrespective of the fact that most of them remain unemployed. Our education is such that it does not involve any interest for hand work. The school should and can do it by introducing some creative activities in school programme, if not in curricular activities, in extra-curricular activities.

The educational inequality is a serious inter-social problem. The inequality is increasing day by day, greater and greater. Rich is becoming richer and richer and, poor is becoming poorer. There is a danger, that in due course of time, it will push the countries to totalitarian camp and theological furry bringing tyranny and agony in peace loving societies.

EDUCATIONAL COMPETITION

The battle of 'Eton' was fought in the 'clan of Etom'. The school master defeated France in 1870. With the launching of Russian Sputnik it become clear that high scientific education controls its defence preparedness, its technology and economic potentials. So educational development becomes a top priority of national policy of countries these days and the school and its teachers become the architect for achieving educational and other gains.

THE PRESSURE FOR ECONOMIC CHANGE

Due to industrialization and modernization, the standards of living of the people have sharply risen—entailing rise in prices, progressive taxation by the state, craze for machine made things and adopting alien way of living resulting in hedonism and xenophilin. All this made the society accultured. So, there is a compulsion to have school education as early as possible and thereafter higher education so as to enable the future guardians to fall in the line of competition. Hedonistic materialistic desires and necessities made it necessary for the youngs to be ready to prepare themselves ready to do jobs as early as possible, and to earn. So the present day education is supposed to prepare the man an economically prepared man in the society. Being a well qualified is an evident necessity, these days, due to competitive rules of employment for jobs, that can be only achieved with knowledge, skills, and ability for performance. Demographic rise is reason. The number of young workers in increasing day by day which also entailed cut throat competition in job markets. The educational inequality is a serious inter-social problem. The inequality is increasing day by day, greater and greater Rich is becoming richer and richer and, poor is becoming poorer.

IMPACT OF TECHNOLOGY ON EDUCATION

Importance of educational qualification is the latest manifestation of the employment scenario on which the whole edifice of industrial development has been created. There is an demographic increase in the world. It is said that 1,30,000 faces are increasing in the world every day. We can say that the size of Derby town comes every day. Half of the worlds population is at the starvation level. Energy consumption has also considerably increased in the world. It is highest in U.S.A. and, in India in Asian and in African countries it is much lower. There are chances of energy shortage in the world due to population increase. It is India, China, and in other Asian and African countries which are contributing to demographic explosion. Theology in Muslim countries and to some extent in the Catholic pockets in some countries are a patent force of population growth. It is because of orthodoxy in old beliefs. In Iran there was blacksmith who lived for 155 years. He had married seven times and had a family of 211 children and grand children. His youngest daughter is in thirties. So due to populations increase there is shortage of food, water, energy and also of shelter. This problem can only be solved if a man becomes conscious of these realities. This is only possible if a man is truly educated and is able to realize what is correct and wrong. The teacher can be an instrument for educating man/woman truly in this regard.

The scientists are engaged to find out the substitutes of food and energy. But such approach is not sufficient. Until and unless the man is educated to achieve self-realization and get introspection, the clouds of conflicts and uncertainty will continue. The terrorism will hit the innocent people. The animal nature of the man will dominate. The utmost need of the day is to make the man a rational human being discarding his undue greed and religious fanaticism and dogmatism for bringing a sane economics in the society. Of course there is a real need for producing scientists, technologist, technicians and skilled workers who could boost society's economy, but this should not be done at the cost of sanety and humanity.

TECHNOLOGICAL CHANCE AND EDUCATIONAL CONSEQUENCES

The first phase of industrialization upto first world war shows that three different occupational groups existed in industry, more or less corresponding to the phases of technological development, as skilled workers, unskilled workers, clerical staff and managerial personals were required. Social prestige of these groups reflected closely in their importance in production, training and management. Now the situation is altogether changed because of the advance technology. A worker is slave of the machine these days. He can not use his initiatives. A worker must be provided as raw material, and as directed, he operates the machine and regulates it. To-day the machines have also replaced the tools and, a man who operates and regulates these machines is mere an operator. He operates these machines as he operates his cycle. But, he is also alienated by the owner of these machines.

EDUCATIONAL DEVELOPMENT AND ECONOMIC ASPECTS

We are living in a time when knowledge is exploding—knowledge more knowledge, new techniques, new activities which should entail more gains is the cry of the day. But, without giving his appropriate dues to the operator of his new knowledge and techniques it is not possible. Modern economic activities are changing the world day by day which is entailing educational change accordingly. But the real function of the education is to hand over values, human attitudes, traditions and culture. Along these the education must prepare a person to be economically viable person of the society. These should be the first and foremost priority of education. It must resist the cultural diffusion and acculturation. Education must enculturate the youth. Our educational system is lagging behind in this function. The teacher can do this. He should be trained in enculturaling activities during the course of teacher training.

On the economic front our educational structure aims at preparing the young for government jobs. This is tantamount to realizing the dreams of Lord Macauley who was the initiator of our present formal education. He wanted to change the Indian culture and social set up. On the socio-cultured front it is, implicitly or explicitly still acculturating our youth. It should be immediately checked by those who are in power through the teacher. As an economy develops, the needs for the expert managerial staff, highly skilled and semiskilled workers, and also, for generally educated people increase geomatrically. Consequently, there appears an increasing demand for education. Increase in economy is necessary for better living standard. Therefore, educational development mounts with great rapidity. Due to demographic explosion there is an increase in enrolment in schools. Every order of working folk desire their children to get school and university education. So university enrolment increases every year considerably. Due to greater expenses the lower classes miss their children to send to the universities which is necessary for better economy and upliftment. Only elite class people children could get higher education. But education is an instrument of change. It is an investment and consumption for survival. The teacher can play a vital role in imparting good education and apprising the pupil about the new socio-economic change.

Since times immemorial the human beings, inspite of their animal nature, tainted with greed and lust for undue greed, lust for acquisition human beings have been swilling. The greed factor of human beings character though has ever been dominant, has always been corrected or modified by those human beings who were rewarded by the Nature or Almighty God with big elements of rationality and social sanety. In olden times every society had such rational elements who used to guide the people to be human, rational, co-operative and sane. They used to impose some social restraints upon irrational social elements in the society. They used to study, think and speculate and profitiate new knowledge in the society and motivate people to think reason and comprehend things in social millieu. They used to lay down certain social norms and impose certain rules. As in India, good actions (नेक कर्म), dharma (actions as per religious rules), adharma (actions against religious rules), Naitikta (morality based actions) Anaitikta (actions against morality) were, and are to some extent are, followed to-day. These were and still are, the manifestations of learned old teachers (Gurus) and professors (Acharyas). They could impose certain social manifestations on general public and could control through these social rules or manifestations for the social functioning of the society. The economic development was not their priority. Only they wanted a good social order. They thought if there was good social order the social sane economy will automatically develop and for that they thought the non-formal (पैत्रिक शिक्षा) education is the best.

If the restraints suggested by these rational religious person were ignored the strict rules are used to punish the defaulters. So in the olden days the trauma of greed was controlled because of the old Indian educational systems Now-a-day the economics of corruption has become rampant in the society, be a government office or a higher seat of learning or a mustard oil shop in the market. One can not get any work done without greasing the palm of the person in authority. The educational world is also the prey of this social menace. There is no clarity in the appointment in public as well as in government offices. Same is the condition in the education department. While appointing the teachers the meritorious candidates sometimes are ignored due to favouritism and nepotism. Favoured candidates always ignore their assigned duties. Our markets are prone to adulteration, cheating and corruption. Many times adulteration in food items like edible oils etc take many innocent lives of the people. By fair and foul means the man wants to become rich and richer. Most of our politician are in the dark shadows of courts for heinous crimes. Also many politicians support the criminals and, these criminal are moving safe. It can be said that corruption has become a boon of our socio-economic structure, and a common feature in the whole society. There is no need to go into details, everybody is fully aware about it in the society. Atmosphere of loot chain pulling, pick-pocketing, robbery, burglary, rape of innocent girls and molestation of ladies has become a common feature in the society. There is a need of solution of the menace.

Our educational system in which the teacher is a prime functionary can not bring reforms alone. There is need of social and political will to bring our socio-economic structure on the right track. This requires correct analysation of the whole economic structure. Officers, the teacher can play a prime role. But he/she should be given or restored 'teachers' prestige. The society should give due respect to the teacher. In the materialistic hedonistic age the teacher is considered poor and rich treats him/her not well.

Not only the parents but the students from rich families neglect the teacher. If the parents start giving respect to the teachers their wards will also respect their teachers. The teachers should also respect their profession and should avoid doing tutions. Moreover, the teacher should always try to know about the prevailing socio-economic conditions and, during the course of teaching he/she should apprise the pupils about it.

19

School as an Instrument of State and the Teacher

From the times immemorial since the inception of human society, education has been an instrument of preparation and protection of life, development of civil organization, social and moral values and a source of socio—economic and cultural change. Through education, the society inculcates social and moral values. Be it a development of human rational quality or the development of human other potentialities as moral social and economic development, education has ever been an instrument of chance. So, there has always been a demand for education in the society. In the beginning education was familial. With the passage of time educational agencies and institutions came into being, which entailed the demand for the teachers. Since the value of education is measured by (*a*) to create conditions for a balanced personality and development of well sounded conditions for the individual for living harmoniously in the society (*b*) to prepare a well developed homogenous values system in the society (*c*) to prepare the individual to earn his livelihood judiciously and honestly (*d*) to prepare a person to help in national economic development and productivity and (*e*) visualizing consumption of consumer goods justly in the society. As such the education is imparted for the well being of the individuals and social collectivity, that is, society. If we look to the social aspects of education, it may be treated as a process of—

(*i*) Personality formation of the individuals,

(*ii*) Social restructuring and development,

(*iii*) Cultural development and its perpetuation through enculturation, (*iv*) Acting as an instrument of training of occupations,

(*v*) Preparation a ground for social stratification,

(*vi*) Acting as an instrument of developing social morality,

(*vii*) Acting as an instrument of mutual understanding co-operation, sharing and working for the common course and good,

(*viii*) Elite formation,

(*ix*) Enterpreneurship,

(*x*) Development of attitudes, motives, in incentives towards social change for bringing the technological progress,

(*xi*) Reduction of conflicts and bringing social harmony in the society,

(*xii*) And finally creating good attitudes towards life, .

To achieve all these objectives different educational agencies contribute, sometimes co-operating collaborating in educational activities, state, religious organizations, schools, universities, technical universities and other apex bodies like, UGC, AICTE, NCERT, NCTE, Inter university boards and Secondary Education Boards etc usually are working for educating the young members of the society.

In the beginning the family and community played a vital role in providing education to the youngers. With the growth of population and development of science and technology necessitated more education awareness and consequently avenues of education considerably increased. Earlier the education was totally designed and supported by the community. Very few students used to get higher education in Gurukulas, Academies and Madarsas which were basically residential were free from state control. The Gurukulas, in India, were situated in jungles at the river banks. The students' used to beg and collect food stuffs from the neighboring community. They also used to collect fire woods from jungles and gather fruits from trees.

With the passage of time, demographic scenario changed, man got more equipped for harnessing the natural resources. The society also became more complex. So the demand for education also increased and, agencies like places of religious organizations got involved in educating the younger generation. After sometime, this also slipped into the hands of industrialists who emerged after the industrial revolution. Gradually, the technological and industrial development became complex. The state desired to have a watch on the economy of the state, so also on the development of educational structure. As such, in the long run, the state got hold over the educational structure. Now all of the voluntary private agencies which were having direct control on education, are required to obtain the permission from the state to do so. And the formal education came into being for providing mass education under the state control.

As such, the whole burden of the entire educational structure comprising the schools, Universities, technical institution and medical institution of higher learning including the open schools and apex bodies like UGC, AICTE, NCTE, NCERT and other are financed by the state. In other words the entire financial burden of educational structure is to be beared by the tax-papers.

Before partition, Delhi had only five or six high schools to meet the needs of total five lacs population of Delhi. In 1945 only 18 thousands students had appeared in High Examination conducted by U.P. Board of High School and Intermediate Education. Now the population has crossed the figure of one crore and fifty six lacs in Delhi. So the number of school has also increased in the same proportion, rather more. The number of Govt. run and aided schools is between two to three thousand. As such, the budget for the education, which is a state subject, is multiplied in millions of rupees during the last fine decades. Similar is the situation in others states.

Besides, education has also become a commercial commodity. There are number of creches, nursery schools and public schools being run on commercial lines which are found in every nook and corner of villages, towns and cities. These schools have a good flourishing business. In cities there are many public schools which cater the needs of upper elite class business community. As such these schools create a distinct upper elite class which becomes different from rest of the majority of 98 per cent masses. The product of these public schools serves as bureaucrats in big business organizations, Government of offices and Armed forces. Mostly products of these public schools could only compete and get higher education in engineering, medical and business. And those who get such higher education become, the bureaucrats in government offices also. These schools run on commercial lines and are managed by private bodies, but have to follow the state rules and regulations. These schools charges hi-fi, charges from the students, but pay to the teachers equal to the teacher of the government schools. The public school teachers work more than the teachers of the Government schools.

The management of the educational structure in the past was totally in the hands of the community in al respects. Now it has totally gone in the hands of the state. If you look to the genesis of the school, one would he surprised to see such an affair. The institution of school came into being with the introduction of formal education. This came into existence after industrial revolution in England which consequently spread throughout the world due to Prostent Calvince Ethics in Christian world. This encouraged capitalism and colonization. The phenomenon of colonization added feathers to the institution of school. The colonizers first traced the countries which had immense natural resources and occupied these lesser developed countries and established their rule. After consolidation their rule, they tried to impose their culture through cultural diffusion and acculturation which was not possible without imposing their educational structure. There colonizers first tried to impose their language by educating their subjects through their educational system and prepare them to be loyal to them in the occupied society. As such, the subjects of their colonies became loyal to their masters and became obedient subjects. The colonizers had created an atmosphere in which their subjects considered them as their true guides and protectors. The colonizers planned a strategy whereby the educational structures of the colonies may look novel and gracious to the subjects and serve their propose. So, first in the garb of missionaries they opened schools which could impose their language, culture and religion and also could also establish in-roads in their indigenous cultures of their colonies. Such schools there psuedo-state schools run by the missionaries. These schools reaped rich harvest and the colonizers could be able to (1) change the mind set of the subjects towards their foreign masters and (2) partly the poor subjects could become loyal to the faith of their masters and some of them adopted the faith of their masters.

In India, the educational structure comprised Gurukulas Pathsalas and Madarsas and; when the colonizers mind set developed the idea of changing these original educational set ups, many Britishers were in favour of retaining the old system of Indian education as to allow the Indians to perpetuate their original national culture. But a group of Britishers desiring to change it on western pattern succeeded. The leader of this group was Lord Macauley. Main purpose of such a change was to attract the Indian mind—(1) to words western culture, (2) to get cheap educated clerks for East India Company's British Government and (3) to win the loyalty of the Indians to-word British Government. Main aim of imposing British type of formal education on Indians was to kill the Indian Culture and economy. Lord Macauley believed that if a country was to be kept slave for ever, it was necessary to kill its culture". And Lord Macauley succeeded in his mission. We have lost of our culture. We have lost our language, dress and what not. Lord Macauley's soul might be rejoicing in its grave for such a splendid achievement, Lord Macauley could achieve. He might be eating Indian sweets in his grave.

This experiment very well proved that the institution of school can be very effective instrument for gaining desirable ends. The democracy is the game of numbers. The new rulers came after independence, and they had objectives in mind to perpetuate their hold on state administration. They also wanted faithful followers who support their ideology and, a vote banks could be formed. The new rulers tried to utilize the school as an instrument for the perpetuation of their political culture. Likewise all governments, be it a democracy or aristocracy, or monarchy, or oligarchy or theocracy try to utilize the school as a tool as an instrument for achieving desirable political ends.

The education system is a large consumer of its products, as a large number of its products are employed as teachers in schools and in other educational institutions. The state tries to utilize these elites in such a way that they support the ideology of rulers. So the school curriculum and school text books generally reflect the wish and ideology of the people in power. If a state is democratic in true sense it will permit democrat institutions to grow and progress. If the state is theocrat its only prime aim with be to prove that the particular religion is prominent. In a communist country individualistic initiatives, private enterprises and religious, ideology will not have any place or say in the schools. If a state is capitalist country's Calvinstic ethics will be a subject in the school curriculum. If a country is secular, religious teaching will not get any place in school curriculum. Every ideology tries to cast its shadow in the school structure, in its own mould to perpetuate its ideology for reinforcing its hold on the masses. Not only this, the ideologists also try to cross these boundaries, by changing the text book contents covertly. As such a state generally tries to shake the form of educational structure in such a frame which could enable the schools to achieve what the state has in focus, aspiring to consolidate its position. As such, generally the institution of school is generally functioning as an instrument of state. And it can be said that, old system of education was good.

It is not a new thing. If we visualize the historical perspectives of educational structures prevalent in the world, we find that in the past that this kind of practice was there. In Greece Platonic Academics were designed to educate citizens only about city affairs. In India, in olden days in Aryan period aim of education was to prepare a man for good living, producing and enriching and protecting Indian Culture. Aristotle put forward the dynamic view of education dwelling on nature, its form, matter, activity and potentiality and also ethics. Product of his educational views was Alexander the great who dreamed of capturing the whole world. In Rome Quintilian put forward the interest in Roman Education. Augustine (354-450 A.D.) advocated the Divine Illumination sense perception, and liberal Arts. J.J. Rousseau, Immanuel Kant, Rene Descartes, John Locke, John Dewey, Herbert Spencer, Pestalozzi, M.K. Gandhi, Vivekananda and J. Krishnamurti put forward their own views on education for using it as an instrument of reformation. Since the state in the past, was not contributing well as it had no *'locus standi'* over the then educational structure. Now the state takes full responsibility and bears the financial burden, it wants to influence the educational structure which is implemented by the school. So the school is an instrument of state of which the teacher is always a main functionary of the school.

Now the total educational structure is governed by the state, and all educational institutions are financed by the state. Even the voluntary educational institutions are aided by the state; naturally the state likes to exercise its full control over the overall educational structure in the country. The state always, overtly or covertly tried to impose its will over the educational structure to achieve its desired ends. The teacher, the principals are treated like other government employees. They have to follow the same norms as are followed by other government employees. The universities have autonomy but many times the politicians and the Government try to appoint the vice-chancellors and Registrars of their choice, who fall in the tune with the ideology of the political party in power in the state.

As such, the school which is the main organ of educational structure, moulder of the future guardian and builder of the nation proceeds with the tune of the government and tries to implement the programmes of the government. And nerves of the government remain in the hands of the politicians. The school follows the curriculum prepared by the state. The school and the teachers have no say in curriculum construction. The community also do not have any say in this respect. The curriculum experts committee composed of high level educational bureaucrats prepare the curriculum in such a way that it usually reflects the wishes of the political party in power.

The main role of the teacher is estimated as how many periods he/she takes and how by his/her teaching the students will fare in the annual boards examinations. For this end the teacher is required to do a lot of work. He/she has take extra classes, check the home assignments given to the children. The teacher has to teach atleast six periods per day. As such no time is left to do cultural activities for enculturation. With regard to other academic work as participation in curriculum construction, the school teacher is considered incompetent like a manual worker a brainless man by the elite educationists. The teacher has lost respect in the community. 'Hellow teacher' is the main echo in the school corridors and on the streets and in *Mohallas* and *Galies*. Rich business class families and, their wards who are students of the teacher, treat the teacher as an ordinary worker. When the teacher goes to their homes for tutoring their wards he/she is considered as an ordinary part time earner like a domestic helps.

Our present educational system is only examination result oriented and nothing more than that. It has lost its teleological, axiological, sociological and cultural aims, because it has a lever of good examination results and creating competition in the society. It has totally become a tool in the hands of the bureaucrats for materializing the inherent objectives of the state. Because of the competitive nature of the present educational system which breeds materialistic dichotomy entailing poisonous corruption and frauds, there is a need of educational reforms. These reforms should look to the present condition of the educational structure and present position of the teacher. Major aim of the education should be to prepare youngers, who are our future guardians, for social harmony. The present social harmony is in bad shape due to our present educational system. The teachers, besides teaching for atleast periods a day are also required to do clerical work also. Once a teacher always a teacher is seen in the educational world. There are no promotion avenues for the teachers, therefore, there is no dedication to teaching work. Rapport between the teacher and the taughts is diminishing day by day. Teaching in the rural areas is like a bonus. Most of the teachers in villages first do their home jobs as tilling of land and looking after then cattles, having rounds to their agricultural fields, thereafter, they relax in the school while teaching and negating their fatigues. There is no check because the headmasters also belong to this category. Also, this is because that all primary and middle schools are government run schools. And these schools also carry out the state agenda. No co-curricular activities are arranged in rural schools for enculturation of the students.

It is, therefore, would not be incorrect to assume that the educational structure should never be under state control. It was never before in the past. Only our alien rulers brought the education under state control. No doubt because of large scale expansion of educational structure, it needs state funds. The state should give funds but it should give autonomy also to the schools. The teachers should be given facilities for the improvement of their knowledge.

20

Socialization for Morality, Civilization and the Teacher

Since times immemorial the man has ever been socializing his off-springs enculturating them for culturally prescribed patterns, language, skills, social norms, moral values, customs, traditions for generating in them a capacity to perform many social roles, social relationship and for creating situations for strengthening the collectivity of individuals, that is society. This is all done through socialization of the individuals and by generating into them social norms, values sociability, co-operation and especially morality. This process has deep antiquity used for regulating the human behaviour. If we peep into the history and trace the educational ideas, we will find that our old seers, thinkers and philosophers have always been constantly trying to profitiate new ideas for regulating the human life. This is because the man by nature has ever been egoistic, self-centred, greedy, hedonistic and acquisitive creature. The strong man has ever been exploiting the week man, resulting discontents and conflicts in the society. To overcome this awkward social situations, the wisemen having always been profitiating and prescribing certain sane norms of good social behaviour. The have always been devising ways and means for developing such acceptable human social behaviour in the society. Such patterns of human behaviour and character are generally called morals. And moral building is done through enculturation of the culture of a particular society. Prominent moralists like Immanuel Kant, H.E. Moor, Shopenhaur, Hegel and at home all of our Gurus can be said as moralists. Our present teacher has also to play a prominent role in infusing morality in our youngers.

Culture and civilization are often mixed together, though these have sharp distinctions. Even though these, two are taken in wide, ethnographic sense as similar. But, it is culture which contributes to the development of civilization. The culture is that complex whole which includes knowledge, beliefs, art and crafts, morals, laws, customs, traditions, social traits and many other capabilities and habits acquired by man as a member of the society. Clyde Klukohan and W.H. Kelly say that it only confines to a single cluster of people or a group. A culture is a historically developed system of common ways of living which tend to be shared by the members of a group (The concept of culture Ralph Linton). It encompasses the group languages, traditions, customs, manners and institutions, including the institutions motivating ideas beliefs, values and their embodiments and also artefacts.

The word civilization was used in 19th century in its familiar sense referring to aggregates of characteristics displayed by the members of the society in their life, advanced way of life of people of a historic period for instance Greek civilization at the time of Perciles and Mohan-Jo-Daro and Harrapa civilization. The term civilization as it was used, E.B. Tylor refers it, to show the total achievements of most of the advanced people, to date it, as if the civilizations were unlinear development of the past with later people at different stages of development. To me, "the culture building is an inherent process of inculturing which is always done through non-inclinativeness like a creation a peace of work of art." When this process is engrossed in the material welfare of the society it becomes 'civilization'. This would be wrong to compare or identify civilization with a piece of craft and culture with a piece of art'. As such, a prosperous culture which could inbreed material aspirations for the people, and for their well being, becomes civilization'. Thus it because as we notice, that all civilizations which existed in the past could be possible due to material welfare development of the people.

Due to this fact, in view of human animal nature, we have to consider, 'socialization for moral civilization', and look to the need of morality for a civilization, because civilization has always material overtones. Man being a member of a society builds a civilization, has always selfish ends in view. He will always look to his interests first then good of others. In such a situation there has to be some moral binding on the deviating members of the society. Therefore for a prosperous civilization a sound culture is necessary which could also enculturate the people. It is the function of the culture to devise ethics and morality for the members of the society. It is the functions of the culture to generate ethics and morality in the members of the society through a sound process of socialization. And the school and the teachers can play a prominent role in enculturating the students along with the other agencies of the society.

If we took to the history of ideas, the thinkers have always been contemplating on the tendencies which stop creating disharmony and disintegration in the society and, have been continuously devising some ideas of conduct for its members. They have been continuously suggesting certain social traits, traditions, social sanity and some ideal manners for good behaviour entailing ethical norms which is called morality or moral laws.

Herodotus, a Greek philosopher was the first thinker to suggest ethical values for the society. Thereafter many thinkers like Socrates and his disciples Plato, Isocrates, Crito and many others discussed and showed the need of ethical laws in the society for the solidarity of the society. Their ideas are reflected in dialogues—like Phaedo, Symposium, Laws, Republic etc. Debates in these dialogues are intimately connected with the views about the nature of the society and state and the ends with which the citizens should strive to attain. Their educational theory is based on these ideas so as to bring cohesion and co-operation in the society. Plato's views about the division.citizens of state into classes is designed to emphasize is that three are different kinds of services which the citizens perform should be well organized as (1) to develop reasoning capacity in the individuals through sound education so as to make the individual aware about good and bad, (2) to know about justice and injustice and (3) to know about truth and beauty. This was to subside the self-interest tendencies in the society and to encourage brotherhood, cooperation and good neighbourhood. This kind of thinking had emerged in Greece due to continuous terroristic trouble in their country by the Spartans. This lashing of terrorism on Greeks by the Spartans entailed a war between them which continued about thirty years. India is also facing the same terroristic problem in the form of a proxy war for the fourteen years from a neighbour.

Axiological thinking also proceeded in India simultaneously like Greece, as India was not far from personal greed, social feuds and conflicts. Our classical epics like Ramayana and Mahabharta show how kings fought each other ignoring the common interests of the people. On the other bank, Rishi, Munis and Gurus (teachers) showed the way for common good enunciating good social traits, customs, good life norms, laws and ethical codes. In Indian society many ceremonies like 'Darasthouthan', Yajopavitram, Guru Diksha and Grah pravesh are performed. These ceremonies have been the source of developing moral civilization. In Indian society very few cases of divorce and suicides are still seen. Those such cases occur, due to materialistic influence. Moreover, inspite of rigid Indian caste structure, the Indian social structure is homogenous as it is based on rural agro-economy, which is based on co-operation, self-sufficiency, non-competitiveness, sharing and respect for the neighbours. Still it is considered best in the world. Karl Marx had praised the Indian social structure saying it as communistic.

In the west, many thinkers contributed for the sane social order in the society. Thomas Hobbs (17th century) described the primeval man as solitary poor, nasty, brutish and short of ideas—no art, no culture, no letters and no society. Every thing resulted from human perfectibility which entailed certain norms and values. According to John Gortified Von Herder (German Theologician), man is a divine creation. He must have a purpose on earth namely his own perfection in tune with humanity. Voltur (French philosopher) assumed that enlightnment in mankind for upward progress is necessary. Turgot says that the manners are result of human good behaviour. These draw the nation together, nearer and closer through creating good conditions. He described three stages of human development—savagery, barbarism and civilization.

There have been movements for the equality in human society. French revolution was one of these. Protestant reformation movement was another in Europe. Here at home, in India many reformers tried to improve the condition of the repressed, Guru Nanak, Chaitenya Mahaprabhu, Swami Vivekananda, Swami Dayanand Sarswati and Acharya Vinobha Bhave were among those who tried to socialize people for morality. It is that in 18th and 19th centuries some people tried to generate axiological perspective in the society. It was an important happening in the human history. Man is the product of nature and according to Jean Jacques Rousseau (French thinker) the man is horn healthy, sane and uncorrupt but he is enslaved and made corrupt by the human institution like family, community and society. He said that "the man is born free but finds himself in chains." His saying is an indication of mans greed and selfishness and it needs a change from materialist trends to axiological trends.

Auguste Comte (1798-1857) who gave the social science called 'sociology.' The name of sociology and its basic principles strongly influenced the conception of human progress, which are its basic principles and tenets. The French Revolution had repudiated the monarchy and Christianity and installed the worship of 'reason'. According to it, man's historical development has three stages (1) theological, (2) metaphysical and (3) scientific; and with source of positivism ultimate achievement is secured:

1. *Theological stage*: All cosmic phenomena are thought to be governed by the divine will—much like man, first all things are asciomatic (Fetishn) living and intelligent, secondly the invisible things govern (polytheistic view) and, only God govern (monothrstic view).
2. *Metaphysical stage*: All events are no longer governed by supernatural forces but by the fundamental abstract ideas essences and energies.
3. *Positivist stage*: Finally in positivistic stage phenomena are exclaimed by cause and effect which are diversified by observation, per. se. (perception), hypothesis, experimentation and synthesis.

Out of these three stages of development, man is in the third stage. He should apply his reason and should act for harmony. These ethical values are necessary in human life. E.B. Tylor (1832-1937 England) and Lavis H. Morgan (1818-1881) were the chief exponents of cultural stages, found in the evolution of mankind. Their main concern was culture development in general and individual culture in particular. Man could survive out of the savagery barbarism because he could do and adopt some of the sane social customs, traditions, good manners and morals.

Charles Darwin invented the term "survival of the fittest", which was followed by Herbert Spencer (1820-1930 English thinker). He held that an 'unknown and unknowable absolute force' is continuously operating in the material world and producing variety of coherence, integration, secularism and individualism.

Karl Marx (1818-1883) (German) saw that the principles of economic organization represented by a social class which builds feudalism leads to slavery. This is done by a partisan class of land lords, nobility believing in capitalism, raised by the entrepreneurs and by the masters who are tortures of the slaves. This leads to class war. The two classes are formed 'bourgeous' and 'proleterates'. This situation can be overcome when there is a consideration about the exploitation of proletariats by the bourgeous.

Lester F. Ward (1841-1913, USA) and Albun W. Small (1854-1926 USA) consider man as an animal. There is a need to change such a man as a rational social man through Telic method of social planning. For such a social change sociology has to play a dominant role.

Max Weber (1864-1920 German) saw rationalization as a tool for the change of man to be moral man. He asserted that (1) it can be through charismatic, (2) Leadership developed by traditional way and (3) by legalization.

Emile Durkhiem (1858-1917, French) saw the division of labour as the main cause of disharmony in the society. He advocates for mental dependence, and put forward the theories of collective consciousness for social organic solidarity. This can be done when man becomes objectively aware of social values—such as sharing, adherence to ethical Values and believing in Collectivity. Then only conflicts can be resolved. Mechanical solidarity is followed by organic solidarity. The interests are followed by restraints in the form of laws imposed by the governments. Therefore, collective consciousness is necessary.

Also many other thinkers contributed to moral education. Important of them are Immanuel Kant (France), G.E. More (England), Fred Clark (England), Swami Vivekananda, Swami Dayanand Sarswati, Swami Agnivesh, M.K. Gandhi, Aurobindo, Swami J. Krishnamurti (India) Fred Clark and many Sadhus, Saints, and Sufis contributed to moral education. All of them contributed towards socialization for moral education for making the society a sane society.

Today amongst all other things, there is a need for a fresh outlook at the present condition of moral values in the society in order to carry on harmonies economic and social development in Indian society. The Indian society has a pluralistic corporate composite culture shared by various linguistic religious, and ethnic groups. After 57 years of independence we are still following an alien educational structure which was imposed on us by a foreign British power for their own ends. Their rigorously neutrality was devoid of any suitable educational programme for cultivating spiritual and moral values through formal education, which is basically state imposed. After independence though we followed the policy of neutrality and adopted secularism, but there should have been, along with it, long researching for moral values, necessary for our system of education. The various commissions and Committees on education have strongly recommended the inculcation of moral values in the youngs through education. But the examination system always became a stumbling block in achieving this end. Our teachers do not find time for inculcating moral values in the youngers and encultivating them due to preparation of the students for examination.

As early as in 1815 A.D., Lord Moria had observed this social situation and suggested ethical maxims in education. Education Commission 1948-49 head by Late Dr. Radhakrishnan reviewed the position of religious education in historical perspective, viz., as existed during Ancient, Medieval and Modern periods of Indian history and considered the constitutional position and the practices prevailing in other secular countries as America (USA) and Australia. The commission also considered the thinking of Mahatma Gandhi on this aspect. The commission observed—"What makes a man truly virtuous is the purpose for which he lives and his general outlook on life. If we look to our historical development, and even after this exclusion of spiritual training in our educational institutions, it appears that such exclusion would be untrue in view of our whole history of educational development. Indians believed and to some extent and, still believe that if one has done his duties faithfully as a grahsthi, a house holder, and has been a good father or mother, a good provider for the family, he/she will be a good citizen. The beauty and mystery of life in the universe, lies in knowing the meaning of life and death, the aspirations of the human soul and sad feelings of wishful mindedness that are beyond the ordinary knowledge. Only positive knowledge can provide an insight that, there is a realm of forces unseen which we feel but can never know completely.

If the education of the individual is diversed from the perfection of moral, social and axiological values, it is defective and rather harmful for social harmony. How can it be improved? What we need, is not mere imparting of instruction or teaching. We need transmitting of vitality in humanity. We must civilize the human hearts for harmonious living in the society. Which can only be accomplish by socializing man morally and apprising of unnecessary greed. The teacher while working in a school, which is a state instrument, for achieving the ends of formal education, can accomplish it provided he/she is given opportunity to do this. He/she can to be a saver of the society from the social evils. Education Commission (1948-1949) recommended as stated below in this regard.

SILENT MEDITATION IN MORNING ASSEMBLY AND YOGA CLASS

A silent worship or meditation can lead to morality. Every morning, in school a short period of silent worship or meditation can be fixed every day in morning assembly or in daily yoga classes. A morning assembly should a permanent feature in every school and college time table. For a few minutes we may distract the mind from the daily life and, attend to the forces which determine the meaning and value of life. The morning assembly should be conducted regularly before the teaching starts. It should be managed by a teacher or a team of teachers who should work under the guidance and supervision of the principal of the school. Students should also be encouraged to deliver a short lecture or talk or morality or sociability. This will give them a training in self-expression. Likewise in yoga classes after the 'asana' there should be a 'dhyana' practice, which should include meditation. After this there should be 'Hasya Yoga'. In the school or college there should not be any religious practice nor any kind of religious criticism. All religious should be respected and then annual religious functions like Janamasthmi, Diwali, Holi, Id-ul-fitter and Christmas days should be celebrated, all should take part in these religious functions.

STUDY OF GREAT BOOKS

A reverent study of the essentials of all religious books would be uniquely rewarding as a step towards social harmony and tolerance in different religious sects, long divided due to dogmatic limited views. This, is in consonance with the spirit of 'Unity in Diversity' of the country. I. Tsuing tells that the University of Nalanda was the meeting ground of different sects and creeds with different possible and impossible religious doctrines. University of Taxila had the similar character where many foreign scholars, from the west, north and east used to come to study. A Greek thinker, most probably Parmenides, during the rule of Perciles in Greece had come to Taxila to escape conscription during the thirty years' war between Greeks and Spartans who had spread terrorism in Greece. It is believed that he stayed for 8 years at Taxila. During the period he studied all Indian scriptures, schools of philosophy, epics and Shrimad Bhagwat Gita. He had gone back to his country with the idea of immortably of soul, which could produce dialogue Phaedo on the concept of immortality of soul by Socrates and his disciple Plato. Therefore, the study of different religious as well as philosophical books will be revential. Generally all religious books make man moral tolerant and kind. It is the self-centred dogmatic religious readers who make the society intolerant. Thoughts of the great souls should he made known to the students in schools and other religious institutions through common religious functions at the school or at other educational institutions. The teacher should be broad minded in this regard.

The Secondary Education Commission (1952-53) headed by Dr. A. Lakshmana Swami Mudaliar, considered that healthy trends in regard to religious and moral behaviour spring from three sources—

1. The influence of home which is the dominant factor in life building,
2. The influence of the school, through the conduct and behaviour of the teachers there and the life at the school community as a whole,
3. The influenced exercised by the public of the locality and to which the public opinions prevails in all matters pertaining to religious and moral codes of conduct.

The committee on "Religious and moral instructions", headed by Shri Prakash set up by Ministry of Education Government of India examined (*i*) the desirability and flexibility of making provisions for teaching moral and spiritual values in educational institutions, (*ii*) If it is found desirable and flexible to make such provisions, then the schools and educational institutions should:

(*a*) define broadly the content of instructions in morals at various stages of education,

(*b*) should consider its place in moral education.

The committee reviewed the whole situation and suggested that religious and moral activities should be left to home, since the parents at home very often observe and celebrate various religious functions and rituals. The committee felt that moral and spiritual values are essential in life. These should be inculcated in the individuals right from early age. The family members have to influence the child first. Good manners are very important for moral education. It is not unusual that when people become free after attaining freedom after long years of bondage, suddenly they are inclined to become self-willed arrogant, intolerant and inconsiderate. To meet this situation good manners and ethical values are necessary. Graciousness, charm of social behaviour and good relationship have largely disappeared from the western countries due to materialistic and consequent hedonistic and xenophilic craze, of which we Indians are also prey to large extent. The committee recommended that:

1. The teaching of moral and spiritual values in educational institutions is desirable, but with certain limitations,
2. Creative and sympathetic study of lives and teachings of great religious teachers should be arranged in schools and educational institutions through functions and seminars. For good manners, social services and patriotism should be stressed through talks, display, radio, T.V., cinema by voluntary organisations. In writer's village the trio freedom fighters Late Mahashial Harishchandra Ji, Pt. Late Baburam Sharma (Munde) and Late Thakur Malkhan Singh Ji used to arrange such talks for the removal of untouchability and gender bias from the village P.O. Bhalarwa Ganj, Distt. Haridwar, Uttaranchal. There should

be a compulsory Rastragan in the morning assembly in the schools. There should be two minute silence after the national anthem (Rastragan). The students should meditate during the silence time. Therefore, there should be a talk by the teacher or the school principal.

3. Suitable books on spirituality and aesthetics should be made available in the schools or colleges library so that the students may be encouraged to read about morality sociability and aestheticity. The class teacher should encourage the students to read by giving some concerned assignments which might entail related reading,
4. For inter-religious understanding, religious functions selected from all religions should be arranged and celebrated annually in schools and educational institutions. This would create a spirit of understanding of the other religious and of tolerance.
5. Some form of physical training should be compulsory for all students in schools and other educational institutions at every stage, so as to bring cohesion bonds among students and physical fitness. Now-a-days, physical education is more or less ignored in schools and in teachers training institutes. This is why we fail to do any viable performance in games at the international level. Parents too, do not permit their wards to plays due to examination studies at home.
6. There should be some clubs like literary club, sports club, art club, social service club and crafts clubs for promoting activities which may bring amity and cohesion amongst the students.

Many ills due to which our world and system of education and, also the whole society are suffering these days are because of lack of social and moral values in the society. These result in wide corruption, non-sociability, cheating-frauds and all these are creating a climate of no work culture, greed, disregard for religion and spiritually, disappearance of the institution of joint family and non-rapportistic attitude towards family members and neighbour. All these are making the society dysfunctional. Non-a-days the society is not united and social bonds are disappearing day by day. All these social lackings is a matter of great concern. God knows what will be of our nation in future.

The Emotional Integration Committee headed by Dr. Sampoorna Nand, appointed by Government of India in 1961, looked education as an agency of strengthening and promoting national integration. It recommended that education should faster mutual appreciation of various religious in the country. Every student who has taken up science for study should have a background of humanities compulsorily. Adult education should be organized. Religious education can not be a part of formal education, but without it the education shall remain incomplete.

The education commission 1964-66 headed by Prof. D.S. Kothari also looked into this matter. It recommended for the inclusion of social, moral and religious values in the educational system as under:

The weakening of social and moral values in the younger generation is tantament to creating many social problems. It can create social, ethnical and ethical conflicts as happening in some western countries. The commission felt that ethical and moral values are necessary for social harmony. The commission also felt that modernization does not mean renouncing of social and moral values. These should be promoted for self discipline and social harmony.

SECULARISM AND RELIGION

In a multi-religious society, like Indian society, it is necessary to define the attitudes of the state towards religious and religious bodies. The adoption of secularist policy, that is, in political, economic and social matter's, all citizens irrespective of their religious faiths will enjoy equality of rights that no religious community will be favoured. Secularism implies that there should not be religious education in schools; but it does not mean that there should not be any place for spiritual, moral and social values in the life of a person. The state should make a distinction between religious education and moral education. The former is concerned about the religious traits and the later is concerned about religious values which are essential for good life. They should encourage tolerant attitude towards the study of all tenets of all religious. Ignorance and misunderstanding about it should be removed and clearly about own religion should be given.

SOCIAL MORAL AND SPIRITUAL VALUES IN SCHOOL CURRICULUM

A serious defect in the school curriculum is absence of provision for social, moral and spiritual values in education. In the life of the majority of Indians religion is a great motivating force and, is ultimately is a bound up with the formation of character which can be done by enculturation of ethical values. A national system of education that is related to life, needs to took to the aspiration of the people. It can not afford to ignore this purposeful objective. The commission therefore recommended—

1. Moral education should be imparted through methods such as suggestions, as well as discussion, as well as teaching orally.
2. Congenial school atmosphere, that is, the behaviour and personality of the teachers and the administrators,
3. Every teacher, whatever his teaching subjects are should keep in mind the integrity point of events,
4. Sense of social purpose should always be reflected in school programme as well as in co-curriculum activities.
5. Honesty, integrity and cohesion should be the motto of every teacher,
6. Atleast one two periods should set aside for telling stories.
7. There should be story telling contest in co-curriculum activities programme in the schools. A teacher should look after this.
8. And in addition, the Principal of the school should find time to attend the morning assembly.

Committee of members of the Parliament on National Policy on Education Constituted in 1967 suggested ways and means for inculcating moral, social and spiritual values in the children. For formation of character steps should be taken, which should receive due emphasis in total process of education. Proper study of humanities and social sciences including great universal religions, participation in games sports and hobbies can contribute to the right values and attitudes. Also these can contribute to the development of religious tolerance, cooperation, spirit of sharing among student. The curriculum development by the National Council of Educational Research and Training in 1975 for ten year school programme was a good exercise in this regard. Now the N.C.E.R.T. is again set up a committee for curriculum construction.

THE WARDHA EDUCATION CONFERENCE ON BASIC EDUCATION 1937

Following resolution was adopted for Basic Education:

1. Free and Compulsory education for all for seven years,
2. Medium of instruction should be mother tongue.
3. Education should centre around manual work and production. Production work most probably should be related to control or localized handicrafts. The conference felt that the production would meet the salary of teacher.
4. The school teaching will not contain teaching of religion. Gandhiji believed and affirmed that all religions are same. The teacher must have faith and respect for all religions. The teacher must have an ideal character to influence the taughts.

In the last it would not be wrong to stress that home is the first place where the first lesson in social, moral and ethical values pertaining to one's life starts and where it attains maturity. The parents should show an ideal presentations to their children to the children in social, economical and moral values. If the parents are religious, they should inculcate the religious values and traits in their children. They should inculcate a spirit of forbearance, tolerance, sharing, co-operation and kindness in their children. If the parents are addicted to bad habits as drinking as smoking, drug eating and engaged in some unlawful unsocial activities like corruption, adulteration they should renounce such bad habits bit by bit and should not expose such nefarious activities to their children.

The idea of Basic Education advanced by the father of the nation Late M.K. Gandhi was unique. It was in the line of our national culture based on sane axiology and, a suitable tool for rooting out alien system of formal education. It was aimed at to develop a sound work culture in the country and inculcate sanity, morality and moral values in the youngers. But the then rulers were so much influenced by the western culture that they preferred the alien system of formal education and cremated the Basic education along with the dead body of the father of the Nation Mahatma Gandhi. The Basic education was quite different from the pragmatist education started by John Dewey just after the first world war, which was introduced just for material gains and not for axiological gains. Though we Indians renounced the Basic education but the African country Kenya and Indonesia are still following the Basic Education which aimed at economy based on axiology. In Indonesia in Bali it was introduced by a retired police officer and in Kenya by a Negroes who were influenced by Mahatma Gandhi. On the whole it is true that socialization for sane sociability, morality, co-operation, sharing and enculturation should be the prime aim of education.

21

Relevance of Co-curricular Activities in Education and Teacher

All teachers in schools and universities teach according to curriculum. A curriculum is a chalked out fixed programme of course of study, whereby the stipulated content of general as well as science subjects are taught by the teacher. If the teaching is done continuously without any break or variance, the pupil get bored and also the teacher is tired. Moreover, teaching the general or science subjects is not only education. Education is a wider activity. If the teaching is only done for the preparation for the annual examination and does not inculcate, social and moral values and if it does not entail enculturating activities, it can not socialize the youngers and can not the said true education at all.

Earlier the family and community used to inculcate desirable social moral and cultural values through familial education in the children from the very beginning. Now because of dys-functioning of joint family system and due to over engagements of parents in nuclear family system for money earning, the familial education has become redundant. All the schools are supposed to impart all types of education including familial education, that is, inculcation social, moral and cultural values. And it has become very difficult rather an ardous job to teach and prepare the students for annual examination and also to enculturate the students, in social, moral and cultural values The is because teacher has to carry on teaching through out the day atleast in six periods out of eight periods. Also inculturation of social, moral and cultural values is very necessary, because if the school products do not became rational, the school and the teachers of the school are blamed by the society. This can be done through the co-curricular activities. The school co-curricular activities are generally pleasing, joyful and meaningful. These can ease the students' boredom, burdensome and from tiresome continuous class room teaching. Now-a-days a teachers' job is measured by subject content he teaches in the classroom, how glaring examination results are achieved through his teaching. In many cases the school authorities as well Directorate of Education and also the parents expects the better glaring examination results. This process goes as die-casting process of examination results. This process goes as die-casting process of machine design in a workshop. Both the teacher and the student are victims of this soul killing process. When the students come to school they have to carry an unbearable load of books and classroom exercise notebook to the school. And they come back to have they are extremely tired. Inspite of this, many parents, especially mothers force them to study and do assigned homework. As such, the present process of teaching and preparing for the examination is very tiresome. Some so called progressive schools lay emphasis lay emphasis on progressive methods of teaching because of good examination results. The schools provide excellent teaching aids too. But cumulative efforts of teaching, inspite the use of innovative teaching aids also entail boredom as there is no relief in continuous teaching. The teacher and the school principal are not to be blamed for the agony of teaching boredom of the innocent students. It can also not be true to say that they are aware about it, but they are innovated and motivated by the authorities to do so for examination results. They are aware about the importance of social, moral and cultural values for the society but they generally ignore due to examination results. The result is that the students do not learn anything about these social values. The parents are also enable to carry on these in students due to the rat race of money earning. After passing the annual examination the students knock the doors of many employers. They stand in the queues of competitors. Due to lack of co-curricular activities neither the students enjoy these activities nor learn social, moral and cultural values. The co-curricular activities are necessary for character building personality development and for saneful social living.

Lack of awareness about the co-curricular activities may be due to some extent, to the nature of teacher's own experience at the schools where he was educated and where he is teaching and also at the teachers' training institute where he was trained. There activities were, and are absent, at these educational institutes. Therefore, the teachers are not generally aware about the co-curricular activities and about their social and educational values. Of course the teachers might have heard and read about the co-curriculum activities but many of them might have not got opportunity to experience the co-curricular activities. Though many of the teachers and principal of the schools and training colleges realize and agree that co-curricular activities are very essential for enculturation and culture building but they do not get green signal from the authorities due to examination phobia. It is also unfortunate that many sub-standard training colleges do not have any provision for co-curricular activities in their teacher training programme. Some of such colleges were only training teachers through correspondence courses approved by certain universities. Now the National Council for Teacher Education banned all such colleges.

It is very important that every school, college and teacher training college should make a provision for co-curricular activities. Another most important point is that every teacher should be called upon to join and perform some activity in this direction in the school. He should take charge atleast of one of the co-curricular activities. There is no reason that a pupil should not be initiated and involved in co-curricular activities. Every student should participate if not in all, atleast in some activities of his interest. The co-curricular activities should be one of the important activities. There are great advantages of co-curricular activities. Through these activities exposure to hand work is possible. There can be expression of emotions. Evolvement in out of the class activities can be possible through the co-curricular actives. Regular scheduled programme of these activities create an aesthetic sense in the students, which generates a sense of morality, sociability and togetherness. Visual education in teaching can be a boon for such activities. The students get involved in creative activities while preparing for visual aids.

Doing so they discover beauty in physical things. Even they try to use ugly things. Such activities generally develop special interest for doing creative things in students, and they become creature. When they become creature, they naturally become inventive. Being inventive future guardians, the students become national assets. All this can be done by encouraging the students to do creative work and expression. Emotional release through creative expression is good for balanced personality development. Balanced personality development is only possible when a person also develops himself aesthetically, intellectually, morally, socially along with intellectually. If a student is highly intelligent but, is socially withdrawn egoistic and megalomaniac, he is not fully educated. The society can never function well with such persons. Such person can be elite but they can never be human persons.

Absence of co-curricular activities from the school programme is a tragic event. These activities are joyful, meaningful and bring happiness and harmony in the society. Their missing is tantamount to soul killing. These activities can fill up gap which has been created by the dys-functioning of our institution of joint family system. No development of healthy human attitudes, good manners, healthy habits and emergence of cultural traits are possible in the present social flux in which only material motivations are most prominent. One reason for the non-presence of co-curricular activities in schools, these days, may be lack of awareness about these. The principal and headmaster of the school can also blamed for this. They should not remain blind to the ultra anti-social flux which is making the man materialistic and which may be tantamount to the savagery in society in future.

Co-curricular activities are not conspicous at degrees colleges, teachers training colleges, At and at schools. It is a complete neglect of an important activity. It is found that many technical universities and technical institutions have better co-curricular activities than the other educational institution of national fame. Some teachers training colleges yet to pick up the chords of co-curricular activities. This can be done only educating and apprising such institutes about the important of co-curricular activities and about their role in enculturation and culture building. This can be done by making these institutions and the teachers aware about the effects of motivations of these. Therefore, there should be a comprehensive orientation programme relating to co-curricular activities in teachers training colleges from the beginning of the session, so these activities may be carried out through out the session. These are necessary for character building. The co-curricular activities need to be included as a form of entertainment and to relieve the students and the teacher from the boredom and monotony of the class room. Pedagogic values need these activities through out the year. Maintenance of the pedagogic values should be the concern of the school authorities. The student select these activities themselves according to their taste, interests also according to social taste, interests and aptitudes. The teachers should implement these activities sincerely. They, teachers and the students, should be guided by the Principal and the Headmaster of the school or by some expert senior teachers. The teacher incharge of the co-curricular activities should also guide the students for various activities as solo or mono acting, dancing, acting singing, debates, performing instrumental music and games and sports. On special occasions, if such activities of arranged will be good. And on such occasions some chief guest may be invited for inauguration and valedictory functions. There should be arrangement for stage setting for doing make up of the participants. The art teacher should help in these activities. Above all there should be good lightening arrangement. Actual participation in any of these activities should be compulsory for all students. And such activity should be compulsory in all teacher training institutes.

For optimum presentation of co-curricular activities, these should be a given a place in school teaching programme during the full session. And following co-curricular activities should be organized.

- Debates, lectures, symposium and study circles be arranged,
- Mock courts, mock parliaments, mock panchayats and mock gatherings,
- Weekly wall magazines, periodicals, bulletins, newsletters and annual magazines,
- Dramatics, solo-acting and enculturation.

- Vocal and instrumental music, sports and games and guiding,
- Scouting and guiding camps,
- Excursions educational visits and tours,
- Annual gatherings by arranging melas etc.
- Celebrations of important religious festivals like, Janamasthmi, Pongal, Diwali, Milad-ul-Nabi, Id-ul-Fitter, Guru Nanak day and X-mas day.
- Observation of national days like, Independence day, (15th August), Mahatma Gandhi's Birth day (2nd Oct.) and Republic Day (26th Jan.) every year.
- Parents Day, Alumni Day and Teacher Day (5th Sept.), Red Cross Day
- Birth days of Great Leaders, Tagore Day, Vinobha Bhave Day, Aurobindo Day, Subash Chandra Bose Day, Tolstoy Day and Lincoln Day
- Melas, Fetes and Sports day, Painting competition day,
- Orientation programme in the beginning of the session,
- Valedictory day at the end of the session,
- Decoration on special occasions as Parents Day with Alpna & Rangoli.
- Foundation Day of the institute or school.
- Social activities like cleanliness and decoration before occasions like Foundation Day and Parents Day.
- Hobby clubs likes art club, sports club, craft club and writing club
- And black board writing competition.

All these co-curriculum activities should be arranged on house wise. All students should be divided in houses like Tagore House, Gandhi House, Maulana Azad House, Vivekanand House etc. etc. No student and teacher should be allowed to ignore co-curricular activities. There should be a record of individual participation in co-curricular activities. Hobbies like photography, painting, decoration and gardening should be involved. Each house should have one teaching staff supervisor who should guide the students to organize co-curricular activities. Besides this, special committees should be formed for special occasions as foundation day, teachers days, parents day, Independence day and Republic Day etc.

For the encouragement of co-curricular activities there should be students v/s teachers competition like (1) Cricket match (2) Sports (3) Music and poetry etc. etc. The staff should help in arranging stage setting etc. Teacher should also co-operate and contribute in arranging functions like annual days, sports, Guru Nanak Day, Basant Panchmi (Sarswati day) etc. etc.

There are some odd jobs which generally need active participation of the students on certain functions. These odd jobs are like ushering the guests, doing seating arrangements, serving refreshments, division of visitors to different seating galleries. On the occasional gathering arranging special cultural programmes to be performed by special artists like singers, musical instrument player and *Nautankies*.

There is a need for giving special attention is the co-curricular activities programmes at all levels of teacher training, that is Nursery School Teachers Training and teacher and Sr. teachers training in all teaching institutions. This can only be materialized if the teachers of the teachers training Institutes are enthusiastic for co-curricular activities and know about the value of these programmes. Also this can only be done if authorities are interested in these. Then only these activities will be gainful for the pupils teachers who are going to be appointed as teachers in schools. The school should give equal weightage to these activities. These activities will not hamper in the studies of the students rather the students will be encouraged. But the parents and the educational authorities believe that these hamper the studies on the contrary such activities give moral strength to the students and generate creative innovative spirit in the students which builds a sound personality.

Therefore, the teacher training Institutes, colleges, colleges of art and schools should provide co-curricular activities for their student. These should maintain a record of participation of individual students as performa given below:

Record of Co-curricular Activities

1. Name of the student............................
2. Class .... Section ....
3. Academic year ....
4. Name of the Institute ....

Activities	*Occasion and date*	*No. of Participants*	*Remarks by the Incharge of co-curricular activities*
A. Music			
B. Dance			
C. Dramatics			
D. Specialities			
i. Debate			
ii. Symposium			
iii. Recitation			
iv. Mono-acting			
v. Solo-dance			
vi. Literary activities			
vii. Artistic Activities			
E. Display			
i. Magazine			
ii. Bulletin Board			
iii. Morning thought for the day			
iv. Press Club			
v. Mobiles			
vi. Rangoli			
vi. Alpna			
vii. Sculptors			
F. Art and Crafts			
G. Visual Aids			
H. Excursion picnic tour participation pic-nics			
I. House wise contests as			
i. Black Board writing			
J. Physical Education			
i. Attendance			
ii. Participation on Inter group contests			
iii. Proficiency in sports			
K. Participation in inter-school Activities			

These activities should be judged at the end of the session by the Co-curricular Activities Committee.

22

Artistic Activities in Teaching and the Teacher

The word 'Art' is derivation from the Latin Word 'Ars' which means doing something 'useful'. Various thinkers defined art in different ways. Some of the important references or descriptions relating to art are given below:

1. *Plato*: According to Plato art is an activity or a careful creation, which requires a careful theory and practice while doing it (Ref. 10th Book of Republic). According to Plato art can only be possible through practice which requires imitation.
2. *Aristotle*: According to Aristotle art is one of the science as are physics and philosophy, art provides beautiful things for aesthetical use.
3. *Acquinas*: According to acquinas, "for the creation of right things art is a way of thinking and doing."
4. *Lessing*: According to Lessing every work of art has principles.
5. *Hegel*: Hegel described different aspects of art. These are symbolic, classical and Romantic. According to him art is absolute shining.
6. *Schopenhauer*: According to Schopenhauer, music is the biggest art.
7. *Nietzche*: According to Nietzche art is the manifestation of spiritual soul.
8. *John Dewy*: According to John Dewy art is an experience like other experiences. With the knowledge of art creation of beautiful artafacts, and architecture can be possible. And an aesthetic sense can only be possible with the knowledge of art. The word aesthetic is a derivation from the Greek

word 'aesthesis' meaning a sense of beauty. As such, aesthetics is a sensible experience abut the beautiful things. Because aesthetic things are always beautiful, they always inculcate an aesthetic sense in man. The concept of aesthetics was given by Baumgaiten. Herbert Read also used the term aesthetics. Many philosophers and thinkers have put forward their views in definite ways, and more views are given below:

9. *Platinus*: Art is associated with beauty and creates splendour.
10. *Thomas Acquines*: Beautiful art objects are completely integrated and have perfection.
11. *Jacqnus Maritem*: Beauty as transcendental is a concrete embodiment and is pleasing to the intellect. It is sign of something more.
12. *Shaftbary & Huthson*: Art is the result of inner sense and sentivity to harmony.
13. *Immanuel Kant*: Art is a sense of harmony in whatever is produced.
14. *Borsangot*: He was follower of Hegel. He described art as concrete universal phenomenon.
15. *Croce*: Art in which we find beauty is a specific act of imagination. It is a complete intuition.
16. *Tolstoy*: Art is an impression of emotions.
17. *Santayam*: Art is an objectified pleasure.
18. *Fedric Scheller*: Basic category of life allowing morality and feeling to be existent in art.
19. *Collingwood*: Art is concerned to reality of things and there historicity.
20. *Edward Bullogh*: Art represents psychological distances.
21. *Theador Lipps*: Art is a feeling visualized into objects and experiences.
22. *H.S. Langfield*: Art is a tentative activity with in self and experience.
23. *Sigmund Freud*: Art is a inner drama of the human soul. Human repressed emotions force man to create.
24. *Clive*: Art is a significant form of human actions.
25. *Roger Pry*: Aesthetic emotions leads to artistic activity.
26. *Sushan and Mrs. S.K. Lauger*: Art is a presentation of unconscious symbols.

27. *Ortega Y. Gasset*: Dehumanization due to modernization forces man to create and construct new understandings.
28. *Herbert Read*: Amongst all of the thinkers who put forward their views on art, Herbert Read tried to define art. He said that is art metaphysical concept an organic and measurable phenomenon. Art is deeply involved in actual perception, thought and bodily action. Art is the main source to provide governing principles to life as it is the builder of culture and civilization which balance the human life.

Art is one of those activities, which like our soil is everywhere around us. We rarely step up to counter art. Art is something we not only find in millennium and in art galleries or in old cities like Rameshwaram, Ranthambore, Chennai, Puri Bhuneshwar in India and in Rome, Paris etc. etc. Art is present every where around us to please our senses and desires. There is a hierarchy in art. Many qualities in art activities had emerged in the past and many new qualities emerge now in art to make a work of art of highest type and quality. The process of art activities is a continuous. The work of art which does not appeal to human senses or physical organs of perception can not be termed as art. The quality of art is that which appeals to our senses. An aesthetic element is already in perception itself.

The essences of art are so universal, so open to all kinds of impressions and so interwoven with one another, just because the mind is like an automatic exchange with ringing at every second.

What is art? To begin with it can be said that common to all a work of art is some thing we call 'Form'. Form is a simple, short word. It is a derivation from the Greek word 'Forma' meaning a shape. If same one plays well or runs well, we say he/she is in good 'form'. We mean that his/her body is trim, active, He/she acts quickly and efficiently. We use this word for many artistic activities like singing, playing, dancing and acting etc. Form is used in all artistic activities. We use 'form' as verb as forming hockey club, cricket club, art club, social service club etc. etc. In this sense, the word 'form' means a shape or structure. All natural flora and fauna have special forms. The drops of dew makes a form, Due to flow of winds a 'form' is formed. As such, the form does actually mean to take a shape. And this is what 'form' means in works of art, that is, a shape which means to take a shape which has taken place with deliberate action. Such artistic action is the result of emotions. It does not matter whether it is a building, a statue, a picture, a sculpture, a poem or a sonata, all these take particular specialized shapes; these shapes are forms of works of art. The shape is given by a particular person who is called artist. The artist is not only a man who only paints, but also a man/ woman who composes music, writes poetry, makes creative furniture, prepare new cookies, designs new shoes and dresses.

A good form in art is that which please the senses. The works of art are those which have good forms. Then what are the good conditions which make good forms. These conditions are which give to our senses most pleasure not only in one sense but in two or more senses and finally to the reservoir of all senses which is our mind.

But what pleases one person may displease another. Then what is the touch stone out of the human peculiarities of human beings. Thus, the touch stone exists in human nature. And by nature the 'whole organic process of human life', and the "movement or a process of human organic whole"; is which makes the existence of an individual possible.

The nature is so imminence and multiformal that, at the first sight, it would seem to be difficult to select a general or universal features, which would take them, as the touch stone for the forms of things we are to analyze. Usually artists do not seek or try to find out such a touch stone. They sense it and find it instinctively. They try to provide the artistic elements in the work of art which exist in nature.

What are these forms in nature? They are present in the vast space of the universe. These are inter connected and are found in the most intercellular microscopic cells and molecules of the matter. The artist arranges these intercellular and microscopic elements of the matter and gives them new shapes which are called forms.

Many century ago Pythagoras and Plato had already found in numbers, the clues to the nature of the universe and to the mystery of beauty. Science and philosophy have undergone many transformations since then, but the final result is the same that number is the basis of all forms which matter assumes whether organic or unorganic in kind. That is to say that the growth of particular things in particular shapes is determined by forces acting in accordance with certain inevitable mathematics and mechanical laws.

The bees cell might be taken as an example. Each cell is a honey comb is a close approach to perfect mathematics and proportion which is the basis of a good form. When we see something beautiful, we are really admitting that certain mathematical proportions give rise to emotions in us which we normally associate with the work of art. Like that many other examples can be cited which gives forms.

There are many symmetrical forms in nature which we might see—like we see the bones which make up skeleton, the pelvis bone of legs, hand bones and pair of ribs in the human body are examples. Further symmetry can be seen by observing the anatomical examples. There may be reason to believe in structure, but also in the actual form, it assumes that the bone is mathematical solution to a problem in stress and strain, of tension and pressure. This must be due naturalness of a rational or mathematical structure, the bridge and bone possesses the same fitness and appropriation.

We may conclude that there is not a form is nature which is due to mathematical laws (pp. 14-20 Herbert Read). According to Aristotle (History of Philosophy Bertrand Russeau) form is a shape given to matter. He said (1) we start making a statue out of marble piece. Here marble is a matter out of which the sculpture transforms into a shape and gives a form (2) If a man makes a bronze sculpture, bronze is matter and sculpture is the form. It is the virtue of the form which changes the matter into something definite which becomes delightful substance of thing of art.

A thing must be bounded and, its boundary will constitute a Form. Form gives unity to a portion of matter and this unity is usually not always teleological. Forms are substantial although are not universal. Things increase in actuality by form which is created in matter. Without form the matter is only potential. After the artist, a sculptor has made a statute, it has unity which it drives from its shapes, which actually is a form. Now he essential feature of the body is soul, in virtue of which the form of the body lives. It is the soul which makes the body's form as an organic whole having a purpose as unit. Finally we can say that in art the ultimate is structure, which fulfills and embodies by means of appropriate material. This expression by the artist in terms of new shape is called form. A form is the essence of piece of work of art.

NATURE OF ART

Proportion

We have seen that the nature is the main source of manifestation for the artist. But a deliberate imitation of natural forms like Vessels in the shape of animals, dishes in the shape of leaves etc. of course are delight as well as intelligent effort but do not deserve appreciation. An imitation is never worth of appreciation in the field of art. Natural things develop spontaneity, and basic laws of physics and mathematics. Take for example a person shaped a figure—a form derived from a fruit (pear) which has all the tendencies which make jug beautiful and utilitarian. Like that all organism in nature confirms to proportion, thus have curious mathematical properties. Ideal situation for the artist is that he should learn the principles of proportion and division from the nature.

Composition

Getting inspired by the ideas of Herbert Read that the nature is the main sources of artistic activities, I feel that elements of composition, which are essential elements or characteristics of any work of art are also derived from nature. Nature has opposite elements which co-exist and make the life possible. For example male and female are two opposites, who are topsy-turvy. biologically. But when they are united, it makes their living fruitful and social consistence possible. Because human existence is only possible when they live together and reproduce. In other words social structure is only because of their union and living together life long. There are other things in the nature, which are biologically supplementary like male and female, but they exist and enhance the beauty of the nature. Such things are found in abundance in natural flora and fauna. Like this the artist use many things for making art works. As a human organic whole contains many parts, like bones, flesh, muscles and nerves and an art work also is made by joining many elements like lines, perspective, balance, rythm, colours and hues. By the use of all these an virtual element is created in the work of art which makes things attractive and beautiful. A 'form' is created through all these elements and the process is called composition.

BASIC THEORIES OF ART

It is very difficult to define art. However, many thinkers tried to define art. In India Rabindra Nath Tagore put forward ontological—teleological theory of Art. He said that human emotions are the genesis of art. He said that there are two kinds of persons (1) Physical person i.e. man/woman and (2) spiritual or metaphysical or non-physical person. Physical person exists physically whereas non-physical person does not. It is permanent, non-existent, non-visible, omnipresent and all pervasive. In other words his theory is based on the duality of the soul as mentioned in Sankhaya Yoga theistic school of Indian philosophy. In which it is mentioned that there are two kinds of souls (1) one is permanent, non-existent, all pervasive soul which is called "Paramatma" (परमात्मा), that is, God (2) another is Jivatma (जिवात्मा) which is embodied in human body and is part of 'Paramatma' (परमात्मा) Almighty God. Jivatma or human soul given a form to the human body. Human Soul or Jivatma is also undestroyable since it is part of the universal or bigger Soul. The man when alive faces experiences in many life situations, out of which some are sweet and some are bitter. For all these experiences, the physical man consider God as the giver of these experiences. When he is rewarded or unrewarded in life, he bestow these to God. He becomes emotional and do creative works for divine rewards. The art work produced due to such emotions are considered spiritual or teleological art or spiritual art. Man is henothiestic and Tagore believes that henotheism is the main reason of such emotions. For getting any thing man prays different gods, goddesses and deities and after reward he become grateful to the deities and the God. Consequently emotions emerge, and he creates for expressing his gratitude. A number of sculptures, murals, wall painting and relief-sculptures are found in religious places and temples are the result of such feelings. Indian art is spiritual in nature. It is harmonious and shows social ethos like good social procession on the occasion of the marriages of the girls or valedictory to the bride by the whole village. Such artistic relief-sculptures are generally seems on the outside walls of the temples or Dharamshalas.

Another theory of art which may be termed as individualistic or materialistic or empiricist theory of art was advanced by Mrs. S.K. Langer. She says that the work of art is an activity which has been done for the first time for individual satisfaction. Such an activity should be creative, done for the first time, non-inclinative and also done for self enjoyment. If this activity repeated that will be a craft activity. This kind of artistic activities are done by the western artists who are individualistic by nature. The western art is non-homogenic and heterogenic in nature because of the feudalistic structure of western society.

Another theory which may be termed as "Psychological Theory Art", is advanced by Sigmund Freud, who was basically a medical man. He started treating men and women suffering from fits. He found that fits generally occur due to repressed emotions. He also wrote two books 'Dora' and Wolf (assumed names) elucidating the reasons due to which the individuals suffer from fits. He said that due to undesirable happenings emotions emerge, which remain in the body of an individual and remain at conscious level, sub-conscious level and semi or deep conscious level like an ice piece in water. If these deep emotions are not taken out, these can be very dangerous for the health of a person. Catharsis is the only way to take out these emotions, which can take out only conscious level and sub conscious or middle conscious level emotions. The semi conscious or deep level conscious level emotions can only be taken out by art activities. As such, for taking out very repressed or deep emotions art activities are very necessary in human life. To keep the youngest generation free from repressed emotion, the art should be introduced in the school from the beginning. So artistic activities in school programme are necessary.

Herbert Read also emphasised the inclusion of art—"The general purpose of education is to foster the growth, which is an individual in each human being; at the same time harmonizing the induality thus educed with the organic unity of the social group to which the individual belongs". So according to Herbert Read art activities in education is a necessity. Likewise, Frank L. Wright said that art is a discipline of senses, that is, it is skillful, selective and intensive. To deny the opportunities of artistic activities will be masodistic, that is to deprive the soul of the pleasure of beauty and aesthetic sense.

Because the artistic activities mould the psyche of the child and makes him/her co-operative and active social being, these qualities should be taught or inculcated or nurtured in school.

Every child has some inborn creative qualities, these should be nurtured in early formaline years; then the child can be balanced, sane responsible, intelligent, co-operative diligent and hand working person. The personality of the child can only be moulded as a balanced personality if his/her creative urges be tapped for all round development. When language was not developed art symbols were the only source of communication. Art has developed in various ways of doing creature activities as—Impressionism, Expressionism, cubism, Surelism, Romanticism and Expressionism. Education is knowledge gained through old and new experiences. And art helps in this process.

THE TYPES OF ARTISTIC ACTIVITIES, AND THEIR APPLICATION

1. *Sketching, still life and landscaping*: for learning artistic activities.
2. *Painting (oil and water colour)*: for painting murals, painting stained glass, doing or making portraits, rural and folk arts.
3. *Collage painting*: by using cutpieces and supplementing these with paints.
4. *Designing*: making creative designs of greeting cards etc.
5. *Graphic Arts*: Print making and applied arts.
6. *Applied or Commercial Art*: Textile design, furniture design, making of publicity matter as posters, hoardings, costume designs, make up and stage setting for dramatics, making illustrations for books, etc.
7. *Decorations*: making designs for doing Alpana, Rangoli and moveables.
8. *Lighting*: Shadow play, various kinds of lightening effects such as storm rain, ruins and seascape etc. etc.
9. *Photography*: Film making, slide, making etc. etc.
10. *Display*: Arranging exhibitions on special occasions such as foundation day, Alumni Day, Parents' Day and arranging Exhibitions.
11. *Restoration and Preservation*: Collection of art objects and keeping these in exhibition.
12. House and classroom decorations through alpma, mobiles rangoli and through decorative blackboard work.

13. *Education through Art*: helping the teacher in the preparation of teaching aids.
14. Decoration at special occasions as annual *melas* and get together.

As such art teaching and consequent art activities is the soul of any educational programmes. The general teachings should always be designed for sound education and educational recovery of hidden potentials. For this recovery artistic activities always remove boredom, releases emotions and build up sound personality. But it is observed that artistic activities in schools as well as in teachers training colleges are ignored. Not only this the art and craft teachers are generally considered inferior in comparison to other teachers. This situation is not only a common feature in our society, but it is observed that other societies follow this contempt, which has been in practice since times immemorial. Atleast during the contemporary democratic regions this practice should have been discontinued. But it is still continuing. There should be a soul searching in this regard, and art and craft teachers should be given their due status, and their services should be fully utilized. Also other school teacher should take active part in artistic activities.

These activities are so many which could help the students in their career building, as well as can improve the image of the school. Though these activities have already been mentioned earlier. These is no harm to repeat these activities again. The artistic activities can boost the co-curricular activities which are necessary for enculturation. Enculturation is necessary for national culture building. Cultures is necessary for the security of the nation.

The teacher is the builder of the nation because he moulds the future guardians. Therefore, the teacher should be trained in artistic activities during the course of teacher training. The authorities should first prepare the teachers of teachers training institute in artistic and co-curricular activities, so that they could help the pupils teachers in these activities. When the pupils teachers go for teaching they should be very serious in educating the students in school in co-curricular activities. The school administration, the principal, the head master should try to carry forward the co-curricular activities encourage the teachers. The art teachers of the school have a special responsibility in this regard. They should help the other school teachers and students by doing related art work as stage setting, decoration and proper displays. They should train the students in making alpna, rangoli and displays on bulletin boards.

The artistic activities can prepare the students to be creative, inventive and enterpreneuring in their future life. Artistic activities can also prepare the students for good sane life. These can develop a good aesthetic sense in them. And above all the artistic activities mentally prepare the students to do creative and love beautiful things and make useful things of them in future.

It can be said that artistic activities are a boon for the teacher and students. These should be used in teaching and everyday life.

23

Teaching Aids in Education and The Teacher

Education, the teacher, teaching and the teaching aids all are co-related. Though, having different meanings they are also supplementary to each other. The teaching has emerged out of the Greek word "Taccon" which means 'to instruct', 'to impart' 'to tell', 'to apprise' and to pass on what one knows'. The word 'education' is a derivation from the Latin word' 'Educare' meaning 'to bring up', 'to grow up' 'to take out', 'to prepare'. 'to mould' and 'to dig out'. Teaching is usually done by a knowledgeable person. He passes his knowledge to a person who does not know, but has inner potentialities. As such, teaching is usually done to make person aware what he does not know, and to innovate and help him to bring out his hidden knowledge and, know himself through thinking and reasoning. Education and teaching both have different epistemic aspects, so these are two different concepts, though supplementary but are contrary to each other. In teaching, the teacher who knows the subject matter will passes his knowledge to the student through verbal communication. But if this verbal communication is not supplemented by teaching material which may ignite thinking in the students, it remains one way verbal communication which does not motivate the students to think and rationalize. In such a situation generally students become passive and do not learn and become inactive at all. But education is a process through which one tries to learn himself. If the teaching does not innovate and motivate for self learning, it can never be education, it will be mere passing out of one way information. Mere passing out of information makes the pupil passive. He does not become active because, thinking, reasoning and comprehending do not take place. In the modern sense the term, functionally the word education has many meanings. It is a way of upbringing of the youngs. It is an instrument of modernity, upward mobility in social, economic and political life. Karl Marx said that the education is used by the strong for the exploitation of the weak. Education is used for urbaning of the religion. Prof. M.N. Sriniwas said that education is a transformation of occupational knowledge. Many sociologists assert that education is the vehicle of enculturation, socialization and economic transformation. As such, it may be said that the education is a process of all round development of human potentialities and capacities what are already with in the biological whole and entity of a person.

There are many mythological interpretations, which may be correct or wrong, about the concept of education. Many thinkers have put forward various interpretations. Tagore in his book 'Personality' said there are two kind of phases of man, one is physical man or personal man and another is 'impersonal man' or 'metaphysical person or Soul or 'Paramatma'. Physical man acquires experiences through his senses and metaphysical man or person or soul (Jivatma) of the physical man accumulates these experiences with it. To take out these previously acquired and accumulated experiences for the use of physical man is 'education' or 'shiksha'. J. Krishnamurti endorsed Tagore's views. The concept of education is very old, for its invention credit goes to Socrates. He derives this concept from the immortality of the soul. It is believed that the Spartan neighbourer of Greeks, believed in Terrorism. They used to terrorise the Greeks, as presently some countries do with their neighbours. Spartan education has military oriented. So much so, when a male child was born in their Society, they used to slip the child from the hill top. And if, while slipping down from the hill the child survived, he was fit to live a life. They continued their terrorist activities against the Greeks who ultimately decided to wage a war against the Spartans. The war continued for thirty years. To fight such a long war was not an easy job. The Greeks had limited human resources (about 8 thousand only). Perciles the then king of Greece imposed. Conscription on the Greeks (543 B.C.) and made it compulsory for all members between the age 18 to 40 to go to the war front and fight the Spartans whose population was about three throughout only. Thinkers like Theatetus and Crito were forced to go to war front. But there were also some individuals who were afraid of war. It is said, it might be true or wrong or mere an assumption, that most probably Parmenides escaped conscription and sneaked to Mesopotamia (present Iraq) where he tried to know why people fight against each other. Finding no correct reply he against each other and war is erupted between them. He did not get satisfactory answer from them also. At that time Aryana (present Iran) and Gandhara (present Afghanistan) were Aryan countries and had also Gurukulas like India. But he was advised to go Bharat (India) and know about it in Taxila Gurukula (now in Pakistan). He went to Taxila and stayed there nearly for eight years. He studied there all Indian theistic schools of philosophy—Sankhya-yoga, Naya-Vaishisk and Vedant and Advait-vedant and also Indian atheistic schools—Jainism, Buddhism and Carvak. He also studied all Vedic classical striplures like Upanishads, Purans, Shruties, Shuklas, Brahmans and epics—Ramayana, Mahabharta and Shrimad Bhagwat Gita. After studying these religious scriptures he came to know about the immortality of the soul, that is, human soul being part of the supreme soul, never dies, only human body dies. He went back to Greece and offered himself to fight against spartans. This event motivated the Greeks and finally they eliminated the Spartans and the war ended. Greeks were victorious. However, the Socrates came to know about this revelation that the human soul never dies. He discussed this with his disciples why soul does not die? this dialogue between him and his disciples like Plato, Crito, Parmenides, Isocretes etc. continued in the house lane before his house. It was because Socrates wife Xentippi never allowed to enter in her house. If any body used to come, to her house along with Socrates. She used to pour a full cold water pot over his head.

Finally, Socrates and his disciples found a proof of immortality of human soul. Their discussions are recorded in dialogue 'Phaedo' compiled by Plato after the death of Socrates. In dialogue Phaedo three, proofs were advanced about the immortality of as given below—

LAW OF CONTRARINESS

Every thing is in flux said Hereclitus. Man is born as a child, grows as youth and becomes old and finally dies. Likewise every thing comes and goes. Sun rises, day begins and goes, night follows, and again there is a morning and full day. There is a complete continuous process of change in physical as well as social phenomena. River is not the same because its water is continuously flowing. There is not constant heat nor cold. This rule also applies to flora and fauna. We till the land, saw seed and on maturity get a crop. Again the seed is sawn and we get a crop. As such, there is a metaphysical element in every human body, and also in other living beings which comes, goes and comes again. The soul (जीवात्मा) remains in the body till it finds it fit for living. When the body is old and the soul (जीवात्मा) does not find it worth of living, it discards it like we throw our used old cloths and aprons. But when the soul leaves the body it goes with its acquired experiences, which it had acquired through the human body sense organs. Till the soul acquires another body to live, it remains in Hades (cemetery ground). When the soul gets another body in mother's womb, and this body gets rebirth or transmigration, the soul comes with earlier acquired experiences, when it was embodied in the previous body. Due to the birth pangs the body organs become ineffective to bring out the earlier acquired knowledge. Educating or digging out or pulling out the earlier acquired experiences or hidden potentials of the previous life is a process of 'education'. Socrates gave the word 'education' on this metaphysical assumption. It might be true that Greeks got the idea of immortality as soul from Shrimad Bhagwat Gita. And it also tried that the most of the Vedic Indian Scriptures also reflect about the immortality of the soul—as Sankhya-yoga clearly gives the idea of Atma and Jivatma, Naya-Vaishiska also mentioned that we remember because of immortality of our soul. Lord Krishna had given a lengthy sermon on the first day of Mahabharata war to Arjuna on the immortality of the soul. But we do not have any logical proof of it in our scriptures, as we find in Law of contrariness in dialogue 'Phaedo', in which it was asserted that the human soul is a permanent metaphysical force which circulates in contrary way coming to human body and going out of it.

LAW OF FORM

Law of Form put forward in dialogue Phaedo was an attempt to explain the circulatory metaphysical position of the human soul. It can also be equated with the concepts of Atma or Paramatma

(परमात्मा) and Jivatma (जीवात्मा) as given in Sankhya yoga. Here, in the dialogue it was tried to equate the human soul (जीवात्मा) with an omni-present Form, that is, Atma as also put forward in Sankhya yoga. It also tried to equate the physical phenomena with 'Maya', which is copy of the permanent metaphysical Form. In Law of form it is assumed that every embodied social that is Jivatma (जीवात्मा) is the part of a Form which is permanent. It is nothing but the same which has been put forward in Sankhya yoga, which says that every human soul (जीवात्मा) is part Atma or Paramatma (परमात्मा). When Atma or Parmatma is permanent, non-visible, non-existent, omnipresent its part human soul (जीवात्मा) is part of it and is permanent and immortal.

LAW OF REMMINISCENCE

The third proof of immortality of soul is the law of remminiscence is based on the process of remembering. The dialogue Phaedo says that we remember or reflects due to what our soul has accumulated. In other words accumulated knowledge by the soul comes out. That can be said our memory. When we think, reason and analyze the accumulated knowledge comes out. And progress of communing out of accommodated knowledge or memory is nothing but 'education'. As such, education is nothing but taking or bringing out our previous accumulated experiences or knowledge. In Naya-Vaishiska same theory of reminiscence has been mentioned. So the law of reminiscence proves that remembering is nothing but education. And for educating there is a need of careful teaching.

As such the process of education is a recovery of human potentialities or capacities what are already there is the human body or soul.

Teaching and education are complimentary and supplementary to each other. Education is not possible without teaching, and teaching is useless if it is not done for educating the pupils. As such educational process involves a sound process of transmission of information which is done through various communication methods as given below:

(*i*) gestures, symbols,
(*ii*) through spoken and written words,
(*iii*) by showing concrete things,
(*iv*) by contrived experiences through models etc.

(*v*) Pictures, cartoons, illustration, photographs, posters, charts,
(*vi*) Projection and,
(*vii*) displays, exhibitions and so on so forth,

Teaching is basically done through two kinds of symbols

(*a*) Non-discursive symbols (words spoken or written),
(*b*) Discursive symbols or non-verbal media, like concrete things or through contrived experience of the concrete things like pictures, illustrations, charts or maps etc. etc.

In teaching both kinds of communications, that is, verbal and non-verbal are used. Then only teaching can lead to educating. In olden times, conservative methods of teaching were used. Teaching was aimed at to pass on cultural heritage, religious norms for inculcating moral values and for sane socialization. The teacher used to be proficient and an authority on these areas and, used to pass on information about these to his disciples verbally which was entailed with discussions and debates (वाद-विवाद). On the whole the teaching was more teacher oriented and less student oriented. Also the students had not to accept what the teacher used to tell because of follow up debates or Vad Vivad (वाद-विवाद). In some countries, unlike india or China the situation was different. In India, in Gurukulas, thee used to be a lengthy session of discussions and debates (वाद-विवाद) between the teachers (Gurus) and taughts. After this an agreeable conclusion used to emerge. This whole process was called 'vad' vivad and samvad (discussion, debates and synopsis). This was an important activity of teaching.

In China, teaching was based on showing of actual things. There is a Chinese adage "what we hear, we forget and what we see, we remember". In other countries teaching was basically done through verbal communication. But teaching through verbal communication does not lead to education. It remains merely information.

From the olden days, thinkers have been supporting the showing of connected things in teaching. Socrates said "perception is the better of source of knowledge". Plato said "knowledge is only possible, through perception, comprehension and understanding. Aristotle said that knowledge is only possible through the study of matter. René 'Descartes said that every person has some innate ideas, these ideas should be tapped through thinking, reasoning and comprehending. Thinking can only be possible either by showing actual things or their images. John Locke rejected the Rene 'Descartes' assumption of innate ideas and put forward an empiricist theory of perception. He said that at the time of birth, a child is a 'biological physical whole', he/she does not have any innate ideas. As the child grows his/her sense organs also grow. Initially the mind of the child is empty and is like a Tabula Rasa (blank slate), he/she write on it as he/she perceives things after his/her physical growth. He advocated that sensory experiences provide knowledge. Therefore these should be compulsory for educating the child. Their process should be termed as 'hardening in education'. If a child is to be made aware of snow falling, he/she should be forced out to go out and experience snow falling while it is falling. Likewise the child should be given compulsory experiences in all fields, at every stage of life. A.J. Ayer said that "true is that which can be verified". David Hume said that 'dogmatism' should not have any place in education. True, education is that, which is achieved through sensory, experience. J.J. Rousseau who was the founder of Naturalism said that "the child is born free but he finds himself in chains". The society imposes many restrictions in terms of social traits and traditions which are to be obeyed by the child". Comenius was the first person who first of all thought of the use of pictures in teaching. He also suggested that the textbooks should be illustrated. He had introduced the deductive method in teaching, out of which heuristic methods of teaching emerged. Froeble said that "Childs curiosity for knowing should be exploited by showing him concrete things and pictures of the things. Pestalozzi laid emphasis on childs emotions. He also like J.J. Rousseau, advocated that the child should be educated in natural atmosphere and learning should be based on touch and sensation. M.K. Gandhi said that "all the best should be taken out from the child through handwork and co-relating this with related issues". John Dewey laid stress practical approach (pragmatic) in education. He advocated pragmatism in education. But he did not suggest application of axiology in education as was suggested in Basic education by Mahatma Gandhi. Robin Cook was the first person who utilized his artistic knowledge in teaching. R.N. Tagore laid stress on nature and freedom in educating the youngs. With this he established Vishwa Bharati University at Bolanpur in West Bengal. Fedding up with the bookish and informative teaching based on alien system of formal education, which generate acculturation, J. Krishnamurti established Rishi schools and Rajghat schools in Andhra Pradesh in jungles at river bank and at Varanasi, U.P. on the right bank of Ganga on the pattern of Gurukulas. Shri J. Krishnamurti was fed up with the western type of education imposed by the Britishers, which was bookish. By establishing these schools he aimed at natural experience. These schools are still functioning on Gurukula pattern. As such many thinkers laid stress on the use of Audio-Visual aids in teaching.

The process of education is always a deductive process which entails self-learning. If teaching does not invoke self-learning, it will, make the learner a dummy passive receiver who will never try to think, reason, analyze and comprehend. Such person can never be a creative thinker and a contributor. So the schools should always entail the use of Audio-Visual education or teaching-aids, so as to make or innovate the students to think reason, analyse, comprehend and understand for self-learning and true education.

All great man were prone to self-learning through the deductive approach. A deductive method is that method of teaching in which there is maximum interaction between the teacher and the students. This is only possible when the teacher applies progressive heuristic method of teaching. Heuristic method of teaching always aims at to make the students interactive. The students can be interactive if they are given chance of thinking, reasoning, analyzing, comprehending and responding to the queries made by the teacher. This can be done by involving all sense organs as hearing, touching, seeing, smelling and testing. For this teacher should use verbal and non-verbal ways of communication. The verbal communication should always be used for giving introductory narration of the topic which is being taught. It should be followed by showing related pictures, photographs, posters, charts and models etc. This would motivate the students to think, reason and contribute in the development of the topic which is being taught in the class. All great man like Goethe, Homer, Milton, Shakespeare, Shopenkaur, Immanuel Kant,

Karl Marx, René Descartes, Neitzie in the west and in India Kalidas, Tulsidas, Kabir, Nanak, Tagore, Ramanujam, J. Krishnamurti, C.V. Raman could educate themselves through the deductive approach. Likewise all great thinkers in the field of social as well as physical sciences applied deductive method in educating themselves and their disciples.

As such, teachers' approach while teaching in class room should be creative for a congenital atmosphere while teaching. He should use deductive method for clinching the students' hidden knowledge. He/she should establish a good rapport with the students. It can only possible by applying progressive methods of teaching such as deductive and heuristic methods which provide sensory experience to the students. And for this use of audio-visual aids in teaching is must. This can make the students self-learners. For this the teacher must be aware about pedagogic understandings. Peda (a Greek word) means a child and gogic (a Greek word) means an understanding. For pedagogic three elements should be studied:

(*i*) Pedagogic epistemological standpoints,
(*ii*) Pedagogic psychological standpoint, and
(*iii*) Pedagogic personalistic standpoint.

Epistemological stand point refers to the conditions which promote knowledge. For this a pupil should be motivated to know. And the teacher must be aware what teaching aids can be used for epistemic motivation. The teacher should also be aware about the epistemic conditions for teaching. He/she should also try to know about psychological conditions of the teaching his clientals—their personalities. This can be done by having a sympathetic ear and establishing congenial rapport with the students. To make a pupil psychologically sound the child should be understood as an individual. He should be loved and respected. He should be innovated motivated, stimulated and encouraged to learn. The pedagogic principle implies and aims at knowing the unknown.

Audio-Visual aids provides sensory experiences. Sensory experiences from the basis of self-learning and knowledge. There are five senses—Visual (eyes), Aural (ears), olfactory (nose), gustatory (tongue) and Tactile (skin) and these are called gates of knowledge. To begin with, thinking is restricted to concrete experiences, which form the base of abstract learning. Sensory experiences are concrete experiences. Learning experiences appealing to the senses are more effective their abstract learning. Thus, there is a strong case for using teaching aids in teaching by the teacher.

Though, all of the five senses are important, but in many special cases a particular sense is applicable for knowing, but generally stress is laid on aural and visual because without these two, teaching and learning is not possible. If a teacher does not use verbal media, that is, verbal communication and only use non-verbal communication, the students get it difficult to understand. On the other if the teacher use only verbal communication the students always remain at the receiving end and become passive. If verbal and non-communications are used simultaneously then only learning takes place. Verbal communication is always non-discursive and does not evoke thinking process which is necessary for the acquisition of knowledge. Whereas, non-verbal communication, that occurs with the use of teaching aids is always discursive. It forces the pupils to thinks, reason and contemplate which is necessary for learning and knowledge development. Comenius was the first educationist who used pictures in teaching. Pestalozzi used objects and their, models in teaching. Captain Robin Cook used his landscapes in geography teaching. Madam Montessori laid stress for intensive sense experiences in a play way. During the last two world wars the army generals used visual aids for educating the illiterate army soldiers. Before sixty or seventy years ago, the teaching in schools was basically done through verbal communication. Now the entire field audio-visual educational technology dominates the field of teaching and learning process. Due to the advancement of science and technology the progressive methods of teaching have become mandatory for the teachers. It is, therefore, essential that the teacher should be fully aware about the audio-visual aids, their techniques, methods and their proper use. Audio-visual aids make teaching effective and learning easy. These accelerate the rate of learning and increase the span of retention. "More learning quick learning and longer retention" is the slogan of the audio-visual educationists and technologists.

As the sensory experience form the basis of knowledge Edger Dale (U.S.A.) suggested a cone of experience which can help the teacher in class room teaching-learning situations through audio-visual aids.

EDGER DALE'S CONE OF EXPERIENCE

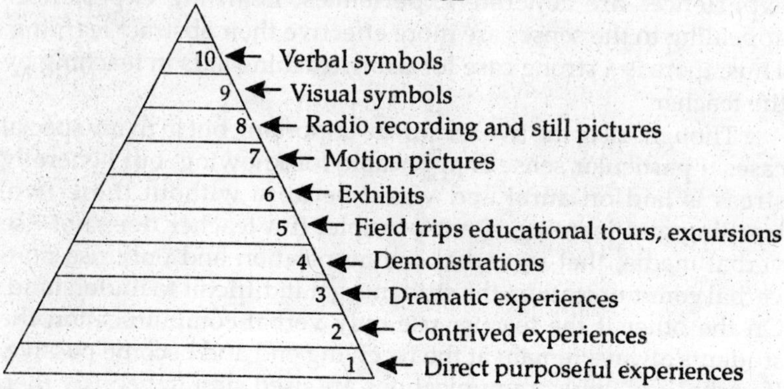

Though all the five senses are important in learning stress is laid on the aural and visual senses as these are widely used in class room teaching. Every physical object can not be shown in the class room while teaching. In the absence of actual things their pictures republicas and models are shown in the classroom by the teacher while teaching absence. In of actual things their pictures republicas and models are shown by the teacher while teaching. The teaching aids or audio-visual aids sometimes give dual perspective and create confusion. A three dimensional model of a thing is also a source of per. se. like that of a picture. It can also be touched and seen. Broadly speaking the audio-visual aids can be divided in two categories—(1) Projected teaching and (2) Non-projected teaching aids. In projected aids the images of things are projective on a screen with the help of projectors like films, film, strips and slides and some other transparencies come under this category. Non-projected aids form the bulk of audio-visual aids. The projected and non-projected teaching aids can be classified as under: (Types of Audio-Visual Aid Chart on page 221)

In projected Aid, the images of things are projected on a screen with the help of projectors. Film trips, Film slides are other transparencies come under this category. Non-projected aids form the bulk of Audio-Visual aids. Charts, diagrams, graphs, maps are major aids. Also chalk board, bulletin board, tag board etc. etc. come under this category. Display boards, dioramas, globes, human skeleton models and dioramas come under the category of contrived experience teaching aids.

TYPES OF AUDIO-VISUAL AID

PROJECTED AIDS

1. Copying Units
(a) Epidioscope
(b) Electro Photo State Machine
(c) Film Strip Projector
(d) Slide Projector
(e) Opaque Projector
(f) Over head projector
(g) Film Strips
(h) Slides
(i) T.V.
(j) Video and V.C.R.
(k) Tlescope
(l) Stero-Scope
(m) reordings,
(n) Relay comic-aids
(o) diagrams etc.

NON-PROJECTED AIDS

Graphic Aids

(a) Pictures
(b) Posters
(c) Cartoons
(d) Charts
(e) Illustration
(f) Land scapes
(g) night scapes
(h) sea scapes
(i) Desert scapes
(j) Drain Pictures
(k) Chalk Board
(l) banners
(m) flash caids
(n) diagrams and
(o) saymgs

Demonstrative Dramatization

(a) Mock parliament
(b) Mork Panchayat
(c) Mock Rly; Slahon
(d) Mock Court
(e) Puppets
(f) Cinema
(g) Tracking

Concrete Things

(a) Spectrum
(b) tools
(c) measuring instruments
(d) Excursion and
(e) concete things

Concrete Experiences

(a) still models
(b) Reliefs
(c) topo graphic models
(d) X-Ray
(e)working models
(f) diagrams

Things

(a) actual things
(b) costumes
(c) stage seting
(d) theatre
(e) dress
(f) make up
(g) sets etc.
(h) tools

UTILIZATION OF AUDIO VISUAL AIDS

Even the most effective aids may become ineffective in the hands of an unexperienced and non-serious teacher. The right use of proper Audio-Visual aids, made of right material, at the right time, at the right place, constitute four Rs. of the use of audio-visual aids. A teacher while using the audio-visual aids must keep in his/her mind (1) the educational outcome or expected elicitations from the student, (2) nature and complexity of the content to be taught or developed, (3) methodology of teaching to be applied and related experience to be given to the students, (4) the choice to the teaching aids should be decided or determined according to the objectives of teaching. How can the aids be related to teaching according to the needs of the learners? There are different scopes of the use of teaching aids according to their viability in different subjects. According to me the teaching aids should innovate and motivate the students to interact and respond without fear in the class room. Getting more elicitations and enabling the students to learn should be the prime objective of the use of teaching aids. The teacher should not use more than one teaching aid at a time. This may create confusion in the minds of the students. Some teachers in order to avoiding the trouble of displaying the teaching one after another, display the teaching aids materials such as role up black board, charts and maps in advance of teaching. This is not correct procedure. This creates confusion in the minds of the students.

While using projected aids like films, film strips, slides the teacher should introduce these aids to the students. After the projection of a particular aid is over, especial points should be elucidated so that students may note down special points about the topic which is being taught. Films are generally of 8 mm, 16 mm, 35 mm and 70 mm size, out of which 8 mm and 16 mm are used for making film strips and slides. A 16 mm sound film has pocket wholes on one margin only, and sound track on the other side. Therefore in 16 mm sound projector the sprockets have cleaves or teeths on one margin only. As 16 mm silent film has sprockets or teeth on both edges. Therefore, a 16 mm sound film should not be threaded a 16 mm silent projector as the sprockets with teeth on both the sides will totally damage the sound track and also the film. Only a sound projector should be used for sound film.

ADVANTAGES OF THE MOTION PICTURES

Both audio and visual teaching aids appeal to (1) both the senses at the same time, (2) because of presentation on an illuminated screen in darkness or semi-darkness. These aids attract attention of the pupils, (3) the pupils generally identify themselves with the events presented on the screen the appeal to the emotions of the pupils, (4) these aids enable the pupils to witness the objects places, events, not ordinarily seen in their day to day lives. Films are close to real life and their motion contribute to realism. But the projectors and films are costly, as such, film suitably made for topics may not be readily available. Teachers sometimes use the films for mere, relaxation from teaching and for entertainment and not for instructional purpose. Many teachers also do not try to know how to use the projectors and use the film in teaching. This attitude makes them dependent on those, who either live far from the school or are few in numbers. Inspite of all these limitations films, that is motion pictures or T.V. programmes are very useful and very effective audio-visual aids. A teacher using theses should arrange a follow up programmes. All students be guided to note down the important events prior to the projection programme begins. These points should be discussed in the follow up discussions.

FILM STRIPS

Film strips are useful teaching aids. One foot to three foot long film is used to prepare the film strips having a series of 30 to 50 still pictures or picture frames as these are termed. There are two size of film strip frames 24 mm and 18 mm. A film strip projector is adjusted to project both kinds of frames. Film strips are cheap and easily transportable. Film strips negatives can be shot on camera and can be framed at home as per size of the film strip projector. For storing, there card board racks can be made at home. These film strips can be projected easily for a desirable time again and again.

SLIDES

Slides are made from 35 mm films (2"×2") and also by using plain glass (3.25"×3.25"). Film slides are photographic slides. Glass may be hand made. These can be used as photographic slides. The slides of 2"×2" can be projected using a film strip projector after fixing the firm slide gate.

The teachers can easily prepare slides with 3.5"×3.25" or 2"×2" glass plates using ink or cellophane paper having printed or written matter. The semi transparent glass can also be used to prepare the slides. One surface of the glass should be painted with a thin solution of gelatine. Writing should be made on this surface. Thereafter, it should be covered by another glass plate of the same size and glued using mixture of resistant glues. The slides are flexible aids, that is, sequence is not fixed. The teacher can arrange these slides serially according to teaching needs. This is the major advantage of the slides over the film strips. Slides need more storage space. The glass slides are breakable. The teacher has to be very careful while putting the slides into the slide gate giving vertical and lateral inversion during projection.

NON-PROJECTED AIDS

Graphic aids are non-projected teaching aids. There are powerful media for teaching and learning. When these are shown and are visualized these convey simply epistemic facts and ideas. These aids represent a judicial bleed of drawing, pictures and words. These are usually two dimensional and many of these can be projected through an opaque projector (epidiascope). An early shown chart, posters, diagrams, illustrations, graphics, cartoons, flash cards, maps are some important graphic aids. "A chart is a combination of graphic material and pictorial media, especially, orderly and logically designed to present the content and elicit knowledge from the students." Charts are useful to show relationships, classifications of the contents by means of pictorial media, figures or statistics to present the material systematically, to apprise the students about the related problems and to stimulate and encourage them to think and respond. Charts can be classified a flow chart, time chart etc. etc. A poster is a pictorial devise to communicate and attract the attention to a story, a social fact or phenomenon, an idea or an image more quickly and clearly. A poster, though generally is used for quick communication and publicize an important fact. It can be useful for communicating community's interest. It can also be useful to communicate a particular fact in teaching. A map is used to show the geographical boundaries of a country. It is very useful in apprising the students about the geographical terrains. A graph is used to show representative qualitative data showing comparisons, ratios and relationships. A cartoon is a kind of metaphysical representation of a thing or a person in the form of tainted picture or posture. Comics are liked by the children. These can be used in teaching languages social features and politics. In teaching, a map is an accurate representation in the form of diagram of the surface of the earth or some part of it. The maps are always drawn according to scale. Maps vary in type and form. These are universally used in teaching history, geography, political science and theology. A flash card is a small compact pictorized card. It is flashed before the students to apprise them about a new idea, a new word, and a new thing. Generally flash cards are used to teach languages to the youngers. Photographs or picture pasted on a sheet of paper or small cards like flash cards are used in teaching. If the pictures are big, the big sheets are used. These are also used in like flash cards. These should not be used for a long time.

DISPLAY MATERIAL

Chalk boards, (moving and static), flannel boards and Bulletin Boards are some of the widely used display boards. Chalk boards, generally called black boards, are extensively used in teaching. A class room is incomplete without a chalk board (black board). A chalk board is the oldest and simplest teaching aids. It was developed during the Protestant religious movement, under the leadership of Martin Luther, in Germany. Later on it was adopted by the church schools in Europe. By the spread colonialism if became an universal teaching aid. Now there are various kinds of chalk boards as wooden chalk board, slide and moveable chalk board, role up chalk board, glass chalk board, cemented chalk board, slate chalk board, rubber chalk board etc. etc. As a teaching aid a chalk board is an important teaching tool in the hands of the teacher these days. A teacher can not proceed without a chalk board (so-called black board). But one of the deadest drawback is that most the teachers are not fully aware about the desirable qualities of the chalk board. Generally the teachers are not made aware about the chalk board or black board during the course of their teacher training. The teachers training institute, in many cases, do not give importance to the use of chalk board during teaching. Following are the important features regarding the chalk board which are to be kept in mind by the teacher while teaching.

1. The lower edge of the chalk board should be at the eye level of the pupils,
2. The black board or chalk should be clearly visible to all students,
3. There should be minimum distance between the first row of the students,
4. The letters and other graphic material written on the chalk board should be written in orderly manner. It should be written in straight lines,
5. Over crowding and incomplete writing should be avoided,
6. Black board writing should be done slowly so as to give the students a chance to follow the teacher,
7. The teacher should never stand before the black board,
8. The teacher should not talk while he is doing the chalk board (black board) work,
9. Never paste or nail any material on the surface of the chalk board. It will spoil the surface of it,
10. The chalk board is one of the most trusted friends in the class room of the teacher. He should give it friendly treatment. The chalk board should be kept clean and unhurt,
11. The chalk board should be dusted before leaving the class otherwise coming teacher may be annoyed,
12. Chalk board is a mistake rectifier. Teacher should not be annoyed if any of his/her mistake is pointed out by the pupil. He/she should rather be thankful to the pupil who noticed the mistake and later on pointed if out,
13. The teacher should advise the students to note down the black-board work. The students should be in tune to have a pace with the teacher,
14. Necessary chalk board accessories and material as good quality white and coloured chalks, good chalk-duster, chalk tray, a piece of wet cloth, also chalk board equipments like templates, compass, set square, scale and an enlarger should be used,
15. The teacher must be aware about the black board paint. Generally all paints are made by (1) Pigment, (2) Binder

and Paint Vehicle. A pigment is a refined coloured clay. For a chalk board, because black board paints is used generally black pigment used for making the black paints. For making the black pigment a sticky, a binder is used. A binder is made by the double boiled linseed oil. The pigment and the binder are mixed in a rotating machine, as cement concrete and sand are mixed in a rotating machine. After this to make this mixture thin a thinner usually turpentine oil is mixed. Then the paint is ready. In black board the quantity of binder is very little just about ten per cent of the whole mix. This is because the surface of the black board should remain rough and not smooth,

16. The role up black is made of a thick cartridge paper on two sides of the paper round wooden strips with a bending chord are fixed, so that the role-up black board may be rolled. The role up black board should be used for making black board work in advance before teaching. Black board paint is used in making role up black board,
17. A flannel board is a dynamic display board. The flannel either can be stapled or tagged on insulation board or glued on a ply sheet. The pictures which are to be stuck on the flannel board should have sand paper background. The sand paper of rough temper should be pasted on the back of the flash card or of the picture which is to be display. Generally the bulletin learned are used for display. In teaching the young pupils when the teacher use of flash card it is necessary that the flannel boards are used. Things can be fixed and removed quickly fix on it.

A bulletin board is used for displaying things as notices, and students contribution in the field of and literature. Bulletin boards are also generally made of insulation boards, as these re soft and drawing pins can be generally fixed easily on then bulletin boards. The bulletin boards should be fixed where its visibility becomes common. As such the corridor of the schools are most suitable place. Atleast one bulletin should be fixed in class room. Pictures, clipping and other paper cuttings should be collected for bulletin boards displays. At one time display only of them should be chosen. Coloured pictures, photographs should have appropriate backgrounds on the bulletin board. Lettering should be done when it is necessary. Bulletin board displays stimulate pupils' interests and motivate them to perform various artistic and creature activities. Bulletin boards are very useful in introducing and explaining and also reviewing the topics to be taught in the school or else where as social service. Also the bulletin boards are very useful in carrying out co-curricular activities in the school.

Besides for the use of all these teaching aids, every teacher must atleast know how to use the epidiascope for enlarging small drawings to big size on drawing sheet, the and use of over head projector for projecting chalk board transparencies. Also it would be good, if the teacher must learn to prepare film strip, slides and chalkboard work transparencies. The schools should jointly arrange some seminars or workshops for apprising the teacher for such activities.

Besides these activities, there are some activity aids like arranging mock parliament excursion, educational tours, inter-school debates and discussions on national burning issues like enculturation to stop acculturation, festival *melas*, exhibition and displays.

It is also necessary to introduce the teaching aids to all students and teachers. The teachers should have keen interest in preparing and using the audio-visual aids. They should involve the students in making the teaching aid. This will motivate the students to do creative work. For this, end the teacher have to be creature minded. The teachers should also involve the students in model making in arranging displays and doing decorative activities like alpna, rangoli and arranging exhibitions. The teacher should involve the students in making dioramas. A model is a true representation of a real thing which is big like earth or very small like an atom. Diorama is a big model housing multiplied spectrum of models. Also, there are situations when providing of contrived experiences through models diagrams, still models, topographic models or relief models are not necessary. Only sample of things as hand saw, tools like hammer, speedometer and some other necessary tools can only be used. In some experience of touch and taste like knowing about *desi ghee* or *dalda* will be known by taste or smell. Salty or sweet puddings will be known by taste. It is true the use of audio-visual aids are necessary in every sphere of teaching.

24

Ideal Roles of the Teacher

Swami Vivekanand said that "the main aim of education is the like wholesome development of the individual". Father of the nation M.K. Gandhi said that "education is drawing out the best from the individual". Prof. E.A. Pires said that "the education should inculcate ideas in the individual for making him self-conscious human being. The individual should be kindly to his fellow beings. His soul should discern common spiritual good. Without good ideas a man can never be a good person. Therefore, essence of education should be self-discovery, self-direction and find out one's own limitations. The goal of education should be wholesome and integrative development of individuals personality and self-built character, ideal development of one's personality." Since the teacher is the beacon light and torch learner of the pupils, some sane ideals are necessary in the life of the teacher. So the teacher should always cherish for all sane, unique important ideas.

It is necessary to give etymological explanation of the term 'ideal' first of all. The word "ideal" is an adverb of the word 'idea'. The word 'idea' is a derivation from the Greek word "Idus" meaning the 'mental form or appearance of a person', 'a thing', 'a kind of species', 'a root', 'a model of thinking in mind' that which is comprehended by the intellectual faculties in philosophized terms. A idea is generally aimed at to designate subjective notions with or without objective validity. An idea is a thought acceptable, appreciable and applicable belief by the majority of the people. There are schools of philosophy like idealism, realism, dogmatism, naturalism, empiricism, communism, pragmatism, terrorism, socialism and capitalism etc. etc. based on specific ideas. Idealism is one such philosophical school which is based on common good.

Acting according to one's inner consciousness, believing in spirituality for the common interest and good, without any personal gain or inclination is a form of action which may be called idealism. As such, the term 'ideal' is that which is noble, good for all and is always non-inclinative. Many governments adopt idealism as a path of their action and adopt similar ideal constitution. Ideal thinking generally always entails a belief which is circumscribed around the wish of common good and not doing anything which may harm or hurt others in the society. An ideal person is one who always has good ideas and works for the common good. Such person is always considered an ideal man in the society. He is liked and loved by the majority of the people. An ideal man is an embodiment of goodness. An ideal person should be a fully developed personality. He/she possess the following qualities:

1. a perfect admirable character.
2. an integrated personality which should always entail (*a*) balanced behaviour, (*b*) non-inclinativeness, (*c*) deep desire for common good, (*d*) respect to the fair sex, and elders, (*e*) an intense deep desire to help the week, poor, ill and fair sex, (*f*) should love every child as his/her own child and (*g*) living a simple living and high thinking life.

And ideal personality be worth respecting by all in the society. Sane sociability, morality and living for the common cause should be the life motto of an ideal person. A fully developed human being is only possible if a person develops socially, morally having sensitivity for the truth, beauty, justice, love, affection, co-operation, tolerance, non-violence, thinking, reasoning, comprehending and having a sense of kinship teaching as sharing. In the modern times of industrialization which entailed modernization which renounced simple living and high thinking, made the man too much greedy, self-centred, utilitarian, hedonistic, xenaphilic and maglomaniac. Due to this social idealism has been renounced by most of the people. Instead of idealist modern man has become a pragmatic for material gains. The old religions beliefs based on spirituality and monotheism has been replaced by henotheism, polytheism and tanterism which are practiced for personal gains. Daily prayers are being discarded generally due to busy materialistic life of man. These have been replaced by weekly satsangs on the pattern of western Calvinistic philosophy of exploitation of natural resources for material gains and, praying in church once a week on Sunday. For material gains the modern man/woman does not spare time even for there own kith and kins. It is seen the wife does not hesitate in killing her legal husband for personal gains. Son does not hesitate in killing his own father for gaining property. Neighbourly relations have almost been vanished. Now the old caste structure is being replaced by class structure. The old norms of social living are vanishing day by day. An elite person does not want to maintain relationship with his neighbourly elite because of maglomaism. An owner of car always likes to talk to a person who has a car. A person having a bicycle, though he may be an intelligent, diligent, honest and an ideal person now is considered a fool by the well established and economically settled person. With the result there is a rat-race for material mobility. This trend, has more or less eliminated sociability, morality and ethnicity from the society. The present man has become totally self-centred, egoististic, greedy, acquisitive and maglomaniastic. This is because of our present formal system of education which has no ideas to generate sanety in the students.

Our present system of education only breeds love for material gains which entails cut through competition. It lacks axiology and moralization which is the soul of integrated social life. The corruption is so rampant in the society that there is hardly any field which can be said free of corruption. Incidents of loot, dacoities, burglaries, snatching, pick pocketing have become a common feature. Acculturation has engrilled the society very badly. Sixty year back there was fear of wolves and other beasts in the country side, now the jungle wolves and beasts have disappeared, more and more human, wolves and beasts are found in abundance in both urban and rural areas. Kidnappings of young children, businessmen, young girls for ransom have become a common feature in the country. Man nas become an animal as cases rapes of women and very young girls have become a common feature in the society. And very unfortunate happenings are these heinous criminal are shielded by the politicians.

In such a pathetic social situation there is an urgent need of idealism in our lives. But there is no congenial atmosphere for building ideals in our younger generation. Because of ostantecious and xenophilic life styles the joint family system has more or less crumbled down. In place of joint families nuclear families have emerged. Both the parents are in the rat-race of money earning. They want to earn more and more. They generally ignore their younger ones. The socialization and moralization which used to start at home and the family members used do it, is now missing. Where are the younger ones are going is neither the concern of the parents, nor of community and society. The rulers always look to consolidation of their governance. Parents, community and the government generally expect school to do every thing for the young generation—education, socialization and axiolization. Also the schools should prepare the future guardian for competitions. The teacher devote most of his/her time to prepare the students for annual examination so as to enable them to face the job competitions. The teacher does not have time to socialize, moralize and enculturate the students. If a younger becomes a criminal generally the school in which he is studying, is blamed and not the parents. So the moulding of the minds of the youngs for enculcating same ideas is not done. This is the prime need of the day. There is no way-out of sane ideas. Only inculcation of good ideas can save our youngers from the materialistic fever which is acculturating our society. The materialistic trends is robbing the society of our culture. In fact the school teacher is over occupied in competence fact in preparing the students for examination results. He/she has no time to do other enculturating activities. Since the parents also have no time to enculturate their children due to their materialistic activities. Inspite of the busy life the teacher has to look after of the enculturation activities too.

The teacher is nation builder, a trend setter and character builder of the youngers. If we peep into the past history of our old Brahmanic education system, we find that our old teachers were the idealistic personalities. They were well read, spiritualistic, monotheistic and were dedicated to teaching profession. The old teachers were sincere, epistemic, non-inclinative, sacrificers, helpers guides to their disciples. They used to act as spiritual and social gurus. They never thought of their personal gains and enjoyment. They always respected fair sex. Main objective of teaching in olden times was social moralization, economic upliftment of the people.

The old teachers used to follow the teaching profession's ethical code. Now the situation has totally changed. It is quite topsy-turvy.

Now the teacher is a public servant, whereas in the past the Guru (teacher) was a true professionist, an idealist and a spiritualist. He was widely respected. The present teacher, because of his minimum economic gains, is not respected by the economically affluent members of the society. But the present teacher should not forget, the teacher's roles. He/she should not forget the ideal roles performed by his/her predecessors the old Indian teachers, the Gurus.

It is the teacher who can raise the people from the social degradation. The teacher should cherish and aspire a well balanced personality. If a teacher has a well balanced personality then only he/she can mould the personalities of the pupils by presenting himself/herself as an ideal model before the pupils. The teacher should constantly build himself/herself for being a constant helper of the children and pupil. This can only be possible if he/she has a sympathetic ear towards the children. The teacher should listen and understand the problems of the pupils and, then should respond to their problems sympathetically. The teacher should see that the pupil is mentally undisturbed and is spiritually bold. Therefore, the teacher should try to take steps to prepare the young pupils as fully developed human being. The full development of the pupils is only possible if they develop socially, economically and morally. For this end the teacher should have a sensitivity about truth, beauty, justice, goodness and a sense of kinship in the pupils. With these qualities an individual can be a true sane citizen who well aspire for the common good and will dedicate to the national development.

No teacher can be said to have a real role of teaching profession, if he/she is not inspired by the ideal roles of teaching profession. The teacher must be aware about the credentials of the teaching profession which are as:

1. A profession is a relationship between an expert and ignorant client. Of course the teacher is supposed to be an expert in the subject he is teaching, but his client, the student, is not an ignorant client like that of a medical man, or of a lawyer and of a priest. So the teacher has to be more expert and proficient in the subject he/she is going to teach. For this he has to continues his studies for becoming proficient in the subject, he is teaching,
2. Therefore, a teacher should continue his studies so that he may be proficient in the subject he is teaching,

3. The teacher should be very sincere to his clients that is students he is going teach. If the teacher is not inspired by the ideals of teaching profession and not dedicated to the pupils and society, he/she can not mould the future guardian. This can be done when a teacher possess:
    1. a sense of good character,
    2. a sense of sympathy and kindness towards the pupils,
    3. a sense of self-introspection and restraint,
    4. a sense of epistemacy and desire of gaining more and more knowledge and practical experience in creative field,
    5. a teacher should be sympathetically appreciative of multi-patterned life situations. He should face the life situation courageously.

In addition to this the teacher should be sympathetic to animal life also. He/she should always keep in mind that as a builder of the future guardians, his/her services are essential for the society. These should be discharged with dedication. The teacher should keep in mind that his duties are not limited with in the four walls of the schools alone. These go for beyond the school. He is the builder and enlighter of the whole nation. Therefore a teacher has to be most active intelligent and diligent and a social minded citizen. So he should be broad minded, kind hearted and socially active person.

A teacher must strictly follow the code of teaching ethics which requires proficiency sincerity to the pupil and to the society as a whole. He should not have any grudge towards to his/her fellow colleagues. The teacher should not commercialize the teaching profession. He/she should not do tuitions. Instead the teacher should create an urge in the students for self-upbringing. He/she should also fully co-operate with his/her colleagues. A teacher should never be a maglomanious, that is, having a belief of knowing every thing. If fellow colleague advises the teacher he should not ignore the advice. A teacher who is maglomanious can never be a good teacher because he/she will not try to know more and add to his/her knowledge. This dictum does not only apply only to the teaching profession but it applies to all other vocations. For example if a cabinet maker or a fabricator thinks that he is the master of his area of action, his maglomony blocks his thinking reasoning and analyzing. This ultimately will put a halt on his creation. So a teacher should always keep his area of action for thinking, reasoning and criticism. A teacher should not be afraid of criticism by his disciples and colleagues. Rather the teacher should welcome and appreciate open criticism and suggestion. This will unveil the doors of his/her brain for self-introspection and thinking. The teacher should apply such methods of in teaching—as hueristic method, project method, discussion method etc. etc. which could motivate and stimulate the student's mode of thinking reasoning, comprehending and analysing. These could help the student in learning. For this process the use of teaching aids is necessary. The teaching aids can initiate the teacher-taught interaction which lead to elicitations. The teacher should be liberal. He/she should allow the students to discuss the other matters such as social, practical, and moral integration, social upward mobility, economic development, social integration and encultivation. The teacher should spend leisure time for the development of creativity.

The culture of any country is its soul. If the culture of a nation disappears, the nation also dies like a human body dies when its (जीवात्मा) soul leaves it. Therefore, for having a wide variety of wholesome interests, the teacher should know fully about the national culture, and should learn about all cultural activists. Then only the teacher can enculturate the pupils.

The democracy is the slogan of the day. In a democratic form of government many people, if not all, participate. A democratic government, "is a government by the people for the people". Because of human animal nature, many political leaders make democracy as their property. And for keeping their hold intact and remain in power, they even do not hesitate to criminalize the political institutions. The teacher has a great responsibility in this regard. He/she should inculcate democrat norms in the students by developing beliefs in democratic institutions. The teacher should prepare the future citizens for ideal democratic living, making them aware about the political criminal dens and other criminals and to fight with such bad unsocial elements. This can be done through co-curricular activities, group discussions, seminars, workshops and symposiums. The teacher should make the pupil aware about the versatility of sociability, truthfulness, honesty, regularity in life such as "early to bed early to rise makes a man healthy and wise". The teacher should also motivate the pupil to be regular and perpetual and also enculcate some habits of good living. All these can be enculcated through a co-curricular activities in the school.

Teaching is a creative process like that of doing the creative arts and fine arts. The teacher should always apply creative process in educating the pupil, which could cultivate the creative spirit in the pupils. Then few of them will be creature thinkers, artists and other professionalists. The teacher should always keep in mind great teachers (Guru) of olden times while teaching. The teacher should make references about the great persons. This will help in the character building of the pupils. The teacher should always keep good rapport with the students and the parents. He/she should apprise the students about evil effects of modernization and acculturation which occurred due to the cultural diffusion with the western culture.

Finally it would not be wrong to assume that roles of an ideal teacher should be honesty, sincerity, simplicity proficiency in the subject sociability, morality and truthfulness, and also dedication to the teaching profession.

Index